Building the Realtime User Experience

Building the Realtime User Experience

Ted Roden

O'REILLY®

Beijing · Cambridge · Farnham · Köln · Sebastopol · Taipei · Tokyo

Building the Realtime User Experience
by Ted Roden

Copyright © 2010 Ted Roden. All rights reserved.
Printed in the United States of America.

Published by O'Reilly Media, Inc., 1005 Gravenstein Highway North, Sebastopol, CA 95472.

O'Reilly books may be purchased for educational, business, or sales promotional use. Online editions are also available for most titles (*http://my.safaribooksonline.com*). For more information, contact our corporate/institutional sales department: (800) 998-9938 or *corporate@oreilly.com*.

Editor: Simon St.Laurent	**Indexer:** Ellen Troutman
Production Editor: Kristen Borg	**Cover Designer:** Karen Montgomery
Copyeditor: Genevieve d'Entremont	**Interior Designer:** David Futato
Proofreader: Teresa Barensfeld	**Illustrator:** Robert Romano
Production Services: Molly Sharp	

Printing History:

July 2010:	First Edition.

RepKover™. This book uses RepKover™, a durable and flexible lay-flat binding.

ISBN: 978-0-596-80615-6

[M]

1277147714

Table of Contents

Preface

This book describes a host of technologies and practices used to build truly realtime web applications and experiences. It's about building applications and interfaces that react to user input and input from other servers in milliseconds, rather than waiting for web pages to refresh.

In some ways, these changes are incremental and fairly obvious to most developers. Adding simple JavaScript-based widgets to a website can be done in an afternoon by any developer. However, implementing a Python chat server, or integrating some server-push functionality based on Java into your PHP-based-stack, takes a bit of advance planning. This book aims to break these technologies down, to ensure that you can take any of the examples and insert them into your existing website.

This book assumes that you're comfortable with modern web application development, but makes almost no assumptions that you know the specific technologies discussed. Rather than sticking with a simple technology, or writing about building applications using a specific programming language, this book uses many different technologies. If you're comfortable with web application development, you should have no trouble following the examples, even if you're unfamiliar with the specific technology.

Conventions Used in This Book

The following typographical conventions are used in this book:

Italic

> Indicates new terms, URLs, email addresses, filenames, and file extensions.

`Constant width`

> Used for program listings, as well as within paragraphs to refer to program elements such as variable or function names, databases, data types, environment variables, statements, and keywords.

Constant width bold

> Shows commands or other text that should be typed literally by the user.

Constant width italic

> Shows text that should be replaced with user-supplied values or by values determined by context.

 This icon signifies a tip, suggestion, or general note.

 This icon indicates a warning or caution.

Using Code Examples

This book is here to help you get your job done. In general, you may use the code in this book in your programs and documentation. You do not need to contact us for permission unless you're reproducing a significant portion of the code. For example, writing a program that uses several chunks of code from this book does not require permission. Selling or distributing a CD-ROM of examples from O'Reilly books does require permission. Answering a question by citing this book and quoting example code does not require permission. Incorporating a significant amount of example code from this book into your product's documentation does require permission.

We appreciate, but do not require, attribution. An attribution usually includes the title, author, publisher, and ISBN. For example: "*Building the Realtime User Experience* by Ted Roden. Copyright 2010 O'Reilly Media, Inc., 978-0-596-80615-6."

If you feel your use of code examples falls outside fair use or the permission given above, feel free to contact us at *permissions@oreilly.com*.

Safari® Books Online

 Safari Books Online is an on-demand digital library that lets you easily search over 7,500 technology and creative reference books and videos to find the answers you need quickly.

With a subscription, you can read any page and watch any video from our library online. Read books on your cell phone and mobile devices. Access new titles before they are available for print, and get exclusive access to manuscripts in development and post feedback for the authors. Copy and paste code samples, organize your favorites, download chapters, bookmark key sections, create notes, print out pages, and benefit from tons of other time-saving features.

O'Reilly Media has uploaded this book to the Safari Books Online service. To have full digital access to this book and others on similar topics from O'Reilly and other publishers, sign up for free at *http://my.safaribooksonline.com*.

How to Contact Us

Please address comments and questions concerning this book to the publisher:

O'Reilly Media, Inc.
1005 Gravenstein Highway North
Sebastopol, CA 95472
800-998-9938 (in the United States or Canada)
707-829-0515 (international or local)
707 829-0104 (fax)

We have a web page for this book, where we list errata, examples, and any additional information. You can access this page at:

http://www.oreilly.com/catalog/9780596806156

To comment or ask technical questions about this book, send email to:

bookquestions@oreilly.com

For more information about our books, conferences, Resource Centers, and the O'Reilly Network, see our website at:

http://www.oreilly.com

Acknowledgments

This book would not exist without Nick Bilton, who thought it was a great idea and had an address book big enough to get the ball moving. I'd also like to thank everybody in the Research and Development group at the *New York Times* for their excitement and for allowing me to focus on these topics during my day job.

I'd also like to thank everybody at O'Reilly, whether or not we had any interactions. This process was remarkably smooth thanks to the people and the system in place there. Specifically, I'd like to mention my great editor, Simon St. Laurent, who has been through this so many times before that a simple email would put an end to even the biggest panic attack.

Also, I had some great technical reviewers, including Kyle Bragger, Zachary Kessin, Niel Bornstein, and Finn Smith. If you have any issues with the code, the fault lies at my door, not theirs.

Most importantly, I'd like to thank my lovely wife, Ara. She spent many sleepless nights on baby duty so that I could spend as many sleepless nights on book duty. I must also thank Harriet, who was born a couple of days before I agreed to do this, and who also serves as an important part in the introduction of this book.

## CHAPTER 1

Introduction

My wife and I recently had a baby girl. As she grows up, I'll teach her all kinds of things. Some of the things that I tell her she'll accept as fact, and other times she'll have her doubts. But the one thing I know for sure is that when I get to the part about the Web, she'll be positively tickled when I describe what it looked like before she was born.

I'll tell her that when we got started on the Web, developers had to be careful about which colors they used. I'll let her know that when I bought my first domain, I had to fax in some paperwork and it cost me $70. But the thing that will blow her mind more than any other detail is that we had an entire button on our web browsers dedicated to refreshing the web page on the screen.

Even as the Web hit "version 2.0," most sites were largely call and response affairs. The user clicks a mouse button, data is sent to the server, and some information is returned. Thankfully, the Web that just sat there and stared at you is gone. What was once nothing more than a series of interconnected documents, images, and videos has become much more lifelike. The Web now moves in realtime.

The realtime experience is arriving and, as users, we are noticing it as a fairly subtle change. Unread counts now automatically update, live blogs seem to update a touch faster, chat moved out of a desktop client and onto the web page. From there, more and more things will start to change. Applications that were once merely static websites are starting to make our cell phones tremble in our pockets. These experiences will increasingly meet us in the real world, where we'll be able to interact with them immediately and on our own terms.

What users are noticing as a snowball gently rolling down the hill is hitting developers much more abruptly. Developers have taken a great deal of time to learn relational databases and complicated server configurations. But when they look to add realtime features, they quickly discover it's a whole different world. It may be different, but it isn't difficult.

What Is Realtime?

Since the explosion of the Web, developers have been inclined to think in terms of building websites. Even in this book, I've spent a good deal of time writing about building websites. But make no mistake about it, a realtime user experience does not exist entirely inside a web browser.

The original web browsers were designed to load and display web pages. The idea of a web page is quite similar to the printed page. It is a static document, stored in a computer, but a static document nonetheless. The interface of web browsers evolved to work within this paradigm. There is a Next button and a Back button designed to take you from the current page to the page that you viewed previously. That makes perfect sense when you're working with documents. However, the Web is quite quickly shifting away from a document-based paradigm to a web-based form of communication.

It used to be that a web page was more or less published to the Web. A page was created and given a specific URI, and when the user went to that page, it was pretty clear what to expect. Now we have sites like Facebook (*http://www.facebook.com*) where the same URL is not only different for each of the hundreds of millions of different users, but it changes moments after a user loads the page.

Changing Interactions

In the past, the interaction between a user and a web application was very simple. When a user wanted content, she would load up her browser, point it at a URL, and get the content (see Figure 1-1). If she wanted to write a blog post, she'd load up her browser, fill out a form, and press submit. When she wanted to see comments, it was much the same.

This has changed. No longer can a website wait for users to navigate to the right URL; the website must contact the user wherever that user may be. The paradigm has shifted from a website-centric model, where the website was at the center of the interaction, to a user-centric model. Now all interactions start and end at the user (see Figure 1-2), whether she is visiting the website or sending in Short Message Service (SMS) updates.

A truly realtime experience exists anywhere the user is at a given moment. If the user is interacting with the web browser, then that's the place to contact her. If she's got her instant messenger program open, she'd better be able to interact with your app from that window. When she's offline and your application has an important message for her, send it via SMS. Naturally, you'll need to ask the user's permission before you do some of these things, but your application needs to offer them.

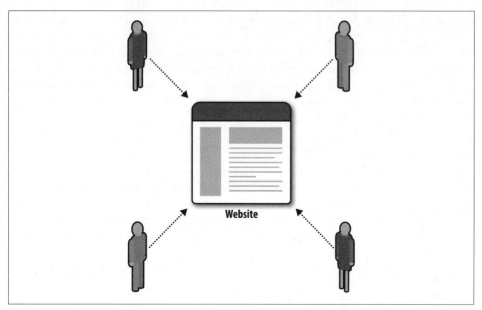

Figure 1-1. In the past, users visited websites

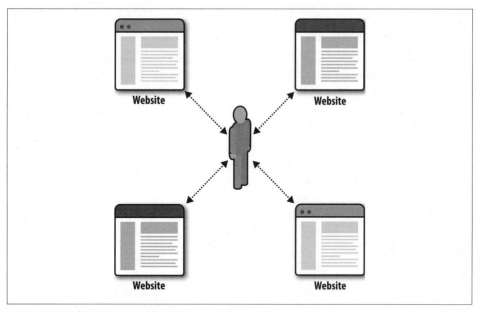

Figure 1-2. Websites must reach out to users wherever they are

I mentioned SMS, but the mobile experience does not end there. These days, users have phones in their pockets with full-fledged web browsers that in some cases offer more functionality than their desktop-based brethren. Among other things, mobile browsers can handle offline data storage, GPS sensors, and touch-based interfaces. Their impressive featureset, coupled with nearly ubiquitous wireless broadband, means they cannot be treated as second class Internet citizens. Applications and user experiences simply must be built with mobile devices in mind.

Push Versus Pull

For about as long as the Web has been around, there have been two main ways of getting content to a user: *push* and *pull*. Pull is the method in which most interactions have worked—the user clicks a link and the browser pulls the content down from the server. If the server wants to send additional messages to the user after the data has been pulled down, it just waits and queues them up until the client makes another request. The idea behind push technology is that as soon as the server has a new message for the user, it sends it to him immediately. A connection is maintained between the server and the client and new data is sent as needed.

In the scheme of the Internet, push technology is not a new development. Throughout the years there have been different standards dictating how it should work. Each proposed standard has had varying levels of support amongst browser makers and different requirements on the server side.

The differing behaviors and requirements of the two technologies have led many developers to use one or the other. This has meant that many sites wanting to offer dynamic updates to their users had to resort to Ajax timers polling the site every *X* seconds to check for new content. This increased amount of requests is taxing on the server and provides a far less graceful user experience than it should have.

Pushing content out to the user as it happens gives the user a much more engaging experience and uses far less resources on the server. Fewer requests means less bandwidth is used and less CPU consumed, because the server is not constantly checking and responding to update requests (see Figure 1-3).

Prerequisites

This book assumes the reader is comfortable with most aspects of web development. The example code in this text uses Java, JavaScript, PHP, and Python. You are encouraged to use the technologies that make the most sense to you. If you're more comfortable with PostgreSQL than MySQL, please use what you're more familiar with. Many of the command-line examples assume you're using something Unix-like (Mac OS X, Linux, etc.), but most of this software runs on Windows, and I'm confident that you can translate any commands listed so that they work in your environment.

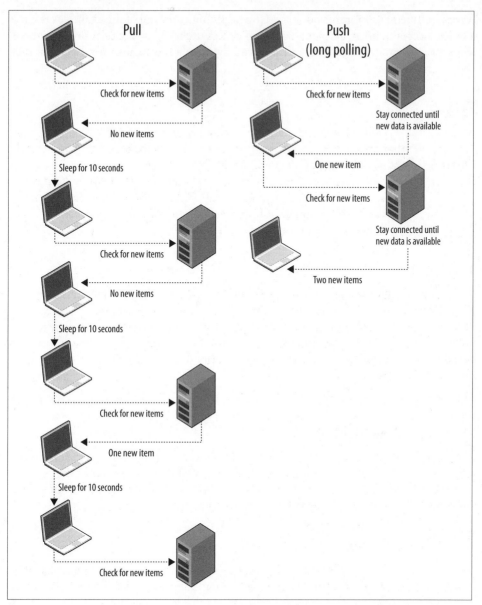

Figure 1-3. Visualizing push versus pull

Building a realtime user experience is language agnostic, and in this book, I've chosen to use several different languages in the examples. Some examples use several technologies chained together. If you're not familiar with one language, don't worry about it. Much of the code is written so you can read it if you're familiar with basic programming practices, plus I've done my best to explain it in the text.

Another prerequisite for this book is a Google account. Several of the examples require a Google account for App Engine, whereas others use it for authentication. Where it's used for authentication, you could fairly easily drop in authentication from another third-party site.

Python

Python is the most-used language in this book for a couple of reasons. Whether or not you know Python, it's a very simple language to read on the page. It also has a couple of terrific libraries that are used throughout this book. During the process of writing this text, one of the pioneers on the realtime web, FriendFeed (*http://friendfeed.com*), was sold to Facebook. After the acquisition, Facebook released a core piece of Friend-Feed's infrastructure as open source software called Tornado (*http://tornadoweb.org*), which is both a collection of libraries and a web server.

JavaScript

This book uses JavaScript in many of the chapters. In most chapters I use a library that helps with some cross-browser issues and enables the examples to contain less code by wrapping up some common activities into simple function calls. This was done to save space on the page and make things easier. If you have a preference of mootools.com (*http://www.mootools.net*) or any other JavaScript library over jQuery (*http://www.jquery.com*), please go ahead and use those. These examples are not based around the languages.

JavaScript Object Notation

This book heavily uses JavaScript Object Notation (JSON) in a number of the examples. JSON is a simple, lightweight data interchange format. It's often used as the payload from Application Programming Interface (API) calls to external services, but in this book it's also used to send messages to the server and back to the browser.

Google's App Engine

Another technology that is used in several chapters is Google's App Engine platform. This service is Google's entry into the cloud computing services industry. It's a fairly unique way of looking at serving applications, and the developer does not have to think about scaling up by adding servers. It's useful here because it gives us a lot of standard features for free. There is a datastore, authentication, and integration with other services, all without paying a cent or writing much complicated code. It was also picked because it requires almost no configuration for the developer. If you're not familiar with the service, that is no problem, because we go through the process of setting up an account in the text.

The Rest

Many of the examples in this book contain a lot of code. I encourage you to type it out, make it our own, and build applications with the knowledge. But if you're not interested in typing it out, you can download every bit of code at this book's official website, *http://www.therealtimebook.com*. In many cases, the code available online is expanded in ways that are useful for development, more suitable for deployment, and better looking than the examples here.

The website has code samples available for download, but also has many of the applications ready to run and test out. So if you're not interested in writing the application and getting it to run, you can follow along with the text and test the application online.

I view this book as realtime experience in its own way. Not only do I plan to keep the code updated, but I also plan to continue the conversation about these topics online through the website, Twitter, and any new service as it pops up. The official Twitter account for this book is @therealtimebook (*http://twitter.com/therealtimebook*). There is a lot of content being created about this topic, and following it online will always be good way to keep up to date.

## CHAPTER 2

Realtime Syndication

Interacting on the realtime web involves a lot of give and take; it's more than just removing the need to refresh your web browser and having updates filter in as they happen. Acquiring content from external sources and publishing it back also must happen in realtime. On the Web, this is called *syndication*, a process in which content is broadcasted from one place to another.

Most syndication on the Web happens through the transmission of XML files, specifically RSS or Atom, from the publisher to the consumer. This model has always been fairly simple: a publisher specifies a feed location and updates the content in that file as it's posted to the site. Consumers of this content, having no way of knowing when new content is posted, have to check that file every half hour or so to see whether any new content has arrived. If a consumer wanted the content faster, they'd have to check the feed more often. However, most publishers frown upon that type of activity and specifically prohibit it in their terms of service. If too many consumers start downloading all of the feeds on a site every minute, it would be very taxing on the server.

Although this has been a problem on the Web for as long as RSS feeds have been around, only recently have people put serious effort into fixing the issue. There are a good number of competing standards aimed at solving this problem. Each of these solutions has had varying degrees of success in getting sites to adopt their technologies. We're going to focus on two of the bigger winners at this point, SUP and PubSubHubbub, but it's worth acknowledging the other standards.

SUP

The Simple Update Protocol (SUP) is a simple and compact poll-based protocol that can be used to monitor thousands of feeds in one shot. It's not a push format like some of the others, but it can save countless amounts of server resources by eliminating the need for frequent polling to many separate feeds, and it allows for much quicker updates of the new data. This protocol was developed by FriendFeed and is supported by a number of sites around the Web, including YouTube. SUP is remarkably easy to implement for both subscribers and publishers. The biggest downside to this protocol is that it's still based on polling. So it's not strictly real-time, but it's darn close.

PubSubHubbub

PubSubHubbub is a publish/subscribe protocol based on web hooks or callbacks. This protocol describes an entirely push-based system designed by a group of developers at Google. It is a totally open standard with a decentralized and open method of providing updates. When new content is posted, the publisher notifies a hub, which then sends out the new updates to each of the subscribers. Subscribers don't have to ping for new content, and the hub sends only the differences in the feed each time, significantly cutting down on the bandwidth transfer after each update. It's a fairly easy protocol and can be added into most existing systems without much effort. The most complicated parts, by design, are contained within the hub.

rssCloud

This protocol was actually developed as part of the RSS 2.0 specification. It works very similar to the PubSubHubbub protocol with very slightly different implementation details. The cloud part of rssCloud, which is very much like the hub from PubSubHubbub, receives updates as they're posted. The cloud then pings each subscriber to let them know that the content has been updated. The problem here is that once a feed has been updated and all the subscribers have been notified, each subscriber will have to request the feed from the server. Depending on how many subscribers there are, this could mean a lot of requests and a ton of traffic on a big feed. Some clouds support hosting the RSS feed directly on the cloud, which relieves some load from the individual server, but the subscriber has to download the entire feed either way. rssCloud isn't covered in detail in this book, but more information on it can be found at *http://rsscloud.org*.

Weblogs.com Pings

Many blogging platforms support "pinging the blogosphere." These work by pinging known URLs as things are published. After being pinged, these services can then download the new feed. However, the basic method of pinging doesn't supply link to the actual feed URL, so the server must parse the site to find the usable RSS/Atom feed. This protocol also doesn't allow for arbitrary subscribers to receive pings or get the data any faster than they would with standard poll requests. More information on this can be found at *http://weblogs.com/api.html#1*.

Simple Update Protocol (SUP)

Although SUP isn't a push protocol enabling true realtime updates, it's a great syndication format and worth a close look. SUP was developed by FriendFeed to solve a problem that plagued them and many other sites on the Web: the need to reduce the amount of polling for the remote feeds and improve the time it took to import new content. SUP enables sites that syndicate their content to aggregators such as Google Reader (*http://www.google.com/reader*) to do so without the need for constant polling of each RSS feed. For this technology, any site that provides RSS feeds is a syndicator and could benefit from this technology.

The order of operations here is simple. The publisher adds a unique SUP ID to each feed. Then, every time the feed is updated, the publisher also updates the SUP feed. When a subscriber wants to get updates from any of the feeds, it only needs to check the SUP feed, which will alert the subscriber to any recently updated feeds. Once the subscriber knows the updated feeds, it downloads only those feeds as it normally would. The subscriber only needs to ping the SUP feed to check for new content, which cuts down the need to ping multiple feeds per site, saving resources for both the subscriber and the publisher.

Without SUP, a consumer of feeds would have to check every feed on a site every time it wanted to check for new updates (see Figure 2-1).

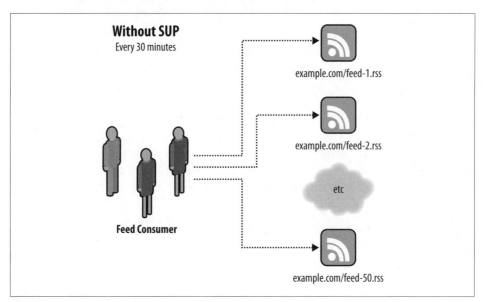

Figure 2-1. Without SUP

When working with SUP, the consumer of the feed knows when each feed is updated by checking the main SUP file. The consumer can easily check the SUP file very often and then check the individual feeds only when they've been updated (see Figure 2-2).

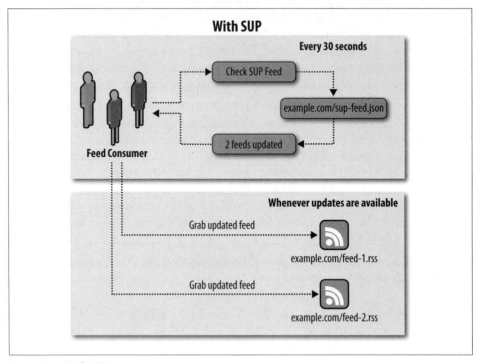

Figure 2-2. With SUP

The SUP file

The crux of this whole protocol is the SUP file. This is the file that alerts subscribers of new content across a site. It's a serialized JSON object containing, amongst other things, a list of updated feeds. The following fields need to be defined:

period
: This is the number of seconds covered by this feed. If any feed on the site has been updated in the last X seconds, it will be listed in this feed.

available_periods
: This is a JSON object that specifies the different update periods supported by the server. The keys defined in the objects are the number of seconds between updates, and the value is the feed URL for that period.

updated_time
: This is the time when the data included in this file was generated (RFC 3339 format).

since_time

> All of the updates defined in this file were created on or after this time. The time between this field and updated_time must be at least period seconds apart, but ideally it would be slightly longer to ensure subscribers see all of the updates (RFC 3339 format).

updates

> This array is an actual list of updated SUP IDs. Each element of the array is another array that has two items: the first item is the SUP ID and the second is called the update_id. The update_id is used to eliminate duplicate pings. I'd suggest using timestamps or anything useful for debugging. Consumers should not try to interpret the update_id for meaningful content. The important thing is to know which SUP ID has been updated.

 Although the spec requires the timestamps be in the format specified by RFC 3339 (e.g., 2009-08-24T00:21:54Z), I strongly recommend that you accept any date format. With everything on the Internet, it's best to follow the axiom, "be lenient in what you accept and strict in what you produce."

Lists of fields are great, but what does this thing look like? The following is an example of a working SUP feed from *http://enjoysthin.gs/api/generate.sup?pretty=1*:

```
{
    "updated_time": "2009-08-21T23:40:27Z",
    "since_time": "2009-08-21T23:39:27Z",
    "period": 30,
    "available_periods": {
        "30": "http:\/\/enjoysthin.gs\/api\/generate.sup?age=30",
        "60": "http:\/\/enjoysthin.gs\/api\/generate.sup?age=60"
    },
    "updates": [
        ["2a356709bd","1250912424"]
    ]
}
```

Subscribing with SUP

To demonstrate subscribing to SUP feeds, we're going to aggregate content from the website *http://enjoysthin.gs*. Enjoysthin.gs is a visual bookmarking site that supports SUP and has an API call to get a list of recently active users. This means that we can grab the feeds of some active users programmatically, even if they change from the time I'm writing this to the time you're reading this. This also means that we'll be able to grab the most active RSS feeds on the site, ensuring that we have new content frequently. Figure 2-3 shows the active users page on enjoysthin.gs.

Figure 2-3. The active users page on enjoysthin.gs

We're going to be aggregating links to new content for any number of users. To do this, we're going to need to create two MySQL tables. If you don't have a test database to use, create one with the following command:

```
~ $ mysqladmin -u db_user  -p create syndication_test
```

Now that we've created the database, we need to create the two tables needed for the example. Run MySQL using your newly created database and create the following tables:

```
~ $ mysql -u db_user -p syndication_test
mysql> CREATE TABLE feeds (
    id serial,
    feed_url varchar(128) not null default '',
    sup_url varchar(128) not null default '',
    sup_id varchar(32) not null default ''
);
mysql> CREATE TABLE entries  (
    id serial,
    feed_id integer not null references feeds,
    date_created datetime not null,
    date_updated datetime not null,
    url varchar(255) not null,
    title varchar(255) not null default '',
    atom_entry_id varchar(56) not null
);
```

This example and the PubSubHubbub example both use a very simple database class. Save the following as `db.php` in your working directory:

```php
<?php

function _escape(&$str) {
    $str = "'" . mysql_real_escape_string($str) . "'";
}

class db {

    private $handle;

    function __construct($database_name,
                         $username, $password,
                         $host="127.0.0.1") {
        $this->handle = mysql_connect($host, $username, $password);
        mysql_select_db($database_name, $this->handle);
    }

    // select a bunch of rows and return as an array
    function select_array($sql) {
        $_ret = array();
        $result = $this->query($sql);
        if($result)
            while($row = mysql_fetch_object($result))
                $_ret[]  = $row;
        return $_ret;
    }

    function insert_array($table, $data=array()) {
        if(!count($data)) return false;

        $values = array_values($data);
        array_walk($values, '_escape');

        $sql = "insert into {$table} (" . join(',', array_keys($data)) . ') ' .
            " values(" . join(',', $values) . ')';
        return $this->insert_query($sql);
    }


    function insert_query($sql) {
        $this->query($sql);
        return mysql_insert_id($this->handle);
    }

    function query($sql) {
        return mysql_query($sql, $this->handle);
    }

}
```

Locating SUP feeds

We're eventually going to build a script that checks a SUP feed for a bunch of different Atom feeds, but before we can do that, we need to get a list of fairly active Atom feeds and their corresponding SUP IDs. Rather than scour the Web for sites that support SUP and then manually finding the users on that site that are still active, we're going to ask enjoysthin.gs for that list. Enjoysthin.gs provides a public API function to get a list of recently active users. That API function returns, amongst other things, the URL of the Atom feed for that user. The following PHP script, `sup-id-aggregator.php`, grabs those feeds, searches for the SUP ID, and saves the result to the `feeds` table we created.

```php
<?php

include_once("db.php");
$db = new db('syndication_test', 'db_user', 'db_pass');

// make an API call to get a list of recently active users/feeds
$url = "http://enjoysthin.gs/api/active.users";
$data = json_decode(file_get_contents($url));
$feeds = array();
foreach($data->users as $u) {
    $feeds[] = $u->atom;
}

echo("Checking for SUP-IDs on " . count($feeds) . " Atom feeds\n");

foreach($feeds as $feed) {
    // sup_discover is at the bottom of this file
    if($sup_link = sup_discover($feed)) {
        list($sup_url, $sup_id) = explode("#", $sup_link);
        $data = array('feed_url' => $feed,
                      'sup_url' => $sup_url,
                      'sup_id' => $sup_id);
        $id = $db->insert_array('feeds', $data);
        echo("{$id} Found SUP-ID: ({$sup_id})\n");
    }
}

echo("Done.\n");

// Pass this function the URL of an Atom/RSS feed,
// and it will return the SUP-ID
function sup_discover($feed) {
    // download the feed as a PHP object
    $xml = @simplexml_load_file($feed);
    if(!$xml) return false;

    $sup_link = false; // initialize the variable

    // loop through the XML
    foreach($xml as $k => $v) {
        // look for the link tag with SUP feed defined
        if($k == 'link') {
            $attrs = $v->attributes();
```

```
                    if($attrs['rel'] == 'http://api.friendfeed.com/2008/03#sup')
                        return (string) $attrs['href'];
                }
            }

            return false;
        }
```

After connecting to the database, this file starts by making the **active.users** API call. That function returns a serialized JSON object with the list of active users. We loop through those users to create an array called **$feeds** containing only the location of the Atom feeds.

The result of the **active.users** API call will give us various pieces of information about recently active users. One of these fields will be the URL to the Atom feed for that user. The full JSON response will look something like this:

```
{"users":[
    {"atom":"http://georgie.enjoysthin.gs/things.xml",
     "url":"http://georgie.enjoysthin.gs/?from=api",
     "username":"georgie",
     "name":"Georgie Hammerton",
     "avatar":"http://...jpg"},
    {"atom":"http://tedroden.enjoysthin.gs/things.xml",
     "url":"http://tedroden.enjoysthin.gs/?from=api",
     "username":"tedroden",
     "name":"Ted Roden",
     "avatar":"http://....jpg"}
],"stat":"ok"}
```

Once we have a list of feeds to use, we need to check each of them to see whether they have a SUP feed associated with them. They all do have a SUP feed defined, but if you run this code against other URLs, this is a good test. Once we determine that the feed does have a SUP-ID associated with it, we save it to the database.

The SUP specification says that the SUP-ID can be specified in one of two ways. Either it can be a `<link>` tag in the feed itself, or it can be served as the `X-SUP-ID` header with the HTTP response. The full SUP-ID is formatted as a string containing both the SUP feed URL and the ID for the feed itself. Whereas the SUP URL is a standard URL, the ID is specified by using a named anchor tag in that URL. The full SUP-ID will look something like this: `http://somesite.com/sup-feed.json#sup-id`.

Calling the `sup_discover` function returns that full URL. So after calling that function, we split apart that URL to get the base and the SUP-ID. Then, we build a simple PHP object to map the fields from the **feeds** table to the Atom feed URL, the SUP URL, and the SUP-ID itself. The `insert_array` function takes this data, turns it into SQL, and inserts it into the database.

The `sup_discover` function is the function that does most of the work in this file. This function uses PHP's very handy SimpleXML extension to download the XML file and parse it into a PHP object. That all happens on the first line of this function. Once that's done, we just loop through the tags in the XML looking for the `link` tag with the proper `rel` attribute. Once we find it, we return the SUP link that we found.

To run this script, run the following command:

```
~ $ php sup-id-aggregator.php
Checking for SUP-IDs on 30 Atom feeds
1 Found SUP-ID: (03654a851d)
2 Found SUP-ID: (033097ff53)
3 Found SUP-ID: (cdeb48b690)
...
29 Found SUP-ID: (4791d29f89)
```

This command may take a little bit of time to finish because it's downloading and parsing a number of RSS feeds, but once does it finish, you'll have a bunch of feeds and SUP-IDs saved locally to the database.

The time it takes to download these feeds should help illustrate the beauty of SUP. Without SUP, you would have to download all of those feeds again every time you want to check whether they've been updated. But from here on out, you don't need to do that. We just need to check the main SUP feed and check the files it tells us to use.

Checking the SUP feed

Now that we have a good number of Atom feeds and we know their corresponding SUP URLs and SUP-IDs, we can starting pinging the common SUP feed to check for updates. Prior to SUP, if we wanted to check all of these feeds for updates, we'd have to grab each and every one and compare them to the data we have. We'd do that every time we wanted to check for new content. With SUP, we simply have ping tell us when things are updated. This process, while fairly straightforward, is a bit more complex than the previous one. So we're going to step through it piece by piece. Open your text editor and create a file called `sup-feed-aggregator.php`:

```php
<?php

include_once("db.php");
$sup_url = "http://enjoysthin.gs/api/generate.sup?age=60";
$sup_data = @json_decode(@file_get_contents($sup_url));
if(!$sup_data) die("Unable to load the SUP_URL: {$sup_url} ...");
```

Getting started is simple; we just need to download the SUP file used by all of our feeds. Normally, you'd want to check the database and get all of the SUP files needed for the data feeds you need to check, but since all of our feeds are coming from the same spot, I removed that complexity. We just download the file and use PHP's `json_decode` function, which builds it into a native PHP object.

 PHP provides `json_decode` and `json_encode`, two of the most useful functions in the language for dealing with web services and data exchange on the Internet. If you're not familiar with them, you should seriously consider giving them a look.

Once we have the main SUP feed, we need to load the SUP-IDs that we know about from the `feeds` table in our local database. This is the SUP data that we inserted in our previous script. To load it, add the following to your script:

```
$db = new db('syndication_test', 'db_user', 'db_pass');
$sql = "select id, sup_id, feed_url from feeds " ;
$local_sup_info = $db->select_array($sql);

$feeds_to_check = array();

// loop the sup entries in our database
foreach($local_sup_info as $local_info)  {
    // and check to see if any of the entries we know about ($local_info)
    // have been updated on the server ($sup_data->updates)
    foreach($sup_data->updates as $u) {
        list($sup_id, $garbage) = $u;
        if($sup_id == $local_info->sup_id)
            $feeds_to_check[] = $local_info;
    }
}

if(!count($feeds_to_check))
    die("No feeds to check, sup wins again!\n");
else
    echo("Checking " . count($feeds_to_check) .  " feeds\n");
```

As you can see, we connect to the database and select all of the SUP data from our table. Then we loop through all the entries and compare it to the **updates** field loaded from *http://enjoysthin.gs/api/generate.sup*. If there were any feeds on enjoysthin.gs that had recent updates, they'll be in the updates field. So all we need to do is compare the SUP-IDs that we know about to the SUP-IDs provided by that file. If we have a match, add the whole database row to the `$feeds_to_check` array.

That last snippet of code had one curious line operating on `$u`:

```
list($sup_id, $garbage) = $u;
```

When used like this, PHP's `list` function pulls apart an array and assigns the different elements in the array to the variables named in the list.

The SUP protocol specifies that the **updates** field is an array of arrays. Those inner arrays declare which SUP-IDs have been updated by inserting them as the first element in the array while providing another string as the second element. We're not expected to interpret that second element, so it's assigned to `$garbage` here, making it clear that it's not needed.

If none of the feeds need to be updated, there is no need to continue with this script. However, if we have `$feeds_to_check`, it's time to check them, so add the following to the file:

```
foreach($feeds_to_check as $feed) {
    $entry_ids = array();
    $sql = "select atom_entry_id from entries where feed_id = {$feed->id}";
```

```
$existing_atom_entries = $db->select_array($sql);
foreach($existing_atom_entries as $e)
    $entry_ids[] = $e->atom_entry_id;

$xml = simplexml_load_file($feed->feed_url);
$kids = $xml->children('http://www.w3.org/2005/Atom');
$entries = $kids->entry;
echo("Feed has ". count($entries) . " entries\n");
foreach($entries as $i) {
    if(!in_array((string) $i->id, $entry_ids)) {
        $link = $i->link->attributes();
        $data = array('feed_id' => $feed->id,
                        'date_created' => $i->published,
                        'title' => $i->title,
                        'url' => $link['href'],
                        'atom_entry_id' => (string) $i->id);
        $entry_id = $db->insert_array('entries', $data);
        echo("Imported {$i->id} as {$entry_id} \n");
    }
    else
        echo("Already have $i->id, not adding it.\n");
}
}
```

Each time through the loop we check and import the entries contained within this feed. However, since SUP only tells us that something has been updated, we can't just blindly save everything we find; we have to check the entries in the feed against our records.

The first thing to do is load up all of the entries for this particular feed. The only feed from our local table that we care about is atom_entry_id. These IDs remain unique to every post in the feed, even if the feed changes servers, so we can be confident about this field signaling new content. We'll cache that for later in the $entry_ids array.

Once we know the feed we're interested in and which Atom IDs we aren't interested in, it's time to actually look at the Atom file. Again, we turn to PHP's SimpleXML. We get all of the entries out of the root element of the XML and loop through each of them.

Each time through the loop we're looking at a single entry from the feed. The first thing that we want to do is see whether that particular entry is in our $entry_ids array. If it's not, save everything that we care about to entries table.

We have everything we need to consume the content feeds via SUP. Let's try running the script to see what we get.

```
~ $ php sup-feed-aggregator.php
Checking 1 feeds
http://nicedream.enjoysthin.gs/things.xml:
ENTRY-id: 1
ENTRY-id: 2
...
ENTRY-id: 29
ENTRY-id: 30
```

Your results may vary widely from mine. When I ran it, the SUP feed indicated that one of the Atom feeds had been updated. However, you may get several of them, or you may get none at all. It's the nature of how SUP works. Sometimes this script will find itself updating many feeds, and other times it doesn't do much at all.

This script works best when run quite often via a cron job. Since the script is requesting the feed with a period of 60 seconds, running it once a minute makes a lot of sense. So to let's set that up with cron. Run the command **crontab -e** and add this line:

```
* * * * * php /PATH/TO/sup-feed-aggregator.php >> /tmp/sup-feed-aggregator.log
```

This tells the cron daemon to run this script every minute of every hour of every day and append the results to a file in the /tmp directory. Watching the entries table grow will let you know that it's working, but you can also check the /tmp/sup-feed-aggregator.log to see what's happening.

 If you're not careful, you could start filling up your database and your hard drive with feed and log data. Be sure to remove that cron job when you're done testing.

Publishing with SUP

We've seen how easy it can be to implement SUP on the subscriber side, but it's also easy to implement for a publisher. Any system that stores the creation date of each entry can add SUP to their site with minimal effort.

Generating a SUP file

To generate a SUP file, we need to make some assumptions about the system for which it's being used. For the sake of simplicity, let's say that you are making a social bookmarking site that provides Atom feeds of each user's bookmarks. Let's also assume that each time a user saves a bookmark, the system automatically updates a field called last_update in the (hypothetical) MySQL users table. Our users table would look something like this:

```
mysql> describe users;
+-------------+---------------------+------+-----+---------------------+-----+
| Field       | Type                | Null | Key | Default             | ... |
+-------------+---------------------+------+-----+---------------------+-----+
| id          | bigint(20) unsigned | NO   | PRI | NULL                |     |
| username    | varchar(32)         | NO   |     |                     |     |
| password    | char(32)            | NO   |     |                     |     |
| last_update | datetime            | NO   |     | 0000-00-00 00:00:00 |     |
+-------------+---------------------+------+-----+---------------------+-----+
4 rows in set (0.00 sec)
```

If you want to try out these code samples and follow along, you can create that table with the following SQL:

```
CREATE TABLE users (
    id serial,
    username varchar(32) NOT NULL default '',
    password char(32) NOT NULL default '',
    last_update datetime NOT NULL default '0000-00-00 00:00:00'
);
```

Every SUP file is tied to a specific period, or number of seconds, that the file represents. When generating the default SUP file, the publisher generally defaults to a period of 30 to 60 seconds. The SUP file should also provide alternate URLs for different spans of time. No matter what time frame is used, the process to generate the file is the same.

To generate a SUP file, all the publisher needs to do is grab all the users who have updated their bookmarks in the specified time frame, generate the SUP-ID, and output the file. This file can be added to our hypothetical PHP-based bookmarking site with a very short script. Create a file called sup-generator.php and add the following code:

```php
<?php

// get the time frame they're requesting, default to 30 seconds
// this is known as the 'period' in the SUP spec.
$age = (is_numeric($_GET['age'])) ? $_GET['age'] : 30);

// we also add 30 seconds to provide a good amount of overlap.
$since_age = $age + 30;

function generate_sup_id($user_id) {
    return substr(md5('secret:' . $user_id), 0, 10);
}
```

The first thing this file does is determine the period to be used for the SUP file. Since this variable represents seconds, I call it age and give it a default of 30 if it's not supplied. Then, we generate the $since_age variable, which is what we'll actually use when it comes time to build the SQL statement. All we do here is add 30 extra seconds onto the age variable. The extra time gives subscribers some leeway when checking the feeds.

The first function in the file, generate_sup_id, is used to create a unique SUP-ID for each user. This function combines a "secret" string along with the user's unique ID and generates the MD5 hash of it. Then it returns the first 10 characters of the hash by running it through PHP's substr function. There is no string length limit on the SUP-ID, and we're free to use the whole MD5 for it, but the point of SUP is to provide quick and lightweight updates to subscribers. Shortening these strings will drastically reduce the size of this file when there is a large number of users.

Cropping the SUP-ID before returning it means that two users could quite possibly have the same SUP-ID. "Collisions" with these IDs are fine because the worst thing that happens is that the subscriber will grab all the feeds that have the same SUP-ID each time a shared ID is updated. Unless there is a huge amount of overlap, this is nothing to worry about. The smaller file is worth the risk.

The next thing we need to do is look at the database and figure out which users have updated content. Add the following to sup-generator.php:

```php
function get_updates($since_age) {
    include_once("db.php");
    $db = new db('syndication_test', 'db_user', 'db_pass');
    $sql = "select id, last_update from users
            last_update > date_format(now() - interval {$since_age} second,
                                    '%Y-%m-%d  %H:%i:%s')
            order by last_update desc limit 100";
    $updates = array();
    foreach($db->select_array($sql) as $row)
        $updates[] = array(generate_sup_id($row->id),
                            (string) strtotime($row->last_update));

    return $updates;
}
```

This function, get_updates, is also the last function needed (I told you this was easy). This function selects out all of the users who have updated bookmarks in the last $since_age seconds. After creating an array to store all of the updates, it populates that array with another array for each user who has updated content. That second array contains the generated SUP-ID and the time of the last update. As I mentioned before, the second value can be anything we want, so I'm just using the timestamp. The timestamp value will allow us to easily debug what is happening if anything seems out of the ordinary. The updates array will end up looking something like this:

```
// This is what the main updates array will look like.
// You don't need to add this to sup-generator.php
"updates": [
    // arrays of single updates
    ['sup-id-01', 'internal-publisher-string-01'],
    ['sup-id-02', 'internal-publisher-string-02'],
    ..
]
```

Now that we can generate semi-unique SUP-IDs and load the data out of the database, we just need to assemble the object that we'll return. The following code is all that remains to be added to sup-generator.php:

```php
$sup = new stdClass;
$sup->updated_time = date('Y-m-d\TH:i:s\Z');
$sup->since_time = date('Y-m-d\TH:i:s\Z', strtotime("-{$since_age} second"));
$sup->period = $age;
$sup->available_periods = new stdClass;
$url = 'http://' . $_SERVER['HTTP_HOST'] . '/' . $_SERVER['PHP_SELF'];
$sup->available_periods->{'30'} = "{$url}?age=30";
$sup->available_periods->{'300'} = "{$url}?age=300";
$sup->available_periods->{'600'} = "{$url}?age=600";
$sup->updates = get_updates($since_age);

header("Content-Type: application/json");
print json_encode($sup);
```

This segment of code builds a PHP object with all of the fields that need to end up in the JSON object. The `updated_time` and `since_time` can just be generated on the fly. The available periods are the URLs that the subscriber can access if they don't like the default period; we just use the same script and change the **age** variable for each period. The protocol recommends providing more than one available period, so we're providing three here, including the default period. Then we just encode the PHP object into JSON and print it out.

Testing our SUP file

Now that we have a script to generate the SUP file, let's test it out. You can upload it to a web server (that has the **users** table already created), or you can simply run it from the command line:

```
~ $ php sup-generator.php
```

That will print out the SUP file in one line. I've formatted it to look a bit nicer here, but your output should look something like this:

```
{
    "updated_time": "2009-08-26T08:43:26Z",
    "since_time": "2009-08-26T08:42:26Z",
    "period": 30,
    "available_periods": {
        "30": "http:\/\/\/ch02-1-sup-generator.php?age=30",
        "300":"http:\/\/\/ch02-1-sup-generator.php?age=300",
        "600":"http:\/\/\/ch02-1-sup-generator.php?age=600"
    },
    "updates": []
}
```

Running this command from the command line means we have no server name for the `available_periods` fields. Once we run this from a web server, those will be fine. The main thing to notice here is that we have no SUP updates. If a SUP client was connecting, it would think there were no updates to grab.

Ideally, the application would update the `last_update` field in the **users** table whenever new content is available. For our purposes, we can just insert several rows and run it again. Run the following SQL as many times as you like; this will populate the **users** table with some data to test.

```
insert into users(username, last_update)
    select concat('username-', round(RAND() * 100)),
           (now() + interval (rand()* 100) minute);
```

Running the `sup-generator.php` script should give us some updates now. On my machine, the updates array now looks like this:

```
"updates": [
    ["be69ff6d4c","1251296083"],
    ["dcfc912115","1251295962"],
    ["f4066352d6","1251293981"],
    ["df97cf82f1","1251292781"],
    ["a29e3fe0d9","1251292362"]
]
```

 Once you've built your SUP feed, you can run it through the FriendFeed validator at *http://friendfeed.com/api/sup-validator*. This validator is an open source Python project, and you can download the code from *http://code.google.com/p/simpleupdateprotocol/source/browse/trunk/validatesup.py*.

The SUP header

As I mentioned previously in this chapter, in order for a subscriber to find the main SUP file useful, it needs to know which SUP-IDs to check. To do this, the subscriber downloads the RSS file and looks for one of two things. It can be specified as either a `<link>` tag in the feed itself, or it can be served as the `X-SUP-ID` header with the HTTP response. Actually adding the SUP-ID to an existing feed is very straightforward. For example, let's assume the script that generates an RSS feed looks something like this:

```
<?xml version="1.0" encoding="UTF-8"?>

<feed xmlns="http://www.w3.org/2005/Atom">
<title><?= $user_name ?> - Atom Feed</title>
<id><tag:my-site.com,1980-01-19:<?= $user_id ?></id>

...

<? foreach($entries as $entry): >
    ...
<? endforeach; >
```

Adding our SUP-ID to this file is very easy. As you can see, we already have the `$user_id`, which in the example is being used to generate the `id` for the Atom feed. When generating our SUP feed, we generated the semi-unique ID from nothing more than that `$user_id`. We've already created the *sup-generator.php*, so all we need to do is add that information to the feed, as I've done in the additions here:

```
<?

function generate_sup_id($id) {
    return substr(md5('secret:' . $id), 0, 10);
}

$sup_base_url = "http://" . $_SERVER['HTTP_HOST'] . '/sup-generator.php';
$sup_url = $sup_base_url . "#" . generate_sup_id($user_id);
```

```
header("X-SUP-ID: $sup_url");

?><?xml version="1.0" encoding="UTF-8"?>
<feed xmlns="http://www.w3.org/2005/Atom">
<title><?= $user_name ?> - Atom Feed</title>
<id><tag:my-site.com,1980-01-19:<?= $user_id ?></id>
<link rel="http://api.friendfeed.com/2008/03#sup" href="<?= $sup_url ?>"
      type="application/json" />
...

<? foreach($entries as $entry): >
  ...
<? endforeach; >
```

This adds the same `generate_sup_id` function that we used when creating the SUP feeds and uses that to generate the full URL to the SUP feed. Using that function, we just created the full SUP URL by appending the ID to the location of our *sup-generator.php* script. Then, we add the SUP-ID to both the HTTP response header and as a link in the XML feed itself.

Earlier in this chapter, we built a script called *sup-id-aggregator.php* that was used to locate valid SUP data in Atom/RSS feeds. Running that script against this feed would find the valid SUP information.

 Much like the SUP feed validator listed earlier, you can also check the validity of your Atom/RSS feed. There are many of these Atom/RSS validators, but FriendFeed provides a validator that also acknowledges that it found valid SUP headers. Check your feed at *http://friendfeed.com/api/feedtest*.

PubSubHubbub

PubSubHubbub differs from the rest of the implementations because it is a fully push-based protocol. All of the content between publishers and subscribers runs through centralized hubs, but this protocol is completely decentralized, open source, and free. Anybody can run a hub and publish and subscribe to content. There is no single entity in control of this system. However, this is a server to server protocol and requires public-facing servers end-to-end. So although this protocol isn't used directly by end users, it makes it possible for end users to get almost instantaneous updates from the publishers.

In the PubSubHubbub workflow, a publisher specifies a hub server in the RSS or Atom feed. Every time a publisher adds or updates content, it pings the hub to announce that the feed has been updated. After receiving the ping, the hub checks the updated RSS file for differences and sends them via POST request to any subscriber that has requested it. During the subscription process, each client specifies a callback URL, and it's this URL that the hub POSTs to as new data arrives.

The Protocol

As the name suggests, the PubSubHubbub protocol has two major components: publication and subscription.

Subscribe

The Sub part of PubSubHubbub is subscription. When your main goal is to collect aggregated content from around the Web in real time, this is the most important part. It's a bit different from subscribing to RSS feeds because it involves two servers, and instead of you pinging the central RSS server, it pings you. Figure 2-4 describes the subscription process at a high level.

Often the Publisher and the hub are two different servers, but this is not a requirement.

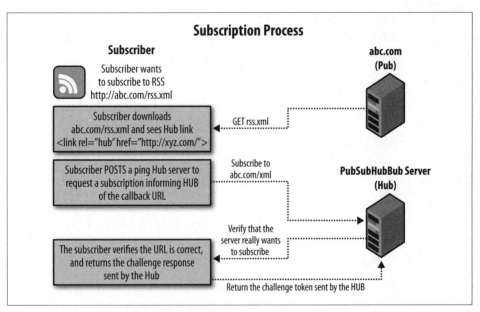

Figure 2-4. Subscribing with PubSubHubbub

The first step in subscribing to a feed with PubSubHubbub is discovery. The subscriber must determine whether the RSS feed is already publishes to a hub. To do this, the subscriber downloads the RSS feed and looks for the proper hub link tag in the XML, specifically a `link` tag where the `ref` attribute is `hub`. In the XML, it looks like this:

```
<link rel='hub' href='http://www.myhub.com/hub'/>
```

This tag informs any subscribers of the location of the hub. While any client can continue to use the RSS feed, services supporting this protocol can use the hub instead. In order to subscribe to this published feed, the subscriber must make a POST request to the hub and request a subscription.

The subscription process takes several steps to complete. Every interaction from the subscriber to the hub is done with a POST request that has a content type of `application/x-www-form-urlencoded`. The subscription request requires two steps to be successful. First, a subscriber requests a subscription from the hub. Then, the hub tries to confirm that the subscription is desired by verifying it with the subscribing server. This requires two HTTP POST requests with several parameters. Most importantly, subscribing to a published feed requires specifying the topic URL and the callback URL. A full listing of the subscription parameters follows. All fields are required unless otherwise specified.

`hub.mode`
> The mode will be either `subscribe` or `unsubscribe`.

`hub.callback`
> This is the subscriber's callback URL. When the hub has an update, it will POST it to this URL. According to the protocol, this URL should not contain a query string of any kind.

`hub.topic`
> This is the topic URL to which the subscriber is subscribing. This is generally an RSS or Atom feed.

`hub.verify`
> This parameter describes the verification mode(s) supported by the subscribing server. This parameter can be listed more than once if the server supports more than one method. There are two possible values. First there is `sync`, which requires that the verification request must happen before the subscription's HTTP request has been returned. `async` specifies that the verification request may happen after the subscription request returns.

`hub.verify_token`
> This is an optional parameter. A subscriber can supply this token, which will be supplied by the hub during the verification request. If not supplied, it will not be present during verification. This can be used to help ensure that the subscriber is receiving valid requests.

`hub.lease_seconds`
> This is an optional parameter. It specifies the number of seconds that the subscription should be active. The hub will ping the URL only during this period; once it expires, the pings will cease. However, hubs may or may not respect this value, depending on their own internal policies. If not supplied, the hub should use a value of 2,592,000 seconds, or 30 days.

Upon receiving a subscription request, the hub will try to verify that the server at the end of the callback URL is actually trying to subscribe to the feed. To do this, it makes a verification request to the callback URL by POSTing a challenge string. If the subscriber actually meant to subscribe to the feed, it will verify the request by echoing the challenge request back to the server in a normal HTTP response. If the subscriber wants to deny this verification request, it should return an HTTP 404 "Not found" response. The parameters that will get posted to the client are the following:

hub.mode
> The mode will be either subscribe or unsubscribe.

hub.topic
> This is the topic URL that was supplied when initiating the subscription request.

hub.challenge
> This is the random string generated by the hub. If the subscriber verifies this request, it must be echoed back in the body of the HTTP response.

hub.lease_seconds
> This is the number of seconds the subscription should remain active. If the subscriber wants uninterrupted pings, it should resubscribe before this period of time runs out.

hub.verify_token
> If this field was supplied during the main subscription call, it will be present in this field. If it's wrong, or supplied but unexpected, the subscriber should reject this verification request.

Publishing content

Publishing content, or notifying the hub of new content, is actually the simplest part of the whole protocol. When the publisher has new content and wants to inform the hub, it pings the hub with the URL. No authentication is needed, because it's only pinging the hub to suggest that it check for new updates. There are two fields in this request:

hub.mode
> The mode will always be publish during the publish notification.

hub.topic
> This is the topic URL that has been updated. After this ping, the hub server will check the topic URL for any updates and notify subscribers if needed.

After receiving the publish ping, the hub server will make a GET request to the topic URL. This is where the hub gets the new Atom/RSS content. This request is a totally standard GET request, except that it's accompanied by the header field X-Hub-Subscribers.

Because the hub is actually handling the distribution to the end users, the publisher would have no way of knowing how many end users are accessing the content. This X-Hub-Subscribers header contains the approximate number of users. This number can be used by the publisher's analytics system to get a better idea of how many end users are accessing your content.

Once the hub has the content, it compares the new feed to a cached version stored on the hub to determine what has changed. The hub then rebuilds the feed so that it contains only new and updated entries. It then cycles through its list of subscribers and makes a POST to all of the subscribers. This POST request contains nothing more than the updated feed in the body.

Subscribing with PubSubHubbub

To demonstrate subscribing to a PubSubHubbub feed, we're going to add items to the entries table created during the SUP part of this chapter. We can reuse the actual database tables and the PHP database class, but we're going to need to create a class to handle the lower-level pieces of the protocol itself. To get started, open a file called *pubsubhubbub.php* and add the following code.

```php
<?php

class PubSubHubBub {

    private $_hub_url = false;
    private $_params = array();

    public function __construct($hub_url) {
        $this->_hub_url = $hub_url;
    }

    private function param($k, $v) {
        $this->_params[$k] = $v;
    }

    private function _post() {

        $query_params = array();
        foreach ($this->_params as $k => $v) {
            $query_params[] = $k . '=' . urlencode($v);
        }
        $data = join('&', $query_params);

        $options = array(CURLOPT_URL => $this->_hub_url,
                        CURLOPT_POST => true,
                        CURLOPT_POSTFIELDS => $data,
                        CURLOPT_USERAGENT => "realtime-pubsubhubbub/1.0");

        $ch = curl_init();
        curl_setopt_array($ch, $options);
        curl_exec($ch);
```

```
            $info = curl_getinfo($ch);
            curl_close($ch);

            if ($info['http_code'] == 204) {
                return true;
            }
            return false;
        }
    }
```

This really is the bulk of the class that we'll be using, and there really isn't that much to it. This defines a class called PubSubHubbub and requires the hub URL when constructing it. Other than that, it has a simple function called _post to POST the content to the hub URL and a param function to add parameters to the POST request.

As it stands, this class could be used by PHP scripts to handle the work of subscribing to feeds and publishing to hubs. However, it'll be a lot easier for the end users of this class if we add some convenience functions to speed the process along. To subscribe to a feed, let's append a subscribe function to the end of the PubSubHubbub class in the *pubsubhubbub.php* file.

```
    public function subscribe($topic_url, $callback_url, $token=false, $lease=false) {
        if (!isset($topic_url)) return; // nothing to do

        if (!preg_match("|^https?://|i", $topic_url))
            throw new Exception('Invalid URL: ' . $topic_url);

        $this->param('hub.topic', $topic_url);
        $this->param('hub.mode', 'subscribe');
        $this->param('hub.callback', $callback_url);
        $this->param('hub.verify', 'sync');

        if($token) $this->param("hub.verify_token", $token);
        if($lease) $this->param("hub.lease_seconds", $lease);

        return $this->_post();
    }
```

This function accepts enough parameters to handle all of the options needed when subscribing to a hub. The two important parameters in this function are the $topic_url and the $callback_url. The topic URL specifies the actual Atom feed URL that we want to subscribe to. The callback URL is the URL that the hub will ping when it has new content.

In the subscribe function, we check the existence and validity of the $topic_url and add it to the parameter list. We also want to tell the hub which action we're doing; we do this with the hub.mode parameter, which we've set to subscribe. Depending on how your system works outside of this class, you may want to change the hub.verify method or change the token and lease parameters, but these default values should be fine for many implementations.

Finally, that function calls PubSubHubbub::_post(), which assembles the POST request from the parameters and contacts the hub server. While most of the response from the hub is ignored, _post returns true or false to signify whether the post has been successful. However, when you're using the sync mode for hub.verify, the callback URL will actually get pinged before this functions returns.

 Although most hubs should return from the subscribe request quickly, you should avoid forcing users to wait for this function to return. It's best to run this function from queue, which will enable you to return immediately and provide the users with a much smoother and more realtime experience.

Now that we have enough of the class built to subscribe to a hub, let's write some code that actually uses it. We'll start with a simple PHP script that can run on our web server and can handle the whole subscription process. Open a file called *index.php* and add the following code:

```php
<?php

include_once("pubsubhubbub.php");

if($_REQUEST['request_subscription']) {
    // define the hub
    $hub = "http://pubsubhubbub.appspot.com/";

    // initialize the class
    $p = new PubSubHubBub($hub);

    // enter your "Shared Items" Atom URL
    $topic_url = "http://www.google.com/reader/public/...";

    // This is the URL the hub will ping (this file).
    $callback = 'http://' . $_SERVER['HTTP_HOST'] . $_SERVER['PHP_SELF'];

    // POST to the server and request a subscription
    $r = $p->subscribe($topic_url, $callback);

    if($r) {
        die("Done... we should be all subscribed. Try sharing something.");
    }
    else {
        die("\n\nSomething went wrong when subscribing.");
    }
}

else if($_REQUEST['hub_mode'] == 'subscribe') {
    // echo the hub_challenge back to the hub.
    die($_REQUEST['hub_challenge']);
}
```

Subscribing to a hub is a two-step process, and this file handles both steps. When hitting the URL for this script, if the query string has `request_subscription=1`, this will use the PubSubHubbub class to request a subscription from the reference hub hosted on Google's App Engine platform. This is the hub that is used by blogger.com and Google Reader, amongst other platforms.

If the request doesn't specify `request_subscription`, but does set the `hub_mode` to `subscribe`, then we respond to the hub challenge. Responding to the challenge requires nothing more than printing out the string supplied by the hub. If we'd specified a `hub.verify_token`, then this part of the file would check to ensure that token was correct before responding to the challenge. However, since we didn't do that, we can safely ignore that step.

> You may have noticed that the hub parameter called `hub.mode` is referenced as `hub_mode` in the code. This is due to PHP's handling of underscores in HTTP requests. PHP automatically converts periods listed in the key of a request parameter to an underscore. So when a URL has a query string that looks like `?hello.world=hello`, the `hello.world` parameter is accessible as `$_REQUEST['hello_world']`.

Before we can test this out on a web server, we need to specify a URL to use as the topic URL for the feed. Luckily, PubSubHubbub is supported by an increasing number of sites around the Web. As I mentioned before, Google Reader supports publishing to a hub with the "Shared Items" feed. So let's grab a valid Atom URL from Google Reader.

Under the settings feed of your Google Reader account, you should see a tab labeled "Folders and Tags"; click on that and locate the "view public page" link for your shared items. Figure 2-5 shows the settings page interface.

Figure 2-5. Finding your "shared items" in Google Reader

Follow that link and it will take you to the public page for your shared items. Amongst other things, that page has a link to the Atom feed for that page. This Atom feed supports publishing to a hub, so note the URL to that feed (see Figure 2-6).

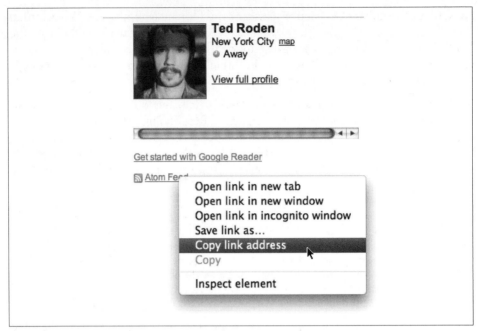

Figure 2-6. The Atom feed for Shared Items

Right-click on that URL and copy the link. That's the `$topic_url` we're going to request a subscription to. In the *index.php* file, change the line specifying the `$topic_url` to the URL you just copied from Google Reader:

```
$topic_url = "your-atom-url";
```

This file is already capable of subscribing to hubs, but in order to really test this out, we want to handle the publish requests as well as the subscribe requests. Adding this functionality is very straightforward. For this example, we're just going to add the shared items from Google Reader as rows to our `entries` table from the section on SUP feeds.

In order to accept the publish POST requests from the hub, we're going to need to add a bit more to our *index.php* file. Append this to the end of that file:

```
else if(@$HTTP_RAW_POST_DATA) { // publish

    include('db.php');
    $db = new db('syndication_test', 'db_user', 'db_pass');

    $xml = simplexml_load_string($HTTP_RAW_POST_DATA);

    foreach($xml->entry as $e) {

        $href = false;
        $links = $e->link;
        foreach($links as $l) {
```

```
            $attributes = $l->attributes();
            if(($attributes['rel'] == 'alternate') &&
               ($attributes['type'] == 'text/html'))
                 $href = $attributes['href'];
        }

        $entry_id = $db->insert_array('entries',
                                   array('url' => $href,
                                         'title' => $e->title,
                                         'atom_entry_id' => $e->id,
                                         'date_created' => $e->published,
                                         'date_updated' => $e->updated,
                                         )
                                   );
    }

}
```

As the protocol specifies, the publish part of the protocol has no special flags. The hub just POSTs the updated feed to the callback URL. To parse it out, we use PHP's "superglobal" variable called $HTTP_RAW_POST_DATA. When working with a POST request, this variable will contain the entire payload of that POST request.

The payload we receive from the hub is an Atom XML feed of the new and updated entries. To parse that XML we use SimpleXML again. For most of the XML entities, we can simply grab them from the SimpleXML object. However, the link back to the original post is a bit more tricky. In the Atom format, there can be multiple links for each entry. We loop the link entities to find the alternate location in text/html format.

To save the data, we're reusing our entries table in the syndication_test database. If you haven't already created that table, go ahead and do that now. We're using the same *db.php* file introduced in the first chapter.

Now that we have everything we need in our *index.php* file, we can copy this file along with *pubsubhubbub.php* to a public-facing server to test it out.

Once you have uploaded these files to a server, point your browser to the file with the query string ?request_subscription=1. This will request a subscription from the hub, which will start pinging this script whenever you share new items. Figure 2-7 shows the result of a subscription request.

Figure 2-7. Subscribing to the Shared Items feed

To test this out, head over to Google Reader and share some items. The hub should POST the new data within seconds of sharing the item. By tailing the logfile, you can watch each POST as it happens.

```
~ $ tail -f /path/to/apache-access.log
12.34.56.78 - - [01/Sep/2009:09:53:22 -0400] "POST /ch02/index.php HTTP/1.1" 200 -
12.34.56.78 - - [01/Sep/2009:10:06:29 -0400] "POST /ch02/index.php HTTP/1.1" 200 -
12.34.56.78 - - [01/Sep/2009:10:16:34 -0400] "POST /ch02/index.php HTTP/1.1" 200 -
...
```

Each POST to the server also means that at least one new row has been added to the `entries` table of our `syndication_test` database.

```
mysql> select id, url from  entries order by id;
+----+-------------------------------------------------------------------------+
| id | url                                                                     |
+----+-------------------------------------------------------------------------+
|  7 | http://www.beingfamous.com/?p=814                                       |
|  8 | http://feedproxy.google.com/~r/LouisgraycomLive/~3/zbknbXICU5k/...page.html |
|  9 | http://tedroden.enjoysthin.gs/226319?from=rss                           |
+----+-------------------------------------------------------------------------+
3 rows in set (0.00 sec)
```

We've now built a script capable of subscribing to and handling publish requests from various hubs around the Internet. If you've built web applications before, you should have no trouble adding these features to your code base. Supporting PubSubHubbub subscriptions is a very simple way to ensure that your users always have the newest content, which should keep them coming back more frequently. However, now that we're accepting pings, it's time to start publishing.

Publishing with PubSubHubbub

Much like SUP, publishing via PubSubHubbub is extremely easy. In fact, publishing with this protocol is the easiest part of the implementation. If your site wants to publish in realtime but doesn't need to aggregate content from other hubs, you can be up and running with PubSubHubbub in minutes.

First things first, you'll need to alert potential subscribers to the location of the hub you're using. You can use any hub you want, but if you don't have one already, a good choice is to use the reference implementation supplied by the PubSubHubbub project at *http://pubsubhubbub.appspot.com/*.

Alerting users to the location of the hub is as simple as inserting one extra line of code into your Atom feed. At the place your feeds are generated, you simply need to add the following line:

```
<link rel='hub' href='http://pubsubhubbub.appspot.com/' />
```

When a subscriber looks at this feed, this line tells the subscriber that we've handed off syndication duties to the hub. The subscriber would then request a subscription from that hub and receive its updates instantly from there rather than constantly pinging the Atom file. However, before a subscriber receives any realtime content, we need to ping the hub when it's time to publish content.

The class we built earlier will work perfectly for publishing content, but let's add one extra function to make the process much easier. Open the *pubsubhubbub.php* file created earlier and add the following code.

```php
public function publish($topic_url) {
    if (!isset($topic_url)) return; // nothing to do

    if (!preg_match("|^https?://|i", $topic_url))
        throw new Exception('Invalid URL: ' . $topic_url);

    $this->param('hub.url', $topic_url);
    $this->param('hub.mode', 'publish');

    return $this->_post();
}
```

This is an extremely simple publish function. First, we do a very basic check to ensure we have a valid topic URL. Then, we add the URL as a parameter along with setting hub.mode to publish. Actually pinging the hub is as simple as calling the _post method. Unlike the subscribe process, we don't have to wait for the hub to ping us back; at this point, we're done publishing. The only thing left is to integrate it with your code base.

On many sites, when you save new content to the database, the content just sits in the database waiting for a request. If the site receives a request for the Atom feed or for the actual website, the server will look in the database and return what it finds. Although that still works, we want any interested parties to get the content as soon as it's published. To do that, we need to add some new code that runs as we're saving content to the database. Let's say your site looks something like this:

```php
if($have_new_content) {
    $post = save_post();
    $post->regenerate_index();
    $post->regenerate_atom_feed();
}
```

To publish to a hub using the class we created earlier, you'd change the code to look like this:

```php
if($have_new_content) {
    $post = save_post();
    $post->regenerate_index();
    $post->regenerate_atom_feed();

    include_once("pubsubhubbub.php");
    $p = new PubSubHubbub("http://pubsubhubbub.appspot.com/");
    $p->publish($post->get_atom_feed_url());

}
```

Obviously this code makes some assumptions about your system that are probably false. However, you should be able to glance at those three lines of extra code and figure out how to insert it into your setup.

One of the design principles of this protocol is that it should be easily "bootstrappable." The protocol was designed to keep all of the complexity in the hub itself and allow subscribers and publishers to implement realtime syndication very easily. Of the guiding principles behind this protocol, the ability to easily get this up and running with existing systems is at the top of the list. The example code here is very simple, but it does some very powerful things, opening up the door for truly realtime syndication.

## CHAPTER 3

The Dynamic Homepage (Widgets in Pseudorealtime)

Moving past syndication, which primarily gives you benefits on the backend, this chapter looks at dipping our toes into realtime experiences on the frontend side of things. We're going to start with an example that uses standard pull requests to build a few dynamic widgets to add to any website or homepage. This example will show the power of realtime experiences and serve as a good example of why new technologies are needed to get the most out of modern browsers.

In a change from the concepts in previous chapters, all of these examples can be built using nothing more than HTML, a bit of CSS, and some JavaScript. Not only are they based in the web browser, but there is no server setup to get them up and running. With minor modifications you can easily put any and all of these widgets onto any webpage.

The Basic Widgets

The first widget that we're going to add to this homepage is a quick view into the trending topics on Twitter (*http://twitter.com*). This widget will do two things. First, it will use Twitter's API to find the trending topics on Twitter. Trending topics are keywords that are currently very active in tweets on Twitter. Then, we'll create a realtime feed of tweets that contain any of those keywords. So if "realtime" is a trending topic, this widget will display any tweet containing the word "realtime" as it comes in.

HTML

Since there is no server-side part to this example, you can put the files wherever it makes sense in your setup. We'll be creating two files total: one HTML file and a JavaScript file. The first step in building these widgets is to write some HTML that will contain them. Create a file called *index.html* and add the following code:

```html
<!DOCTYPE HTML>
<html>
  <head>
    <style>
      DIV { width: 300px; }
      DIV.widget { display: inline-table; }
      DIV.title {
          background-color: #ccc;
          font-weight: bold;
          padding-top: 3px;
          padding-bottom: 3px;
          text-align: center;
      }
      DIV.line {
          display: block;
          overflow: hidden;
          width: 100%;
          border-bottom: solid 1px #ddd;
      }
      DIV.content { overflow: auto; height: 450px; }
      IMG.profile_image { max-width: 48px; max-height: 48px; }
    </style>
  </head>
  <body>

    <div class="widget"><!-- The Trending on Twitter widget -->
      <div class="title" id="trending-title">Trending</div>
      <div class="content" id="trending-on-twitter"></div>
    </div>

    <div class="widget"><!-- The FriendFeed widget -->
      <div class="title" id="friendfeed-title">FriendFeed Updates</div>
      <div class="content" id="friendfeed-updates"></div>
    </div>

    <div class="widget"><!-- The Widget showing live images posted on twitter -->
      <div class="title" id="images-title">Live Images</div>
      <div class="content" id="images-on-twitter"></div>
    </div>

    <script type="text/javascript" src="homepage.js"></script>
  </body>
</html>
```

The first thing this file does is define a number of CSS style entries. These take care of the look and the layout of the elements we'll be building programmatically through JavaScript. These widgets will have a simple appearance, and I've left a lot of room for improvement, but the basic layout is that each widget has some basic fixed dimensions, a title pane, and a line for each realtime update.

The basic shell of each widget is created in the markup of the HTML. This example will create three widgets that can be placed on any page. The first widget will contain a steady stream of tweets that are trending on Twitter (*http://twitter.com*). The second widget is a realtime window into updates that are happening on FriendFeed (*http://friendfeed.com*). Finally, the last widget will show a view of the images that are being posted onto Twitter.

Each widget has a `DIV` for the title of the widget in addition to a place to put the content of each widget. The `id` attributes are important because the JavaScript for this example references these elements by `id`.

Setting Up the JavaScript

For this example, we rely on server-side APIs from a few different services, but we don't actually have to create any ourselves. In this example, the entire application runs on the client side, in the browser.

Initialize

All of the work in this example is done in JavaScript. To do this work, we'll build a simple JavaScript object that can keep track of all the moving parts. In the same directory as *index.html*, create a file called *homepage.js* and add the following code:

```
var Home = {
    trends: [],              // what is trending on twitter?
    twitter_since_id: 0,     // keep track of the twitter entries we've seen
    live_images_since_id: 0, // keep track of the twitter images we've seen
    friendfeed_entries: []   // keep track of the FF entries we've seen
};

// Get everything started
Home.init = function() {
    // load the trending topics from twitter
    Home.appendJS('http://search.twitter.com/trends.json?callback=Home.catchTrends');
};

// a simple method to append JS files to the DOM
Home.appendJS = function(url) {
    url += "&" + Math.random(); // ensure the browser doesn't cache this
    var scr = document.createElement('script');
    scr.setAttribute('src', url);
    scr.setAttribute('type', 'text/javascript');
    document.getElementsByTagName('head').item(0).appendChild(scr);
};
```

The `Home` object will contain all the logic for this application. The first thing we do is initialize some variables that we'll be using in the code. Next, we define an `init` method that will be used to run any initial functions and start the script in general. Although this method will grow along with the functionality of this application, at the moment it has only one call. The `Home.init` method makes a call to `Home.appendJS` to a Twitter search (*http://search.twitter.com/*) URL. This URL will return a list of the currently trending topics across Twitter, which will be used in the first widget to get a feed of tweets about those topics. In addition, the standard Twitter search URL, we add a callback parameter to the URL. When this request returns from the server, the data will be passed to this callback method.

The `Home.appendJS` method appends a new `script` element to the DOM. It takes in a URL parameter and adds a random number to the end. Simply adding a random number to the end of the URL won't have any effect on most JavaScript includes, but it does ensure that every request has a different URL. This will ensure that the browser doesn't automatically return cached content for the request. This URL is then used as the `src` for the `script`. This method doesn't do anything with the output of the included script; it's assumed that each included file can execute any code that is needed. In this case, all of the scripts we've included are JSONP requests that execute callback functions once the content is fully loaded.

A word about JSONP

The widgets that we are building will not use any external JavaScript libraries or even Ajax-style XMLHttpRequest (XHR) calls. To load data from the external APIs, this example uses JSONP or JSON with padding to make our requests. JSONP is a super simple method of fetching JSON data from remote servers. Initially introduced by Bob Ippolito (*http://bob.pythonmac.org/archives/2005/12/05/remote-json-jsonp/*), it has been implemented by many APIs when making JSON-based requests. Using JSONP allows you to essentially make API requests to remote servers by simply adding new JavaScript includes to the DOM, which can be done programmatically.

For example, if you were making an API request for a list of videos from Vimeo (*http://vimeo.com*) in JSON format, the URL for the JSON format would be `http://vimeo.com/api/v2/ted/videos.json` and the output would look something like this:

```
[{
    {"id":"7466620","title":"Party Time", "url":"http:\/\/vimeo.com\/7466620"},
    {"id":"6955666","title":"Speaking","url":"http:\/\/vimeo.com\/6955666"}
    ...
}]
```

That gives you the data you requested, but there is no simple way to use the data if you are requesting the URL via a `<script>` tag. With JSONP, most APIs allow you to specify a callback URL along with the API request, so that when you include the URL, you're able to specify a JavaScript callback function and the whole response will be passed as a parameter to that function. On Vimeo, that same data could be accessed by requesting `http://vimeo.com/api/v2/ted/videos.json?callback=parseVideos`, which would give you a response similar to the following:

```
parseVideos([{
    {"id":"7466620","title":"Party Time", "url":"http:\/\/vimeo.com\/7466620"},
    {"id":"6955666","title":"Speaking","url":"http:\/\/vimeo.com\/6955666"}
    ...
}]);
```

When the browser sees this, it treats it as any other bit of JavaScript code and executes it immediately. This allows us to use the data as it comes in from external sources by including the API requests as JavaScript includes and then waiting for our callback functions to be executed.

Catching the trends

When the Home object was initialized, we ran Home.appendJS to fetch the currently trending topics from Twitter. That request specified a callback method called Home.catchTrends. Add that method to the file:

```
Home.catchTrends = function(data) {
    // save the name of the trends to the local trends array
    for(var i = 0; i < data.trends.length; ++i)
        Home.trends.push(data.trends[i].name);

    // now that we know the trends, start grabbing tweets with those terms
    Home.getTrendingTweets();
};
```

When http://search.twitter.com/trends.json is finished loading, Home.catchTrends will be executed and the parameter will be a JSON object that contains an array of trend objects from Twitter. These objects have two fields, name and url. This method only needs to know the name of the trends, so it loops through all of the trends and saves each name to the Home.trends array that was created in Home.init.

Loading the trends themselves is only part of this widget; the main goal is to show a realtime feed of tweets that are talking about these trends. In order to do that, we need to search Twitter for those trends. So now that all of the trends are saved to the Home.trends array, it's time to start gathering the tweets themselves.

```
Home.getTrendingTweets = function() {

    // setup the base url
    var url = 'http://search.twitter.com/search.json?' +
                'callback=Home.catchTweets';

    // randomize the trends array
    Home.trends = Home.trends.sort(function() {
                                return (Math.round(Math.random()) - 0.5);
                            });

    // search on five trending topics
    url += '&q=' + encodeURIComponent(Home.trends.slice(0,5).join(" OR "));
```

```
        // only since the last time we searched.
        url += "&since_id=" + Home.twitter_since_id;

        Home.appendJS(url);

        // wait for a few seconds and then run this method again
        setTimeout(Home.getTrendingTweets, 7000);
    };
```

To search for individual tweets, this method uses a different URL endpoint of the Twitter search API than it did to list the currently trending topics. We'll be using the same `Home.appendJS` method to make the request, so as we set up the base `url`, we specify the callback function name that we'll be using later.

This method will actually search for individual tweets, so we need to set up a search query and add it to the URL. We're only interested in seeing the tweets that are currently trending, so we can just use our trending array. However, much like posting updates to Twitter, the full length of the search criteria can be no more than 140 characters in length. To ensure we're using less characters than that, this method uses five random trends each time it is called instead of searching for all of them. To do that, this method rearranges the `Home.trends` array into a random order every time it's called.

The search API takes a number of parameters, but this method only needs to provide two of them. The first, and most important, parameter is the query string itself. We concatenate the first five of the newly randomized trends array onto the URL separating each one with the boolean `OR` keyword. These trends are encoded via JavaScript's `encodeURIComponent` function.

Since we're going to be calling this method over and over again, we only want to grab tweets that we have not yet seen. To make this easier, Twitter provides a parameter called `since_id`. When supplied, Twitter will respond only with tweets that have been created since the specified `id`.

Once we run `Home.appendJS`, the code is then waiting for a callback request to the `Home.catchTweets` method. While we wait, we run `setTimeout` in order to run this same method again. This will create a loop that runs as long as the page is loaded. This method will keep running and calling itself over and over again.

Catching the tweets

When running, the application is looping through `Home.getTrendingTweets`, which is including new JavaScript files, each one with a callback method that is executed when finished loading. That method was specified as `Home.catchTweets` and its job is to accept the tweets and update the user interface of the widget. Add the following code to *homepage.js*:

```
    Home.catchTweets = function(data) {

        // loop through the tweets
        for(var i = data.results.length - 1; i > -1; --i) {
```

```
        var tweet = data.results[i];

        // add the tweet to the UI
        Home.addLine('trending-on-twitter', { 'username': tweet.from_user,
                                              'html': tweet.text,
                                              'profile_image':
                                                  tweet.profile_image_url
                                            });
    }

    if(data.results.length)
        Home.updateTitle('trending-title', data.results.length);

    // cache the max_id so we know which tweets we've seen
    Home.twitter_since_id = data.max_id;
};
```

When this callback method is called, its parameter is a data object that contains an array of tweets matching the search criteria. Each object contains the `text` of the tweet along with other information such as the username and even the language of the tweet. As this method loops through each of the tweets, it calls a method called `Home.add Line`, which will add the tweet to the interface.

In addition to adding each individual tweet to the widget, it's also a good idea to inform the user of how many tweets were just added. To do that, we're going to use a method called `Home.updateTitle` that can be used by all of the widgets, not just the trending widget. That method will update the title pane of the widget to display "X new results." In calling that method we need to provide only the `id` of the `div` and the amount of new updates.

Back in the method `Home.getTrendingTweets`, we use the variable `Home.twitter_since_id` to limit the tweets in our request to tweets that we haven't yet seen. We could keep track of each variable ID that we've seen and calculate the highest number, but Twitter makes it easy by providing `max_id` with each result set. We can use that `max_id` variable to populate `Home.twitter_since_id`.

Displaying the updates

In the callback function `Home.catchTweets`, we're looping through all of the tweets and calling `Home.addLine` to display each one in the widget. This method does not use external JavaScript libraries to manipulate the DOM; instead it uses the standard DOM manipulation functions provided by the browser. We could have saved some lines of code using one of these libraries, but using the standard methods ensures that these widgets can easily be integrated into existing websites without causing JavaScript conflicts with existing frameworks. Add the following code for the ability to add updates to the widgets:

```
Home.addLine = function(targetDivId, data) {
    var doc = document;
```

```
    // create a div and give it the line class
    var line = doc.createElement('div');
    line.setAttribute('class', 'line');

    // if data contains a profile image, add it to the line div
    if('profile_image' in data) {
        var img = doc.createElement('img');
        img.setAttribute('align', 'right');
        img.setAttribute('class', 'profile_image');
        img.setAttribute('src', data.profile_image);
        line.appendChild(img);
    }

    // create a P tag to hold the content
    var p = doc.createElement('p');
    p.innerHTML = "";

    // if there is a username, show it
    if('username' in data)
        p.innerHTML += '<strong>' + data.username + "</strong>: ";

    // if there is html content, show that
    if('html' in data) {
        p.innerHTML += data.html;
    }


    // add the p to the line div
    line.appendChild(p);

    // add the line onto the widget itself
    var targetDiv = doc.getElementById(targetDivId);
    // prepend it to the top of the widget
    targetDiv.insertBefore(line, targetDiv.firstChild);

    // clean up the DOM
    var dom_limit = 60;
    var elements = targetDiv.getElementsByClassName('line');
    for(var i = elements.length - 1; i >= dom_limit; --i)
        targetDiv.removeChild(elements[i]);

};
```

This method will end up being used by all of the widgets that we're building, so it has to be generic enough to be used for a few different purposes. Rather than give this method tons of optional parameters, this makes do with only two. The first parameter is the id of the div in which to append the content. The second parameter is a JavaScript object containing any of the fields that this method may use:

profile_image
    The URL to a profile image or avatar to show with this line.

---

46 | Chapter 3: The Dynamic Homepage (Widgets in Pseudorealtime)

username

> If supplied, this method will show the username in bold before the actual update.

html

> This is the actual content of the update. This may be a line of text, an image, or any combination of HTML elements.

As we move through this method, we test the `data` object for these variables and create the interface for each piece. After creating the main `div` element, `line`, we check the object to see whether we should add a profile image. Adding that is as simple as creating an image element with the right attributes and appending it to the `line` element. Then, we create the paragraph element, which will be used to display the username and HTML if they are provided, and append it to the `line`. Once we've built the entire line, we just prepend it to the top of the widget. This will display the tweets in reverse chronological order, with each new update being displayed at the top.

This method is called from inside a loop in the `Home.catchTweets` method, which runs in a loop as well. At the end of every time through that method, it sets a timeout to call itself again. After a few times through these loops, this `Home.addLine` method could potentially add a huge number of elements to the DOM in no time at all. This would take up quite a bit of RAM and turn a realtime experience into a sluggish nightmare. To ensure that things don't get out of hand, we clean up the DOM each time through this method. The next bit of code loops through elements with a CSS class named `line` and removes all but the most recently added.

After displaying the updates themselves, the widget should make it clear exactly how many new updates have been added. To do that, the `Home.catchTweets` method calls `Home.updateTitle`. Add it to your *homepage.js* file:

```
Home.updateTitle = function(divId, number) {
    var titleDiv = document.getElementById(divId);

    // update and highlight the title
    titleDiv.innerHTML += ": " + number + " new results";

    // Wait a beat and then return the title to the way it was
    setTimeout(function() {
                titleDiv.innerHTML = titleDiv.innerHTML.replace(/\:.+/, '');
            }, 1500);

    // Breifly highlight the title, turning it yellow and fading it back
    var highlightLevel = 1;

    // each time this method is called, it slightly changes the color of the title
    var highlightStep = function () {
        var hex = highlightLevel.toString(16);
        titleDiv.style.backgroundColor = '#cccc' + hex + hex;

        // if we're not already light grey (12), increase the highlightLevel
        // and run this method again
        if (highlightLevel < 12) { // 12 == "c" in base16 (hex)
```

```
        highlightLevel++;
        setTimeout(highlightStep, 50);
    }
};

// start highlighting
highlightStep();
};
```

This method will be used by all of the widgets, but it doesn't have a very complicated job to do, so the parameters are totally simple. The first parameter is the `div` of the title pane for the widget, and the second parameter is the number of new updates.

Right at the start, this method updates the `titleDiv` and appends a string to reflect the number of new updates. Then it sets up a timeout to undo the changes. This `replace` statement searches for a colon and replaces it and everything after it with an empty string. This process will update the title from something like "Trending," change it to "Trending: 5 new results," and then finally change it back to "Trending" after a short delay.

To really call attention to the change, this method also highlights the title pane, changing the background color to yellow. Rather than blinking back light gray, it steps through the colors, providing a smooth transition from yellow back to light gray. This section is totally optional; feel free to leave it out or change the colors and timing of the fade.

We now have all the code to run the widget, but with one important exception: nothing ever gets the code started. To initialize everything, add the following code to the bottom of *homepage.js*:

```
// Get everything started.
Home.init();
```

At this point, the trending code widget should be fully operational. Since there is no server-side code to this, you can simply open *index.html* in your web browser to see the widget in action. It should look something similar to Figure 3-1.

FriendFeed in Realtime

FriendFeed (*http://friendfeed.com*) is a web service that aggregates updates from many different social media sites, social networking sites, and plain old blogs. Not long after the site launched, the developers started introducing realtime features into the site. SUP, as described in the previous chapter, was developed for their realtime needs. Although the site has since been purchased by Facebook (*http://facebook.com*), it still has an active community and a full-featured API that will work well for creating a realtime widget.

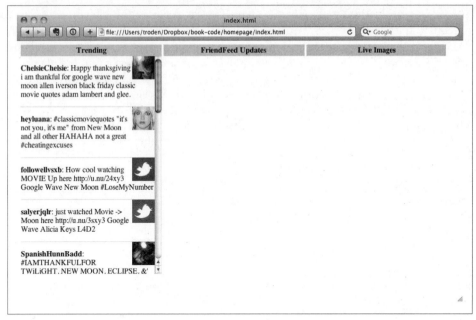

Figure 3-1. The trending widget in action

In building the trending widget, we set up the basic HTML structure along with many of the convenience methods needed to create a basic widget for this application. So to build the FriendFeed widget, we just need to write the code that talks to the server, and we can pass off much of the work to the existing code. To get everything started, modify the Home.init method to look like the following code:

```
// Get everything started
Home.init = function() {
    // load the trending topics from twitter
    Home.appendJS('http://search.twitter.com/trends.json?callback=Home.catchTrends');

    // Start getting updates from friendfeed
    Home.getFriendFeedUpdates();
};
```

When everything gets started via the Home.init method, the FriendFeed code will get started as well as the trending code. Add that method as well:

```
Home.getFriendFeedUpdates = function() {
    // get updates from friends of "scobleizer"
    var url = "http://friendfeed-api.com/v2/feed/scobleizer/friends?" +
            "callback=Home.catchFriendFeedUpdates";
    Home.appendJS(url);

    // start a loop by calling this mehtod again in 5 seconds
    setTimeout(Home.getFriendFeedUpdates, 5000);
};
```

This is a simple method with only two steps. First, it makes an API. Then, it sets up a timeout to start doing it again. You may notice one peculiarity with the URL to the API, particularly that we're requesting data for a user named scobleizer. You can certainly use any username for this URL; I picked this user because of the sheer number of people he follows. This is the username of Robert Scoble (*http://scobleizer.com/*), a well-known blogger. At the time of this writing, he was subscribed to 28,066 friends on FriendFeed, which means his feed always has new content in it. This makes for a much more compelling demonstration of the FriendFeed API for this realtime widget.

Just like the Twitter API, the FriendFeed API (*http://friendfeed.com/api/*) offers output in JSONP format and allows you to specify the callback function with a parameter named callback. In this case, the callback is to the method Home.catchFriendFeed Updates, which does exactly what it sounds like:

```
Home.catchFriendFeedUpdates = function(data) {

    // keep track of the amount of upates we're adding
    var cnt = 0;

    // loop through the friendfeed updates
    for(var i = data.entries.length - 1; i > -1; --i) {
        var entry = data.entries[i];

        // check to see if we've seen this update already
        if(Home.friendfeed_entries.indexOf(entry.id) == -1) {
            // add it to the page
            Home.friendfeed_entries.push(entry.id);
            Home.addLine('friendfeed-updates', { 'username': entry.from.name,
                                                 'html': entry.body
                                               });
            cnt++;
        }
    }

    // update the title
    if(cnt)
        Home.updateTitle('friendfeed-title', cnt);

};
```

This method should look fairly similar to method Home.catchTweets, which we created earlier. Both the Twitter API and the FriendFeed API respond with very similar formats. Where this method differs from Home.catchTweets, it's only to accommodate those differences. One of the main differences between the APIs is that FriendFeed does not accept a since_id parameter. So this method has to look at each result manually to ensure we haven't seen it before. To do this, we keep a cache of the entries we've seen and check against that. If we haven't seen a particular update, it gets inserted into the cache. Each new update gets added to the widget using the Home.addLine method.

It may seem like overkill to cache each of the IDs that we receive from the API and check against them each time through the loop. However, we can't simply check the last ID that we receive from FriendFeed and then grab everything after that on the next time through. FriendFeed updates get reinserted and reordered when another user comments or performs any other action on the update. If we stopped adding lines after finding one that we've seen, we'd end up missing a good deal of updates. This method should clear out old entries after a certain point instead of caching them indefinitely, but that is left as an exercise for the reader.

As we loop through each entry, we increment a counter variable. This variable is used to keep track of exactly how many updates are added to the widget. Once the loop is finished, we update the title of the widget with the new count using the `Home.update Title` method.

Once again, we have a finished widget. Open up *index.html* in your browser to check the results. It should resemble Figure 3-2.

Figure 3-2. The Twitter trending and FriendFeed widget running

Live Images

Until now, the widgets primarily show text updates in realtime. So in this widget we're going to limit it to a realtime view of images that are streaming into Twitter at any given moment. To get this bit started, once again we'll need to modify the `Home.init` method. Adjust yours to look like the following:

```
// Get everything started
Home.init = function() {
    // load the trending topics from twitter
    Home.appendJS('http://search.twitter.com/trends.json?callback=Home.catchTrends');
```

```
// Start getting updates from friendfeed
Home.getFriendFeedUpdates();

// Start grabbing the images
Home.getLiveImages();
};
```

Like the existing code in this method, this part just initializes the code for the live trending widget. The `Home.getLiveImages` method just starts searching Twitter for tweets with images:

```
Home.getLiveImages = function() {
    // search twitter for popular image hosting URLs
    var url = 'http://search.twitter.com/search.json?' +
              'callback=Home.catchLiveImages&q=yfrog.com+OR+twitpic.com';
    url += "&since_id=" + Home.live_images_since_id;
    Home.appendJS(url);

    // set a timeout to run this method again
    setTimeout(Home.getLiveImages, 7000);
};
```

Much like `Home.getTrendingTweets` and `Home.getFriendFeedUpdates`, this method just starts a loop to make the same API request. To search for images on Twitter, we'll simply search for tweets containing the domains of well-known image posting services. Twitpic (*http://twitpic.com*) and yfrog (*http://yfrog.com*) are both services that are commonly used by Twitter users to host images that are then posted on Twitter. This code makes the reasonably safe assumption that any tweet containing these URLs will contain an image.

This uses the same Twitter search API that was used for the Trending Tweets widget. Rather than expanding the `Home.catchTweets` callback method used for that widget, this one specifies a new one called `Home.catchLiveImages`. Add that method to your code:

```
Home.catchLiveImages = function(data) {

    // setup the regexp to be used in the loop
    var image_regexp = new RegExp("http://(yfrog\.com|twitpic\.com)/([0-9a-zA-Z]+)");

    // loop through all the tweets returned by Home.getLiveImages
    for(var i = data.results.length - 1; i > -1; --i) {
        var tweet = data.results[i];

        // run the regular expression on the tweet
        var matches = image_regexp.exec(tweet.text);

        if(matches) {
            // yfrog.com or twitpic.com
            var domain = matches[1];
            // the image ID to be used in the URL
            var image_id = matches[2];

            // setup the thumbnail URL for the different services
            var image_url = '';
```

```
        if (domain == 'yfrog.com')
            image_url = 'http://yfrog.com/' + image_id + '.th.jpg';
        if (domain == 'twitpic.com')
            image_url = 'http://twitpic.com/show/thumb/' + image_id;

        // generate an HTML string to show in the widget
        var image_str = '<a target="_blank" href="' + matches[0] + '">' +
                            '<img src="' + image_url + '" />'+
                            '</a>';

        // show the image (leave out the username and profile icon)
        Home.addLine('images-on-twitter', { 'html': image_str });
    }
}

if(data.results.length)
    Home.updateTitle('images-title', data.results.length);

Home.live_images_since_id = data.max_id;

};
```

The main job of this method is too inspect each tweet that it receives, search for an image in the text, determine the thumbnail URL for that image, and show it in the widget. Luckily, aside from the domain, the linked URLs from each of the services will look nearly identical; both URLs appear in the format of `http://image-service.com/ImageID`. Because the URL format is the same for each service, we can use the same regular expression to search for both types of images. The first thing this code does is set up `image_regexp` to match for these types of URLs.

After creating the regular expression object, it's time to start looping through the tweets. The regular expression is executed against the text of the tweet, and if matches are found, it's time to determine which image service was used to host the image. `matches` contains an array of the distinct parts of the regular expression. The first element in the `matches` array is the entire string that matched against our query. The second element in the array, `matches[1]`, contains the domain, and `matches[2]` contains the ID of the image.

Once we have those values, it's easy to construct the final URL to the thumbnail for each service. The URLs to the profile page of each service are different, and the URL to the thumbnails are slightly different. To link to the thumbnail image on yfrog, the format is `http://yfrog.com/ImageID.th.jpg`. On Twitpic, the thumbnail URL is constructed with the following pattern: `http://twitpic.com/show/thumb/ImageID`.

Next, we build some simple HTML to show the image and link to the original. This widget isn't going to show the text of the tweet, or even the profile image of the user who posted it. We're mostly interested in seeing a live stream of images. So the only data passed to the `Home.addLine` method is the HTML of the image itself. Finally, we cache the `since_id` so that the `Home.getLiveImages` method can request only the newest images.

With this widget finished, all of the widgets should be complete. Open your browser to *index.html* to see all of the widgets in action. Figure 3-3 should resemble the finished product.

 The Live Images widget can be entertaining and addictive to watch, but keep in mind this is an unfiltered view of images that are posted to Twitter. Occasionally this widget may contain images that are not safe for work.

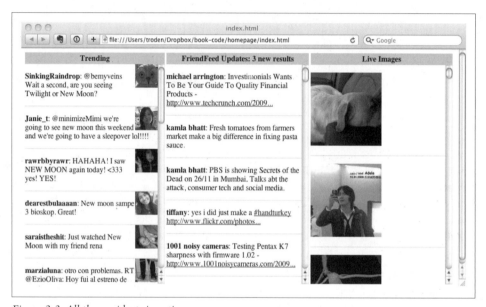

Figure 3-3. All three widgets in action

It Was All a Setup!

These examples used a simple Ajax-like implementation to constantly ping the server for new updates. In this case, it used the best tool for the job to provide constant updates from various places around the Web. However, watching this example come together, you've probably noticed a couple of things.

The first problem with this approach is that although content may be updated quickly, it would be a stretch to call this a "realtime" user experience. All we're doing here is checking for new updates, displaying the updates, waiting for a while, and then repeating the process all over again. What happens when an update is ready on the server while our script it just waiting in the timeout loop? No matter how fast we speed up that timeout, there is still going to be a delay. Figure 3-4 shows the messages queuing up while our code waits in the timeout loop.

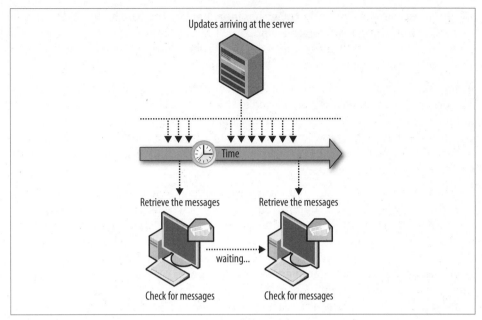

Figure 3-4. Not realtime: new messages queue up on the server instead of arriving at the client

Another problem with this approach is that it just cannot scale. In order to get more feeds on the page, we added more HTTP requests. In order to get updates faster, we would need to add more HTTP requests. The script now runs three HTTP requests per user per timeout, and adding a second user would double that. Every user who connects would increase amount of HTTP requests needed on the server side by three. It gets more interesting as you start to add more users.

This whole exercise also makes another big assumption: that there will be data on the server. You could quite possibly run into the situation where you have thousands of users pinging the server every few seconds for no reason at all. If there is no data on the server, there is no reason to make that transaction. However, with the old technologies, that is pretty much the only option.

The Old Versus the New

Since its inception, the Web has been powered by technologies that have gone relatively unchanged. The specifics of the server software have slowly been updated, but the fundamentals are the same. The major servers, such as Apache's httpd server (*http:// httpd.apache.org*), were designed to provide HTTP services as they were initially envisioned: to serve documents across the Internet.

However, as a perfect storm of technology changes hit, it changed the way the Web was being used. Connectivity is faster and more reliable than ever before. Client-side technologies such as JavaScript are powerful enough to run sophisticated applications while browser support for the language has more or less kept up. This has led to people using HTTP in ways it was never intended. HTTP, which was initially designed as a protocol for serving linked documents, has morphed into the de facto protocol for almost all network applications.

As the Web has started to move from a document-serving platform to a message-serving platform, the old web servers have started to show their age. Old web servers were built to accept a request, serve the request, and close the connection as quickly as possible. Older servers have a fairly low limit to maximum number of connections they can have open at any one point in time. Closing connections as quickly as possible frees up space for more connections.

So new web servers are being built from the ground up to handle the new ways developers are using HTTP. To support long polling, new servers are being designed to handle much larger numbers of simultaneous connections, allowing them to stay connected for extended periods of time. New software stacks are being built to handle message routing between hundreds of concurrently connected users. The rest of this book deals with these new paradigms and new types of technologies. Creating applications with these new technologies is not necessarily more difficult, just different. If you've made it this far, both as a reader and a developer, you'll be just fine.

## CHAPTER 4

River of Content

The previous chapter talked about dynamically updating your home page to show the latest updates long after the page had been loaded. The examples used many of the same technologies most web developers have used for years. Although this works well for some things, it has limitations that quickly become clear. If you want to give your users a truly realtime experience in the web browser, you need to push content to them. In this chapter, I'll show you how to build a simple river of content feed. The most obvious use for this would be for a truly realtime live blog application.

During big events, many blogs will provide a link to a separate page where they will "liveblog" the whole thing. They'll post quick text updates, "this new product could save the company, too bad it doesn't support bluetooth." They'll also post images as quickly as they can take them. However, the pages serving these "live" blogs tend to be nothing more than a regular web page that automatically refreshes every 30 seconds. Users will often refresh their browser by hand to ensure they're seeing the latest content. Getting your content to users faster, even if it's just a couple of seconds, can mean the difference between users staying on your site all day and leaving as soon as they feel they're getting old news.

Using a liveblog as an example, I'll show you how to build a river of content that pushes out updates as soon as they are available. This will help keep users from clicking away, save wear and tear on your server, and most importantly, it's not that hard to build.

A Crash Course in Server Push

There are several forms of server push technology. This idea is not new and has existed in several different forms throughout the years. However, these days when people talk about server push technologies, they tend to refer to a technology called long polling.

Long Polling

Long polling is a method of server push technology that cleverly uses traditional HTTP requests to create and maintain a connection to the server, allowing the server to push data as it becomes available. In a standard HTTP request, when the browser requests data, the server will respond immediately, regardless of whether any new data is available (see Figure 4-1). Using long polling, the browser makes a request to the server and if no data is available, the server keeps the connection open, waiting until new data is available. If the connection breaks, the browser reconnects and keeps waiting. When data does become available, the server responds, closes the connection, and the whole process is repeated (see Figure 4-2).

Technically, there is no difference between this kind of request and standard pull requests. The difference, and advantage, is in the implementation. Without long polling, the client connects and checks for data; if there is none, the client disconnects and sleeps for 10 seconds before reconnecting again. With long polling, when the client connects and there is no data available, it will just hang on until data arrives. So if data arrives five seconds into the request, the client accepts the data and shows it to the user. The normal request wouldn't see the new data until its timer was up and it reconnected again several seconds later.

This method of serving requests opens up a lot of doors to what is possible in a web application, but it also complicates matters immensely.

For example, on an application where users can send messages to one another, checking for new messages has always been a rather painless affair. When the browser requests new messages for Peter, the server checks and has no messages. The same transaction is made again a few seconds later, and the server has a message for Peter.

However, in long polling, when Peter connects that first time, he never disconnects. So when Andrew sends him a new message, that message must be routed to Peter's existing connection. Where previously the message would be stored in a database and retrieved on Peter's next connection, now it must be routed immediately.

This routing and delivery of these messages to clients that are already connected is a very complicated problem. Thankfully, it's already been solved by a number of groups. Amongst others, the Dojo Foundation (*http://www.dojofoundation.org*) has developed a solution in the form of the Cometd server and the Bayeux protocol.

The Bayeux Protocol

At its heart, Bayeux is a messaging protocol. Messages (or events, as they're sometimes called) can be sent from the server to the client (and vice versa) as well as from one client to another after a trip through the server. It's a complicated protocol solving a complicated problem, but for both the scope of this book and most use cases, the details are not that important.

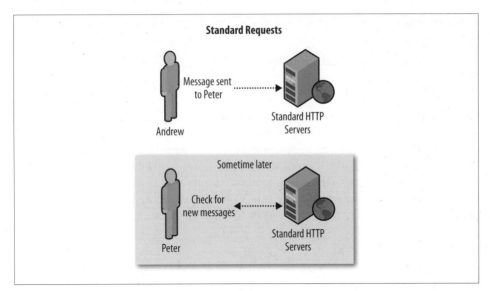

Figure 4-1. Standard HTTP message delivery

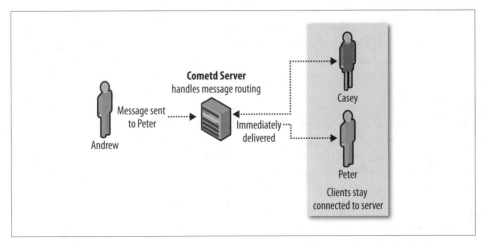

Figure 4-2. Cometd HTTP message delivery

Aside from the handshakes and housekeeping involved, the protocol describes a system that actually is quite simple for day-to-day uses. A client subscribes to a channel by name, which tends to be something like /foo, /foo/bar, or /chat. Channel globbing is also supported, so a user can subscribe to /foo/**, which would include channels such as /foo, /foo/bar, and /foo/zab.

Messages are then sent to the different named channels. For example, a server will send a message to /foo/bar and any client that has subscribed to that channel will receive the message. Clients can also send messages to specific channels and, assuming the server passes them along, these messages will be published to any other clients subscribed to that channel.

Channel names that start with /meta are reserved for protocol use. These channels allow the client and server to handle tasks such as figuring out which client is which and protocol actions such as connecting and disconnecting.

One of the fields often sent along with these meta requests is an advice statement. This is a message from the server to the client about how the client should act. This allows the server to tell clients at which interval they should reconnect to the server after disconnecting. It can also tell them which operation to perform when reconnecting. The server commonly tells the client to retry the same connection after the standard server timeout, but it may request that the client retries the handshake process all together, or the server may tell the client not to reconnect at all.

```
"advice": {
    "reconnect": "retry",
    "interval": 0,
    "timeout": 120000
}
```

The protocol specifies a number of other interesting things that are outside the scope of this book. I encourage you to find out more about the protocol and how to leverage it for more advanced applications, but you don't actually need to worry about how it works underneath the hood during your day-to-day coding. Most client and server libraries, including the ones listed in this text, handle the vast majority of these details.

Cometd

The Dojo Foundation started this project in order to provide implementations of the Bayeux protocol in several different languages. At the time of this writing, only the JavaScript and Java implementations are designated as stable. There are also implementations in Python, Perl, and several other languages that are in varying stages of beta.

The Java version includes both a client and a server in the form of the org.cometd package. This package has already been bundled with the Jetty web server and, no doubt, other Java servers will implement this as well.

Setting Up Your Cometd Environment

The Java implementation of Cometd comes as a completely self-contained web server and associated bundled libraries. The web serving is done by an embedded version of Jetty, which is an incredibly scalable Java-based web server. Get the latest version from *http://cometdproject.dojotoolkit.org/* and unzip it into any place on your computer. It comes ready to run and, for development purposes, there is nothing to install on your computer.

There are two different versions you can download, a source-only version and another with the Java code fully compiled. Both downloads provide implementations in all of the supported programming languages.

The compiled version is a much bigger download than the source-only version, but it provides everything you need in an easy bundle that is read to run.

Once Cometd has been downloaded and unzipped, you'll notice that there are a lot of files in there for the different language implementations. For now, we're mainly interested in the *cometd-java* and *cometd-demo* directories.

Depending on your system, you may need to install some supporting libraries before running the server. Thankfully, installing these libraries is dead simple, and so is handling the build process. To handle all of these project management tasks, we're going to use a build tool called Maven (*http://maven.apache.org/*). Maven is a project management tool that handles everything from building an application and creating documentation, to downloading dependencies. To use it, open your terminal window and navigate to your recently unzipped directory. Run the following command, which will take some time and print out a lot of information:

```
~ cometd $ mvn
[INFO] Scanning for projects...
[INFO] Reactor build order:
[INFO]   Cometd :: Java
...
```

With this command, Maven will look at the *pom.xml* file and do a number of different things. Maven is project management tool for software and the *pom.xml* file is the most basic unit of work in Maven, sort of like a Makefile. The main reason we're using it here is its ability to compile our software project. However, in addition to compiling any updated source files, it will run some unit tests, generate documentation, and install any additional Java libraries needed by your system.

Included in the distribution are a couple of examples of what this package can do. To run those, we're going to use Maven again. This time we're going to give it specific instructions to run the Jetty server. In the same *cometd-demo* directory, run the following command:

```
~ cometd-demo $ mvn jetty:run
```

This will start up the Jetty server and start serving some example programs. Point your browser to *http://127.0.0.1:8080/* and have a look at the examples (see Figure 4-3).

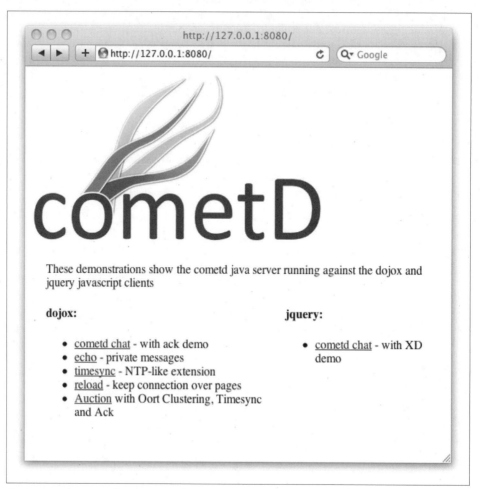

Figure 4-3. The Cometd Demo page

Putting Everything in Its Place

After looking around at the examples and glancing at the directory structure of Cometd, you've probably noticed a couple of things. There are a lot of files in that package, and there is no clear place to put your code. The entire package is geared toward showing off a couple of examples, not building real applications. So the first thing I recommend is to get some of those files out of the way and put everything we need into one self-contained directory. Amongst other things, this will allow us to build the distributable WAR file much easier.

What we're really after is a cleaned-up version of the *cometd-java* directory. That's going to require a couple of very easy tasks. First of all, we need to tell the project to use the Jetty plug-in. By default, this plug-in is included up the chain a little bit, but since we're getting rid of the extra folders, we need to do it here.

This may look like a lot of work, and paradigm shifts take a bit of server-side configuration, but it's just a bit of housekeeping. I've taken the liberty of repackaging the files to ease the development process. Feel free to save some time and download that version from *http://therealti mebook.com*. Once you do that, you can skip ahead to the next section.

First, we're going to create an directory to house our realtime code. We'll make two different directory trees following the standard Java servlet conventions. From inside the *cometd-java* directory, run the following commands to create the directory structure we'll use:

```
~ cometd-java $ mkdir -p apps/src/main/java/com/tedroden/realtime
~ cometd-java $ cp examples/pom.xml apps/pom.xml
~ cometd-java $ mkdir -p apps/src/main/webapp/WEB-INF
```

The path *com/tedroden/realtime* will end up as the namespace in the Java source code. It will also be used in various forms throughout the codebase. You're encouraged to use your own namespace instead of one with my name on it; just be sure to keep it consistent in the code.

The next thing we want to do is create the *apps/src/main/webapp/WEB-INF/web.xml* file. This is the file that provides both configuration and deployment information for web applications. If you're familiar with Apache's httpd software, this file serves a similar purpose to the *httpd.conf* file. This is fairly straightforward. Create the file listed above and add the following:

```xml
<?xml version="1.0" encoding="ISO-8859-1"?>
<web-app xmlns="http://java.sun.com/xml/ns/javaee"
         xmlns:xsi="http://www.w3.org/2001/XMLSchema-instance"
         xsi:schemaLocation="http://java.sun.com/xml/ns/javaee
                             http://java.sun.com/xml/ns/javaee/web-app_2_5.xsd"
         version="2.5">

    <display-name>Realtime User Experience - LiveBlog</display-name>

    <context-param>
        <param-name>org.mortbay.jetty.servlet.ManagedAttributes</param-name>
        <param-value>org.cometd.bayeux</param-value>
    </context-param>

    <servlet>
        <servlet-name>cometd</servlet-name>
        <servlet-class>
          org.cometd.server.continuation.ContinuationCometdServlet
        </servlet-class>
        <init-param>
            <param-name>timeout</param-name>
            <param-value>120000</param-value>
        </init-param>
```

```
<init-param>
    <param-name>interval</param-name>
    <param-value>0</param-value>
</init-param>
<init-param>
    <param-name>maxInterval</param-name>
    <param-value>10000</param-value>
</init-param>
<init-param>
    <param-name>multiFrameInterval</param-name>
    <param-value>2000</param-value>
</init-param>
<init-param>
    <param-name>logLevel</param-name>
    <param-value>0</param-value>
</init-param>
<init-param>
    <param-name>refsThreshold</param-name>
    <param-value>10</param-value>
</init-param>
<load-on-startup>1</load-on-startup>
</servlet>

<filter>
    <filter-name>Continuation</filter-name>
    <filter-class>org.eclipse.jetty.continuation.ContinuationFilter</filter-class>
</filter>

<filter-mapping>
    <filter-name>Continuation</filter-name>
    <url-pattern>/cometd/*</url-pattern>
</filter-mapping>

<servlet-mapping>
    <servlet-name>cometd</servlet-name>
    <url-pattern>/cometd/*</url-pattern>
</servlet-mapping>

</web-app>
```

This file describes simple things like the name of the app, along with simple parameters configuring basic variables needed to serve the content. There are tons of options to this file and we're using only a small subset. Via the `servlet-mapping` tag, we've told the server where to find the cometd code (appropriately enough, at the path */cometd/*). The following are some of the more important parameters that are of interest to most cometd applications, including this chat application:

timeout

> The length of time (in milliseconds) that the server will maintain a connection with the client while waiting for new data. This is the heart of long polling.

interval

> If the client disconnects for any reason, this is the amount of time to wait before connecting again. We've set this to zero because the client should essentially always be connected.

maxInterval

> This is the maximum amount of time to wait for a client to reconnect. If the client doesn't receive a connection in at least this many milliseconds, the server will consider them disconnected.

multiFrameInterval

> If the server detects that a client has connected more than once, meaning the user has more than one browser window or tab open, the server will instruct the client to back off. This value tells the client how long to wait before reconnecting in that situation.

logLevel

> Configure how verbose the logging should be. 0 is None, 1 is for logging informational messages, and 2 is for "Debug" logging.

refsThreshold

> This is used internally by the server to determine when the server should generate each message on the fly and when it should regenerate the message being sent to multiple clients.

You'll also notice that there is a `filter-mapping` and a `servlet-mapping`, which look suspiciously similar. They both have identical `url-pattern` values. These are to handle two different types of servlet containers. Having both of them in there will ensure your code is more portable when you are getting ready to actually deploy it.

The next thing we need to do is make some minor modifications to that *pom.xml* file we copied from the examples directory. We want to instruct Maven where to find the files and ensure that everything is running from the right spot once we start the server.

Open up the *apps/pom.xml* file and change the `artifactId` setting from `cometd-examples-java` to **tedroden-realtime-apps** and the `name` setting to **TedRoden :: Realtime :: Apps**.

Since we're slimming things down and leaving out many of the other directories, we need to update another file that would normally be included upstream. Inside that same *cometd-java* directory, open up *pom.xml*. Be sure to note that this is not the same file as the *pom.xml* listed earlier. Search the file for the opening XML tag called `<plugins>` and insert the following inside:

```
<plugin>
  <groupId>org.mortbay.jetty</groupId>
  <artifactId>maven-jetty-plugin</artifactId>
  <configuration>
    <scanIntervalSeconds>1</scanIntervalSeconds>
    <webAppConfig>
      <contextPath>/</contextPath>
```

```
        </webAppConfig>
      </configuration>
    </plugin>
```

Adding this tells Maven to load up the jetty server, downloading and installing the proper JAR files if needed. Jetty is used to serve the files for our project and can be run from within a library inside our own project, making our app a totally self-contained web realtime application.

We still need to make one more change to that file, so with *pom.xml* still open, update the `modules` section and rename the `examples` module to `apps`. The `modules` section should end up looking like this:

```
<modules>
    <module>api</module>
    <module>server</module>
    <module>client</module>
    <module>oort</module>
    <module>apps</module>
</modules>
```

The `modules` section of the *pom.xml* file tells Maven where to find each module that is needed for the project. We don't actually need all of these modules for our purposes, and I've removed them in the packages I mentioned earlier, but they're not hurting anything, so we'll leave them alone for now. Some of these changes may seem like cosmetic differences, but they'll make it much easier when it comes time to publish your code to production environments.

A Realtime Live Blog

Now that everything is in its place, it's time to actually write some code. At this point the only programming skills required are HTML and JavaScript. We're going to build this base of this liveblog application without any server-side code at all.

To get started, use your favorite text editor and create a file in *apps/src/main/webapp/river.html*. Add the following code to your file:

```html
<!DOCTYPE HTML>
<html>
  <head>
    <script type="text/javascript" src="http://www.google.com/jsapi"></script>
    <script type="text/javascript">
      google.load("dojo", "1.3.2");
    </script>
    <script type="text/javascript" src="river.js"></script>
  </head>
  <body>
    <h3>Live Feed</h3>
    <div id="stream">
    </div>
  </body>
</html>
```

As you can see, we're borrowing some bandwidth from Google by using their Ajax libraries API (http://code.google.com/apis/ajaxlibs/) to host all of the Dojo Java-Script that we're going to use. After including their main API script (http://www.goo gle.com/jsapi), we load the latest version of the base Dojo framework.

The rest of the file is pretty straightforward. Aside from the last JavaScript include, which we will be creating in just a bit, this is just all standard HTML. The most important bit is the DIV tag with the stream id. This is the place on the page where we're going to be posting our live updates.

Now that we have a page that will display the feed, we need to be able to post content to it. Create a file called *apps/src/main/webapp/river-post.html* and add the following code:

```html
<html>
  <head>
    <script type="text/javascript" src="http://www.google.com/jsapi"></script>
    <script type="text/javascript">
      google.load("dojo", "1.3.2");
    </script>
    <script type="text/javascript" src="river.js"></script>
  </head>
  <body>
    <div>
      <p>
        <label for="author">Author</label> <br />
        <input type="text" id="author" value="" placeholder="Your Name" />
      </p>
      <p>
        <textarea rows="10" cols="50" id="content"></textarea>
      </p>
      <p>
        <input type="button" id="river-post-submit" value="Post" />
      </p>
    </div>
  </body>
</html>
```

This file has all of the same JavaScript as the *river.html* file, but it also has some HTML form elements. Although this is where we'll post the content to the realtime feed, we're not actually POSTing or submitting the form. We'll be sending all the data through JavaScript using cometd.

While the Cometd software and the Bayeux protocol handle all of the complicated parts of this process, a small bit of JavaScript is needed to get everything running. Open *apps/src/main/webapp/river.js* and we'll add the needed code piece by piece.

```javascript
function submitPost(e) {
    dojox.cometd.publish('/river/flow', {
        'content': dojo.byId('content').value,
        'author': (dojo.byId('author').value ?
                    dojo.ById('author').value :
                    'Anonymous')
```

```
    } );
    dojo.byId('content').value ='';
}
```

The first function to add to the file is `submitPost`. This is what is used to send the content to the server, much like submitting a standard web form. However, rather than POSTing the data, we grab the values of the form fields created in *river-post.html* and publish them via `dojox.cometd.publish`.

The function `dojox.cometd.publish` is what is used to publish (send) data to a named channel. The channel is the first parameter and is always a string, in this case `/river/flow`. The second parameter is for the JSON data that gets sent to the server.

```
function setupRiver() {
    dojox.cometd.init('cometd');
    var catcher = {
        handler: function(msg) {
            if (msg.data.content) {
                var p = dojo.create("p", {style: 'opacity: 0' } );
                dojo.create('strong', { innerHTML: msg.data.author }, p);
                dojo.create('p', { innerHTML: msg.data.content }, p);
                dojo.place(p, "stream", 'first');
                dojo.fadeIn({ node: p, duration: 300 }).play();
            }
        }
    };

    if(dojo.byId('river-post-submit'))
        dojo.connect(dojo.byId('river-post-submit'), "onclick", "submitPost");
    else
        dojox.cometd.subscribe("/river/flow", catcher, "handler");
}
```

This simple little function is the most complicated part of the JavaScript that we need to create for this application. This one function handles the main setup for both the liveblog viewer and the content creation process.

The first thing that happens is the call to `dojox.cometd.init`, which initializes the connection to the cometd server. This handles the handshake required by the Bayeux protocol along with details such as determining the best transport method for your browser, reconnecting if something goes wrong, and everything else that we'd rather not worry about. The lone parameter is the path to the cometd server itself. This is the same path we set up when we put the `servlet-mapping` tag into *web.xml*.

Next, we create a small object called `catcher`, which is what receives any messages sent from the server. These messages are passed to the `handler` function as JSON objects. The full Bayeux message response is sent from the server, but the only part we're concerned with is the `data`. This data object is the very same JSON object published previously in the `submitPost` function. You'll remember there were two members in that object: `author` and `content`.

In this function, we use the base dojo framework to create some DOM elements to display the posted content. After creating a couple of P elements and a STRONG tag to show the author name, we use dojo animation to make the HTML fade in. It's just an extensible way of printing the HTML content to the page.

Since this file gets included by both *river.html* and *river-post.html*, this function may execute two different actions depending on which page is loaded. When a user is looking at the *river-post.html* file, we'll be able to access the "Post" form button via JavaScript. We simply connect that button's onclick event to the `submitPost` function we created earlier. When we don't have that form element, we assume that we're going to view the liveblog feed and subscribe to the `/river/flow` channel.

Finally, we need to add the code that gets this whole process up and running. Add the following code to the bottom of your *river.js* file:

```
google.setOnLoadCallback(
    function() {
        dojo.require("dojox.cometd");
        dojo.addOnLoad(setupRiver);
        dojo.addOnUnload(dojox.cometd, "disconnect");
    }
);
```

Because we're loading the dojo files from remote servers, we need to wait to run our setup functions until all of the code has been loaded. Luckily, the Google Ajax libraries API provides the callback function `google.setOnLoadCallback` to let us know when that has happened. In that callback function, we tell Dojo which features we're going to need, which in this case is only the cometd extension. Then, we instruct dojo to call our `setupRiver` function when it is ready to continue. The very last step is to instruct the cometd library to disconnect when we unload (or navigate away from) this page.

At this point we have all the code in place for a fully functional liveblog, so I try it out. Running the app is simple. From a terminal window, navigate to the *apps* directory and enter the following command:

```
~ cometd-java/apps $ mvn jetty:run
```

Now the server should be up and running. To fully test this out, you'll want to open one browser, say Safari or Internet Explorer, and point it to *http://127.0.0.1:8080/river .html*. Then, open another browser, say Firefox, and point it to *http://127.0.0.1:8080/ river-post.html*. Figure 4-4 shows a liveblog session in action (see Figure 4-4).

Once you've loaded up the browsers, you should see the two web pages we created. As you start posting content, you should notice how quickly the content shows up in the other browser window. Keep in mind that this involves a trip through the server, and it's not just drawing content from one window to the other dynamically; all of the content is posted to the Web and loaded back in the browser in realtime. If you opened up another browser, say Opera or Chrome, and pointed it at *http://127.0.0.1:8080/river .html*, you'd see the content refresh in two browsers just as quickly as the one.

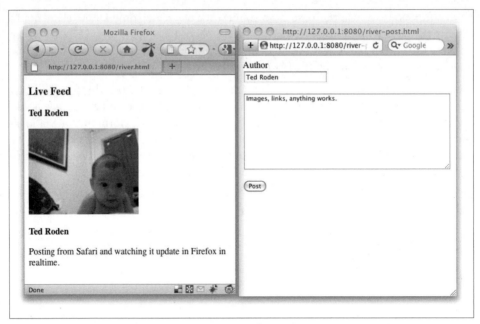

Figure 4-4. Realtime updates from one browser to another

So what is happening here?

In our JavaScript file, when we called `dojox.cometd.init`, we made a connect request to the cometd server. This request handles all of the dirty work of Bayeux's fairly complicated handshake process. At this point the server instructs the client (our JavaScript file) on how to interact with the server. This is where the server declares the timeout, interval, and all the other variables we set up in our server configuration. As programmers, we can safely ignore all of those things now because the dojox.cometd framework takes care of everything.

The next thing we did was call `dojox.cometd.subscribe` and subscribe to the `/river/flow` channel. This function starts making requests to the server using long polling at the intervals described earlier. If the server ever tells us to back off, the framework will handle that appropriately. Once again, we can focus on building our application and not the housekeeping required by the protocol.

The handshake and subscribe processes are detailed in Figure 4-5.

At this point, our browser-based client is maintaining a long-polling-based connection to the server. When data is available, it will be sent through the existing connections.

In the demo, we use a second browser to send messages to the server, which then routes the messages to the subscribed clients. To send a message to the server, pass the data encoded as a JSON object to the `dojox.cometd.publish`. This function just requires the JSON object and the channel name of where the data should be delivered. Then, we clear out the content field to allow the blogger to quickly post more content.

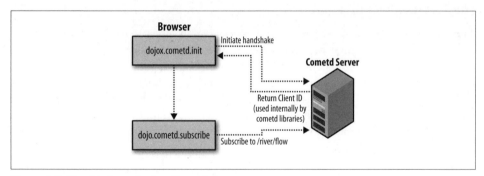

Figure 4-5. Handshake and subscribe with Bayeux

When that message makes it to the server, the server then routes it back to all of the subscribed clients. In this case, it's sent back to the `handler` function of the `catcher` object, which we specified when we subscribed to the channel. This simple function just draws the HTML to the screen and returns.

The whole publish to message routing process is illustrated in Figure 4-6.

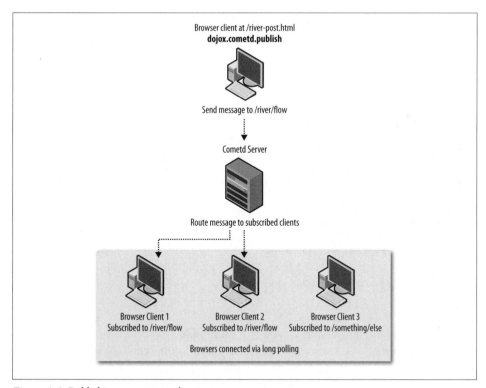

Figure 4-6. Publishing message to clients

The Two-Connection Limit

There is big a reason you need to open these files up in separate browsers and not just different tabs in the same browser when testing. Most modern browsers limit the amount of concurrent connections to just two connections per server. This means that if you have two connections open to the server and try to open another connection in the same browser, even if it's in a new tab, the browser will wait until one of the original connections disconnects. When we're doing long polling, that means we'll be waiting a long time between connections.

Cometd actually helps with this issue by using the `advice` part of the protocol to instruct the client to fall back to regular polling at standard intervals. Although this helps keep connections alive, it means we're not getting truly realtime content because of the length of time between requests. In practice for normal users, this isn't as much of an issue, but when building sites, it poses a bit of a problem. The solution is simple: use totally different browsers.

You can easily check to see if the cometd libraries have fallen back to standard polling at long intervals by examining the transfers with the Firefox extension Firebug (*http://getfirebug.com*). Firebug has many features that make debugging web applications much easier, such as the ability to examine the network activity, including connections that are still active. When you load up and enable Firebug, the `Console` tab will show you the different POST requests currently active (see Figure 4-7). If one of them is constantly active, long polling is working. If the connection returns immediately, it's fallen back. To fix this, navigate away from the page for a minute; it should go right back to long polling when you return.

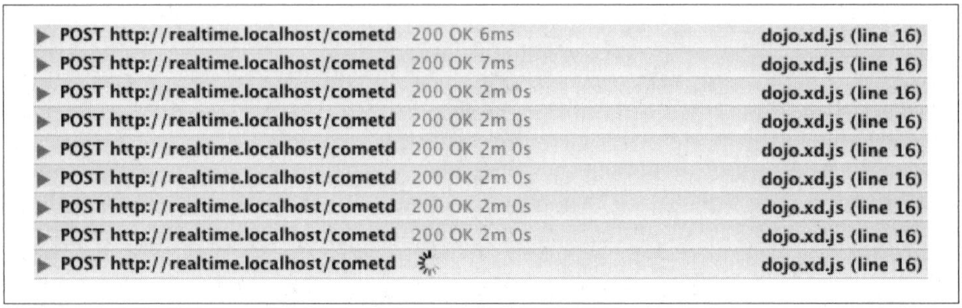

▶ **POST http://realtime.localhost/cometd** 200 OK 6ms		dojo.xd.js (line 16)
▶ **POST http://realtime.localhost/cometd** 200 OK 7ms		dojo.xd.js (line 16)
▶ **POST http://realtime.localhost/cometd** 200 OK 2m 0s		dojo.xd.js (line 16)
▶ **POST http://realtime.localhost/cometd** 200 OK 2m 0s		dojo.xd.js (line 16)
▶ **POST http://realtime.localhost/cometd** 200 OK 2m 0s		dojo.xd.js (line 16)
▶ **POST http://realtime.localhost/cometd** 200 OK 2m 0s		dojo.xd.js (line 16)
▶ **POST http://realtime.localhost/cometd** 200 OK 2m 0s		dojo.xd.js (line 16)
▶ **POST http://realtime.localhost/cometd** 200 OK 2m 0s		dojo.xd.js (line 16)
▶ **POST http://realtime.localhost/cometd**		dojo.xd.js (line 16)

Figure 4-7. Firebug during a long polling session

While the browser is looking at a page in a long polling section, you may notice the status bar say something to the effect of "completed 5 of 6 items," as if the browser is still loading an asset. It is! It's waiting on your long polling operation to finish, and it will keep waiting until it does. Although the status bar may claim the page load is incomplete, for all intents and purposes, everything is ready to go.

Server-Side Filters (with Java)

Our liveblog application will allow any number of clients to connect and view the content in realtime, but it also will allow any number of people to publish content. We don't want to rely on the hope that the users will never find our content creation URL, so we're going to have to lock it down. This is a great opportunity for us to test out some Java code. If you're not familiar with Java, don't worry. It won't hurt a bit.

To limit posting access to authorized users, we're going to require a password to be sent along with each publish request. If the password is correct, we'll publish the content; if it's wrong, we'll silently ignore the request. On the server side we can check for this password in a number of places, but we're going to do it from within the server-side content filter.

Server-side filters are Java-based classes that work very simply. As messages get sent to specific channels on the server, the server checks to see whether those channels have any filters set up. If a filter is configured, the request is sent to the filter before doing any other processing on the request. Inside the filter class, the data may be modified and returned to be operated on by the server or passed back to the clients. But if the filter returns `null`, the message is dropped and not delivered any further up the chain, and certainly not back to clients who have subscribed to the channel. This makes it a perfect place for us to check for the correct password.

The first thing we need to do is set up the filter configuration file. These files are just JSON data structures linking channels to Java classes, stored near the configuration file in the *WEB-INF* folder of the servlet. Open the file *apps/src/main/webapp/WEB-INF/filters.json* and add the following data structure:

```
[
    {
        "channels": "/river/**",
        "filter"  : "com.tedroden.realtime.FilterPasswordCheck",
        "init"    : { "required_password": "12345" }
    }
]
```

This file is pretty straightforward. While this example has only one filter in it, the data structure is set up as an array, so as you add more filters, simply append them as JSON objects into the existing array. The fields in the object are as follows:

channels
> The channel name (or names) that this filter applies to. The channel names follow the same conventions as everywhere else, and we can use a channel glob as we've done here. This will allow us to filter any content sent to any **/river** channel.

filter
> This is the actual Java classname that is used as the filter. When a request matches the channel listed in that field, the request is sent through this class as soon as it is received.

init

> This JSON object gets sent to the `filter` class listed in the previous field upon initialization. You can use this space to pass any variables to the class that apply to this specific instance of the filter.

Next, we need to create the filter class that is called when a publish request is made to /river/flow. Open the file *apps/src/main/java/com/tedroden/realtime/Filter PasswordCheck.java* and add this:

```
package com.tedroden.realtime;

import java.util.Map;
import org.cometd.Client;
import org.cometd.Channel;
import org.cometd.server.filter.JSONDataFilter;

public class FilterPasswordCheck extends JSONDataFilter
{

    String required_password;
    @Override
    public void init(Object init)
    {
        super.init(init);
        required_password = (String) ((Map)init).get("required_password");
    }

    @Override
    public Object filter(Client from, Channel to, Object data)
    {
        try {
            if(((Map)data).get("password").equals(required_password))
                return data;
            else
                return null;
        }
        catch (NullPointerException e) {
            return null;
        }
    }
}
```

The top of this file just declares that it's part of the `com.tedroden.realtime` package, or whichever namespace you've decided to use. After that, we import a few Java libraries that this file uses. Then, we just create our filter class, which extends the `JSON DataFilter` class provided by the cometd distribution.

When we set up the *filters.json* file, we specified certain data that got passed to the `init` function of the filter. As you can see, it's the first and only parameter this `init` function accepts. We pass it along to the parent class and then grab the `required_password`, which will be used for the lifetime of this filter.

The only other function in this file is the actual filter function. On top of the `data` parameter, which is the JSON data passed in from the client, there are also two other parameters. The first parameter is the `Client` object, otherwise known as the sender of the message. The second parameter is an object representation of the destination channel.

The `data` parameter is the JSON object we pass in from JavaScript when we publish to the server. All we do is check to see that the provided password matches the `required_password` that we set up in the `init` function. If it does, we return the data; otherwise, we return null. This is a very basic filter that does one of two things. It either blocks the data from getting through to the client or passes it along unchanged.

Before this filter is picked up by the server, we need to tell the *apps/src/main/webapp/ WEB-INF/web.xml* file about it. Open up that file and add the `filters` parameter to the `<servlet>` section:

```
<servlet-name>cometd</servlet-name>
        <servlet-class>
          org.cometd.server.continuation.ContinuationCometdServlet
        </servlet-class>
        <init-param>
            <param-name>filters</param-name>
            <param-value>/WEB-INF/filters.json</param-value>
        </init-param>
    ...
```

Finally, we need to collect the password from the author and pass it along with the Bayeux publish request. We need to make two minor changes to get this to work. First, let's add the password field to *apps/src/main/webapp/river-post.html*:

```
<p>
    <label for="author">Author</label> <br />
    <input type="text" id="author" value="" placeholder="Your Name" />
</p>
<p>
    <label for="password">Password</label> <br />
    <input type="text" id="password" value="" placeholder="Password (12345)" />
</p>
```

Then, inside *apps/src/main/webapp/river.js*, we add one additional line to send the password to the server:

```
function submitPost(e) {
    dojox.cometd.publish('/river/flow', {
        'content': dojo.byId('content').value,
        'password': dojo.byId('password').value,
        'author': (dojo.byId('author').value ?
                    dojo.byId('author').value :
                    'Anonymous')
    ...
```

We've added all of the code needed to secure this form with a password, so now we need to start the server and test it out. From the *apps* directory, instruct Maven to start the server:

```
~ cometd-java/apps $ mvn jetty:run
[INFO] Scanning for projects...
[INFO] Searching repository for plugin with prefix: 'jetty'.
...
```

This will compile the newly created filter and then start the server. When you point your web browser to the same *river-post.html*, you'll notice the newly added password field (see Figure 4-8). The password we set in the *filters.json* file was "12345". Try submitting the form both with and without the correct password. When the correct password is supplied, the form submits like normal. If the password is wrong, the publish request is silently ignored.

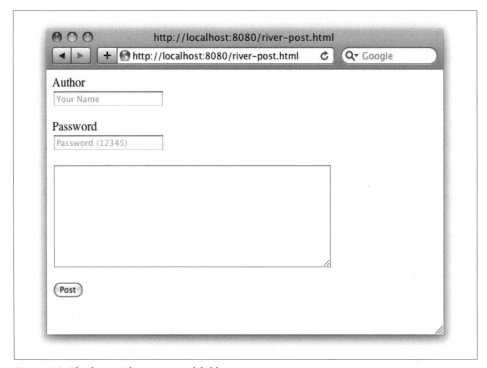

Figure 4-8. The form with its password field

Integrating Cometd into Your Infrastructure

So far, we've seen a fairly interesting example of how Bayeux and Cometd change things for both users and developers. This is great stuff, but unless you're starting a project from scratch, there is a good chance that these examples have used different technologies than your existing infrastructure. Moving over all of your existing code doesn't make a lot of sense. The good news is that incorporating this into a standard web environment is remarkably easy.

For the sake of simplicity, I'll demonstrate how to set this up with Apache's httpd server, which is extremely popular and runs on just about every platform. This idea should work on most other server platforms as well; you'll just need to use their configuration methods.

On Apache, you'll need to install the proxy module if it's not installed already. If you installed Apache through your operating system's package manager, you should be able to install it that way. On Ubuntu, this should do the trick: **sudo apt-get install libapache2-mod-proxy-html**. If you compiled Apache from source, this is as simple as reconfiguring with **--enable-proxy=shared** and recompiling.

You'll also need to update your *httpd.conf* file to load the proxy module. To do that, add the following lines near any other LoadModule statements:

```
LoadModule proxy_module           modules/mod_proxy.so
LoadModule proxy_http_module      modules/mod_proxy_http.so
LoadModule proxy_connect_module   modules/mod_proxy_connect.so
```

Now, before you restart your Apache server, you want to add the proxy directives to your (virtual) host configuration. Open up your host's configuration file and add the following:

```
<Location /cometd>
    ProxyPass http://localhost:8080/cometd/
</Location>
```

This Location directive tells apache to take any requests that it receives for /cometd and pass them along to http://localhost:8080/cometd/. Any response from http://local host:8080/cometd/ is proxied back to the web client through Apache. The web browser never knows anything about the proxy or port 8080. All of the content appears to come from the same server.

This configuration sets up Apache to use the exact same relative path as our Java-based Cometd code. This means we can actually drop in the client-side code, unchanged, and it will just work. To test this out, copy *river.html* and *river.js* to your standard document root and bring up *river.html* in your web browser. When posting content from *http://127.0.0.1:8080/river-post.html*, it should work exactly the same as if it were being served by the Jetty server. This allows you to easily integrate this functionality into new and existing pages on your site.

## CHAPTER 5

Taming the Firehose with Tornado

In the previous chapter, we built an application that gets the data to users as quickly as possible. However, that application is limited by how fast the authors can post new content. This chapter is about speed and about handling huge amounts of data. We're going to build an application that shows off just how fast the realtime web can work. We'll be combining one of the best sources of big data that is publicly available with a truly great piece of software designed for creating realtime web experiences.

Using Twitter's streaming APIs, we're going to build an application to make sense of the firehose of information they make publicly available. Instead of Cometd, this example will use a web server and framework called Tornado (*http://www.tornadoweb .org*). Tornado is a set of Python libraries that were originally created by FriendFeed (*http://www.friendfeed.com*) and open sourced shortly after they were acquired by Facebook (*http://www.facebook.com*).

Tornado

Tornado is a really fantastic piece of software that is both a web framework and a nonblocking web server written entirely in Python. The nonblocking architecture of the web server allows it to scale up to handle thousands of simultaneous connections. On top of being able to handle so many connections, it can also keep them open for long periods of time, making it perfectly suited for realtime web applications. The server was built specifically for the realtime aspects of FriendFeed, and it enables each user to maintain an active connection to the server.

Installing Tornado

Before we can install or use the Tornado web server and framework, we need to install the required Python libraries. The main requirements are `pycurl` and `simplejson`, so if you have those, you may be in the clear. Running the following command should get you up and running on a recent Mac:

```
~ $ sudo easy_install setuptools pycurl==7.16.2.1 simplejson
```

If you're using an Ubuntu-based distribution, run the following command (other Linux distributions will be similar enough):

```
~ $ sudo apt-get install python-dev python-pycurl python-simplejson
```

Now that we have the prerequisites, we need to download the latest version of Tornado itself from the official Tornado website (*http://www.tornadoweb.org/*). Once downloaded, unzip it and install it with the following commands:

```
~ $ tar zxf tornado-0.2.tar.gz
~ $ cd tornado-0.2/
~tornado-0.2 $ python setup.py build
running build
running build_py
creating build
creating build/lib
...
~tornado-0.2 $ sudo python setup.py install
running install
running build
running build_py
running install_lib
copying build/lib/tornado/__init__.py -> /Library/Python/2.6/site-packages/tornado
...
```

> Tornado is written purely in Python, so it should run on any system that you throw at it. However, parts of it are optimized to run on Linux, which means when you deploy your Tornado-based applications, it's best to use a Linux server.

The Basic Framework

Web applications built with Tornado will look familiar if you have experience using web.py (*http://webpy.org/*) or even Google's Python webapp framework (*http://code.google.com/appengine/docs/python/tools/webapp/*). If not, you have nothing to worry about, because building an application with this framework is remarkably simple.

Tornado applications are built using a very basic Model-View-Controller (MVC) framework. Each application provides a simple mapping of URLs or URL patterns to specific classes. These classes can define methods to handle both GET and POST requests to the URL. As requests hit the server, the web framework looks at the requested URL and determines which class should respond to the request. It then calls either the `get()` or `post()` function of the class, depending on the method of the HTTP request. See Figure 5-1 for an example of how requests are handled in Tornado.

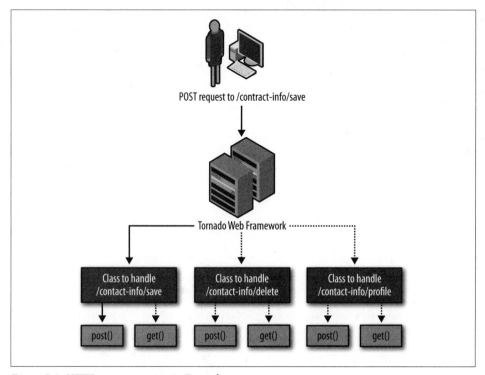

Figure 5-1. HTTP request routing in Tornado

Tornado also has built-in support for long polling, or as it is called in Tornado parlance, "hanging" requests. Just like in Bayeux, when the browser makes a request to the server, the server waits to respond until data is actually available. However, when writing a Tornado application, the developer makes a request to an asynchronous function and provides the framework with a callback function. When the data is ready, the server executes the developer's callback function which finishes the final request. Figure 5-2 shows the callback process in Tornado.

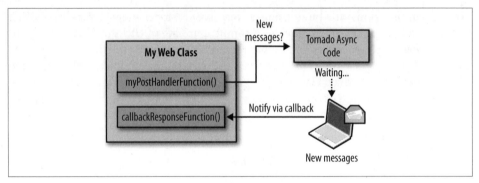

Figure 5-2. Tornado hanging requests via callback functions

Building an Application

So before we can build any realtime features with Tornado, we need to put together an app that responds to basic requests in using this framework. Create a file called *runner.py* and add the following code.

```python
import logging
import tornado.httpserver
import tornado.ioloop
import tornado.web
from tornado.options import define, options
import os

# Define options that can be changed as we run this via the command line
define("port", default=8888, help="Run server on a specific port", type=int)

class MainHandler(tornado.web.RequestHandler):
    def get(self):
        logging.info("Request to MainHandler!")
        self.write("Great, now let's make this app speak in realtime.")


local_static_path = os.path.join(os.path.dirname(__file__), "static")

application = tornado.web.Application([
    (r"/", MainHandler),
], static_path=local_static_path)

if __name__ == "__main__":
    http_server = tornado.httpserver.HTTPServer(application)
    tornado.options.parse_command_line()
    http_server.listen(options.port)
    tornado.ioloop.IOLoop.instance().start()
```

Like all Python scripts, this script first imports the libraries it needs to run and does a bit of housekeeping. In this case we define the port on which this server should run. Using Tornado's options library, we set it to port 8888, but that can be changed at runtime via the command line. Automatic handling of command-line options is a neat little feature of Tornado that allows you to create apps without config files. This script could be started several times on the same server, each one running on a different port that is specified at runtime. This type of configuration is very useful for running big scalable applications in the cloud.

The next thing in this file is the `MainHandler`. This class, along with the call to the `tornado.web.Application` function, are the main bits of web code in this example. We create a Tornado application with the latter function and assign it to the `application` variable. In creating the application object, we define the URL patterns and their matching classes. Defining these patterns is the main purpose of creating an application with this call. This defines the URL routing that we'll be using, as described in Figure 5-1. In this case, when Tornado receives a request to /, it will call either the `get()` or `post()` method in the `MainHandler` class.

When creating your Tornado application, you set up the URL mappings that are needed as well as any special settings that are needed by your application. There are several settings you can specify when creating your application, including a secret key to be used when securing cookies and even the login URL that users are redirected to when they are not authenticated. In this case, we're only configuring the `static_path` setting. This setting is used to tell Tornado the full filesystem path for our static assets. We'll be using this path when we start setting up our templates.

Finally, we get to the code that is called when we're actually running the application. We pass the application object to the `HTTPServer` constructor. This will let the server know about the URL options we've defined and anything else that goes into the application object. Next, we ask Tornado to parse the command-line options. At this point, the user can override the `port` defined earlier. Many other options can be defined and parsed at this point. To get things up and running, we instruct the server to listen on a specified port and start the I/O loop. At this point, the server will call our methods as requests are made to the server.

Let's start up the server and test it out. Open your terminal window and run the following command:

```
~ $ python runner.py
```

Now the server is up and running on port 8888. Open your browser and take a look at the results (see Figure 5-3).

Another nice thing about the Tornado server that you may have noticed is the nicely formatted output from the server as it responds to HTTP requests. This comes from the logging module. Certain actions, such as HTTP requests, get logged automatically along with HTTP errors. But we also can add logging info, as we do in `MainHandler` with the call to `logging.info`. As each request comes in, our message is printed nicely to the screen (see Figure 5-4), which can help make debugging much easier.

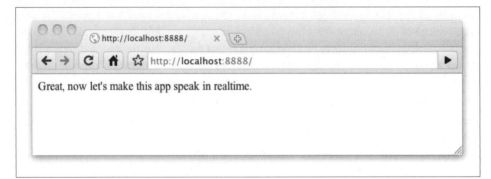

Figure 5-3. "Hello World!" from Tornado

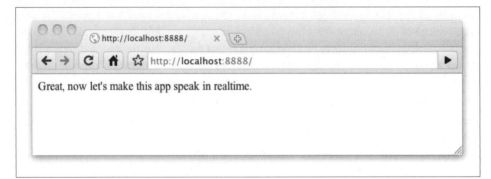

Figure 5-4. Formatted logging output provided by Tornado

Asynchronous Tornado in Realtime

While Tornado can be used to create standard dynamic websites like the example shown earlier, it really shines when creating realtime applications. The framework allows for developers to iterate fairly easily, so we'll just modify the previous script to turn it into our realtime Twitter application. In your *runner.py* file, add the following code just after the existing `import` statements:

```
# Tornado imports
import threading
import re
import simplejson as json

# Setup the queue
import Queue
tweetQueue = Queue.Queue(0)
```

This just imports some extra libraries that we'll be using and sets up a queue that we'll be using to store the tweets. Some of the modules that we're importing here will be used later when we get into the thick of working with the Twitter stream itself. The rest are needed for some of the functionality we'll be using inside the Tornado parts of our app. This queue is made with Python's `Queue` module, which is a multiproducer and multiconsumer queue. The key part is that it works wonderfully across multiple threads. One thread can add items while the other removes them. All of the locking and heavy lifting is handled by the class itself.

Next we're going to add the most complicated part of this file, the main `Tweet` class. This class will handle the routing of specific tweets to the different web clients. In your *runner.py* file, add the following code after the `MainHandler` class:

```python
class Tweet(object):
    waiters = []      # a list of clients waiting for updates
    cache = []        # a list of recent tweets
    cache_size = 200  # the amount of recent tweets to store

    def wait_for_messages(self, callback, cursor=None):
        cls = Tweet
        if cursor:
            index = 0
            for i in xrange(len(cls.cache)):
                index = len(cls.cache) - i - 1
                if cls.cache[index]["id"] == cursor: break
            recent = cls.cache[index + 1:]
            if recent:
                callback(recent)
                return
        cls.waiters.append(callback)

    def new_tweets(self, messages):
        cls = Tweet
        for callback in cls.waiters:
            try:
                callback(messages)
            except:
                logging.error("Error in waiter callback", exc_info=True)
        cls.waiters = []
        cls.cache.extend(messages)
        if len(cls.cache) > self.cache_size:
            cls.cache = cls.cache[-self.cache_size:]
```

This code defines the basic functionality that will be used when web requests come in looking for new tweets. We haven't written the code that uses this class, but it's worth looking into how it works at this point. First, we specify a few member variables that are used by the class. The `waiters` list will be populated with each of the callback functions used during the asynchronous requests. When we have no data to provide to a web client, we'll store them in this array until data becomes available. We also define the `cache` and the size of the cache. This specifies where we're going to store tweets that are waiting to get sent to clients and how many of them we're going to keep around.

As for the functions, there aren't too many required for this example. The first function, wait_for_messages, is supplied with a callback function and an optional cursor. The callback function is the function that we should call when new data is available, whether it's available now or in a couple of minutes. The cursor is used to let the server know the last tweet received by the client. Using this cursor, we can search through the cache of tweets and serve anything that's arrived since the last time the client made a request. If there's no cursor, we add the callback to the list of waiters and call the function as soon as data becomes available.

The other function defined here is new_tweets, which is called immediately when new tweets arrive from Twitter. This is fairly simple; it loops through the waiters list, calling each callback function with the messages it receives as a parameter. This is realtime, so that's the first thing it does. The next thing it does is update the cache. This will allow any client that is currently reconnecting to get the tweets that it missed while disconnected.

The next thing to do is handle the actual requests from the web browsers. We'll be adding one new class and modifying the array that we pass when creating the application object. Inside your *runner.py* file, insert this code right after the Tweet class:

```
class UpdateHandler(tornado.web.RequestHandler, Tweet):
    @tornado.web.asynchronous
    def post(self):
        cursor = self.get_argument("cursor", None)
        self.wait_for_messages(self.async_callback(self.on_new_tweets),
                               cursor=cursor)

    def on_new_tweets(self, tweets):
        if not self.request.connection.stream.closed():
            self.finish(dict(tweets=tweets))
```

This class is much simpler. This is the code that is actually called when we get an Ajax request from the browser. The first thing you'll notice is the @tornado.web.asynchronous decorator. Adding this bit of code tells Tornado that we want the HTTP connection to remain open even after returning from our request handler method. Inside that handler method, we call our wait_for_messages function supplied with on_new_tweets, our callback function.

 Decorators, while outside the scope of this book, are a really nice feature of Python. They enable you to "decorate" functions and classes to give them extra code or to make them act differently. You're actually able to inject new code or modify the existing functions themselves.

The method on_new_tweets is what finally gets called when we have new data. There isn't much to do in this method other than printing out the tweets to the client. After checking to ensure that the client is still connected, we need to "finish" the connection. Because we're in the middle of an asynchronous request, Tornado relies on us to close the connection to the client. We do that by calling `finish` with the output that we want to send to the browser. Simply supplying a Python dictionary structure to the `finish` method is good enough because the Tornado framework will convert that to JSON automatically.

Now that we've prepared Tornado to accept and serve an influx of updates from Twitter, it's time to start collecting them.

Twitter's Realtime Streaming APIs

Twitter has a lot of data. Every second, amazing numbers of tweets are created by users and sent to Twitter. Users are constantly reporting everything from their latest meal to firsthand accounts of airplanes landing in the Hudson River. Almost as frequently, and with almost as many different purposes, applications repeatedly ping Twitter's APIs and web browsers pound their servers in hopes of grabbing the latest content.

For a long while, Twitter has offered up fairly complete but also standard API functions to developers wanting to grab the Twitter feed. For example, if a developer wanted to get some tweets from the public timeline, she would make a request to the public timeline API, which would return 20 or so of the latest tweets. Recently, though, Twitter has started providing streaming APIs to developers. So instead of grabbing 20 updates per request, the developer can make one web request and just leave it open. Instead of sending out a set number of updates, Twitter will keep sending them until the developer closes the connection.

Twitter offers several different streaming methods for several different purposes. Each of these methods requires a certain level of access by the user. The basic methods can be used by anyone, but if you want the totally full feed, you're going to have to talk directly with Twitter to set that up. For us, though, there's plenty of data to work with. The different streaming API methods are listed next.

`statuses/filter`
> This allows you to get a subset of the public feed while filtering out specific keywords. The developer can specify keywords to `track` and users to `follow`. Anybody can filter up to 200 keywords; more than that requires special permission.

`statuses/firehose`
> The firehose is the largest feed of all. This is an unfiltered view of the public timeline. This is not generally available to developers and requires a special level of access.

`statuses/links`
> This returns all of the public statuses containing strings that look like links. If a tweet has `http://` or `https://`, it'll be in this stream. This method is also restricted and requires special access.

`statuses/retweet`

The retweet feed returns all of the updates that contains all of the retweets on the public timeline. Like several other methods, access to this one also is restricted and requires special access.

`statuses/sample`

This is a public feed that contains a small sample of the main firehose feed. Developers who are granted higher access levels can get more data out of this feed, making it a more statistically significant sample and appropriate for data mining and research applications.

For this application, we'll be using the `statuses/sample` streaming API method. Although this is just a small (and therefore statistically insignificant) subset of the main firehose feed, it's a lot of data, and certainly enough for our purposes. It also requires no special permission from Twitter, aside from a standard user account.

 This example will require an active Twitter account. If you don't have an account, head over to the Twitter website (*http://twitter.com*) to sign up. Once you've done that, feel free to follow the Twitter account of this very book at `@therealtimebook`.

The Tornado web server runs as a single process on a single thread. Its nonblocking architecture ensures that it can quickly respond to certain requests even while many other connections are open and waiting. However, even though Tornado runs in a single thread, we're going to need to create some other threads to handle the work from Twitter. The Twitter streaming API feeds will essentially stay open forever, as long as we can keep up with them. To ensure that we do keep up, we're going to separate the work into separate threads. The first thread just catches the data as it arrives and queues it up. Any processing work to be done on the tweets should be in a separate thread, to ensure that we're able to keep up with Twitter. Our example doesn't do any complicated processing of the data, but I've separated the work out anyway, to ensure we can easily modify it in the future.

In its simplest form, creating new threads in Python is as simple as creating a class and defining a `run` method. When you ask Python to start the thread, it will automatically call that method and you're on your way.

 Python has a bit of a reputation for poor handling of multithreaded applications. However, the threaded aspects of our application aren't very complicated, so it should be fine.

The first thread we're going to create is the thread that handles the communication with Twitter. In your *runner.py* file, add the following code after the `UpdateHandler` class:

```
class TweetFirehose(threading.Thread):
    import urllib2
    import base64
    def run(self):
        status_sample_url = 'http://stream.twitter.com/1/statuses/sample.json'
        request = urllib2.Request(status_sample_url)

        # Be sure to use your own twitter login information
        auth_basic = base64.encodestring('USERNAME:PASSWORD')[:-1]
        request.add_header('Authorization', 'Basic %s' % auth_basic)

        # open the connection
        firehose = urllib2.urlopen(request)

        for tweet in firehose:
            if len(tweet) > 2:
                tweetQueue.put(tweet)

        firehose.close()
```

You can see this creates a class called `TweetFirehose`. This class is defined as a subclass of Python's `Thread` class and defines only one function: `run`. In this function we start out by building an HTTP request to Twitter using `urllib2`. At the moment, the only method of authentication to the streaming APIs is via HTTP Basic Auth. To do that, we join our username and password together with a colon, encode it using Base64 encoding, and add the `Authorization` header to the HTTP request.

Having built the request, the only thing left to do is open it. If you've ever used `url lib2` to download a file from the Web, this works a lot like that but with one key difference: it doesn't end. After calling `urllib2.urlopen` with our request, we'll start receiving tweets one line at a time, each one encoded into JSON. The following is an example tweet as received from the streaming API feed:

```
{"text":"Hah! I just ...","in_reply_to_status_id":false, ... "truncated":false}
```

In the code, we just start looping through those lines as fast as we get them. Assuming we don't get any blank lines, we add them to `tweetQueue` that we created at the top of the file. We pretend to close the handle to the `firehose`, but in all honesty, the code will probably never get there.

That's all the code it takes to stream the data in from Twitter in realtime. All it really takes is making one request to their streaming URL and finding some place to put all the data. In our case, the place we found to put the data is a simple queue. It's up to another thread to pull the tweets off of the queue and process them.

To actually process these tweets, we're going to create another thread in the same way we created the previous one. Underneath the `TweetFirehose` class, add the following code:

```
class TweetProcessor(threading.Thread):
    import re
    import simplejson as json
```

```python
def run(self):
    # pre-compile some regular expressions
    links = re.compile("(http\:\/\/[^\ ]+)")
    hashtag = re.compile("(\#[0-9a-zA-Z]+)")
    ats = re.compile("(\@[0-9a-zA-Z]+)")
    retweets = re.compile("RT|via\ ")

    while True:
        tweet = tweetQueue.get()
        if tweet:
            t = json.loads(tweet)
            try:
                stats = {}
                stats['hashtags'] = hashtag.findall(t['text'])
                stats['ats'] = ats.findall(t['text'])
                stats['links'] = links.findall(t['text'])
                stats['retweets'] = retweets.findall(t['text'])
    # pack the message up
                message = {
                    "id": str(uuid.uuid4()),
                    "stats": stats
                    }
                message["html"] = "<div class=\"message\" id=\"m" +
                message["id"] +
                    "\"><strong>" + t['user']['screen_name'] + ": </strong>" +
                    t['text'] + "</div>"
                Tweet().new_tweets([message])

            except Exception, e:
                # ignore any exceptions...
                pass
```

Once again, we have a couple of newly imported libraries and a single run method. When a new thread is created with this class, that method is called and it jumps right into a never-ending loop. The only thing we do outside that loop is compile some regular expressions so that they run quickly as possible when we need them.

These regular expressions are designed to pull out some items that are commonly found in tweets. Aside from a very basic check for URLs in the tweet, this also looks for hashtags, something called "at replies," and retweets. If a tweet has a pound sign and some text—"#realtime", for example—we'll pull it out as a hashtag. We also pull out any reference to other users in the tweet, so if someone writes a message to "@tedroden," this regular expression will find it. Also, retweets are commonly denoted with either "RT" or "via" and so this will find those instances as well. Keep in mind that these regular expressions will miss some of the data and probably turn up some false positives, but it's good enough for our example.

After we set up the regular expressions, we move into the unending loop. This loop will keep going until we shut down the server. Each time through the loop we check the queue for new tweets and parse the JSON object using Python's simplejson module. We're going to use the precompiled regular expressions to create an object that contains all of the stats we'll be filtering on in the web browser. Python's regular expression module, `re`, has a method called `findall`. This method returns an array of any matches found in the string we provide. This way, on the client side we can just check the size of the array to determine how many matches we've made, if any.

Next, we build the `message` object that we'll be sending out to the browser. This object contains a unique field called `id`, which we'll be using as our cursor. It also contains basic information such as the tweet itself and who sent it. The `stats` object is also passed through. To save time, we even build the HTML string that will be displayed by the browser. When the browser gets the data, it can simply display this `html` value to the client.

To send it to the browser, we call the `Tweet().new_tweets` method that we built earlier. As you'll remember, that method loops through all of the connected clients and outputs the Python object encoded as a JSON string. The whole workflow of this method is pictured in Figure 5-5.

This processing workflow ends up calling the `new_tweets` method. As a quick refresher, that method then loops through the list of connected clients to run the callback method associated with each request. That callback method then outputs the data in JSON format and finishes the connection.

The server side of this script is totally complete, though if you run the server from the command line, you won't see much of a change. At this point we're accepting web requests, collecting tons of data from Twitter, parsing it up, and sending it back to any client who cares to connect. There's a big missing piece, though: the web page. So let's build that next.

From the Firehose to the Web Browser

We're already collecting the data we need, and Tornado is ready to respond to requests for updates. Basically, all we have left to do is build the web page and write the JavaScript.

Templates in Tornado

The template language in Tornado is based on the templates in Django (*http://www .djangoproject.com/*). Both of these projects contain rich templating languages where standard HTML files get parsed based on logic written in a subset of Python. However, a big difference between the templating language that inspired Tornado and Tornado itself is the ability to include arbitrary Python code. In Django, you're restricted to variables, filters, and standard flow control statements. To go beyond the most basic logic, you must create new template filters and run those. With Tornado, you're allowed to use any valid Python expression, including functions and list comprehensions. As long as it's a valid Python expression, it will work in these templates.

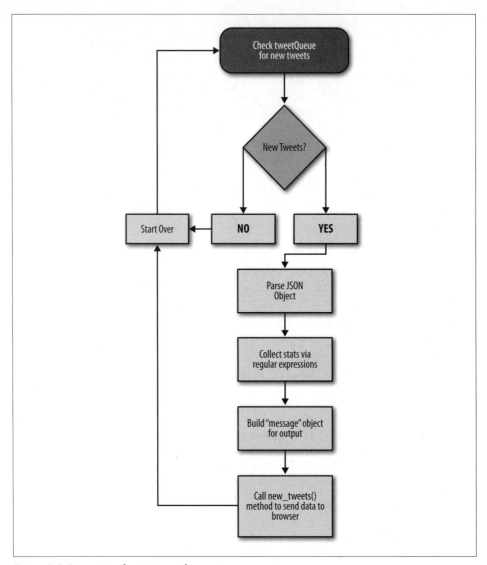

Figure 5-5. Processing the tweets as they arrive

Tornado offers a straightforward mapping of most of Python's standard flow control statements. You can specify `for` loops, `if` statements, `try/catch` blocks, and many of the basic control statements that come to mind. These control statements are wrapped between {% and %}. Developers can also specify arbitrary expressions; those are marked up by wrapping the code with {{ and }}. The expression is evaluated and the result is then placed directly into the HTML. The following is an example template that contains both flow control and a simple Python expression. This template would show different welcome messages after testing for the existence of a variable called `username`:

```
<body>
  {% if username: %}
    <h1>Welcome, {{ username.strip() }}!</h1>
  {% else %}
    <h1>Sign Up Now!</h1>
  {% end %}
  ...
</body>
```

Creating a Template for This Project

In the basic "Hello World" example that we built, our output was a static string printed out to the screen. Normally, when displaying anything more than JSON output or single strings, you'll probably want to make a template and show that. Setting up our current project to use templates requires making two changes. First, we need to specify the template that we want to use, and then we need to create the template itself.

To specify the template, we need to change our `MainHandler` class ever so slightly. To replace our static string with a dynamic template, replace the last line of your current `MainHandler` with the boldface code:

```
class MainHandler(tornado.web.RequestHandler):
    def get(self):
        logging.info("Request to MainHandler!")
        self.render("templates/main.html")
```

In the first iteration of this function, we used Tornado's `self.write` method to write a specific string to the client's browser. In this version, we tell the framework to render a template as a string and then send that to the client.

Our new `MainHandler` class specifies a template relatively located at *templates/main.html*. When Tornado sees this call, it opens that file, parses it by executing any Python code in it, and prints it to the client. To build this template, create a *templates* directory in the same directory as *runner.py*, open a file called *main.html*, and add the following code:

```
<!DOCTYPE html>
<html>
  <head>
    <title>Twitter / Tornado</title>
    <script type="text/javascript" src="http://www.google.com/jsapi"></script>
    <script type="text/javascript" src="{{ static_url('twitter.js') }}"></script>
    <style>
        BODY { margin: 0px; padding: 0px; }
        #content { width: 50%; margin: auto; }
        #toolbar {
            text-align: center;
            border-bottom: solid 1px grey;
            margin: 0px;
            background-color: #dfdfdf;
        }
```

```
        #toolbar UL { margin: 0px; }
        #toolbar UL LI { display: inline; }
        #waiting { text-align: center; font-style: italic; }
    </style>
  </head>

  <body>
    <div id="toolbar">
      <ul>
        <li>
          <input checked="yes" type="checkbox" id="all" value="1" />
          <label for="all">All</label>
          (<span id="all-count">0</span>)
        </li>
        <li>
          <input checked="yes" type="checkbox" id="hashtags" value="1" />
          <label for="hashtags">#hashtags</label>
          (<span id="hashtags-count">0</span>)
        </li>
        <li>
          <input checked="yes" type="checkbox" id="ats" value="1" />
          <label for="ats">@ats</label>
          (<span id="ats-count">0</span>)
        </li>
        <li>
          <input checked="yes" type="checkbox" id="retweets" value="1" />
          <label for="retweets">retweets</label>
          (<span id="retweets-count">0</span>)
        </li>
        <li>
          <input checked="yes" type="checkbox" id="links" value="1" />
          <label for="links">links</label>
          (<span id="links-count">0</span>)
        </li>
      </ul>
    </div>

    <div id="content">
      <div id="waiting">Waiting for content...</div>
    </div>

  </body>
</html>
```

This is a fairly standard and simple HTML file. It lays out a basic web page, has the most minimal of CSS styling, and includes two JavaScript files. Again, we're including the `jsapi` from Google's JavaScript hosting, which we'll be using to include jQuery. To include the other JavaScript file, we're using one of the template functions defined by Tornado. Anything inside of these curly braces is evaluated, and the output is inserted in place. In this case, it's our lone Python expression, the function call to `static_url` (`'twitter.js'`). This function expands the full URL to one of our static assets. We set up the filesystem path for this function when we initially created the application object.

Tornado offers a couple of neat features when serving static content. First of all, it aggressively tries to get the client to cache any content that is served from the static directory, going as far to suggest that the content won't expire for at least 10 years. To ensure that browsers do see the newest content, it also appends a unique version string to each URL served using the `static_url` function. So in our template shown earlier, the full path to a JavaScript file may be `/Users/tedroden/realtime/static/twitter.js`, but it will be translated to the following by `static_url`:

```
http://localhost:8888/static/twitter.js?v=aa3ce
```

The parameter `v` is calculated by generating a hash of the content of the static file. So it will remain the same until the actual content of the file is changed. All this means that Tornado will enable unchanged files to remain cached on the client for a very long time. This type of performance gain is a definite part of providing a realtime experience to the user.

The template itself specifies some basic markup that will enable us to do some basic filtering and show some statistics on the data we're receiving from Twitter. By checking the boxes on the page, the users will be able to specify whether they want to see tweets that are retweets, contain hashtags or links, or even if they just reference a specific Twitter user. We've also specified a place in the template to show the number of each type of tweet that we've received.

Let's start the server to see what that page looks like when it's served by Tornado. This isn't going to show any tweets (we need to set up the JavaScript for that to happen), but let's start it up and take a look at our work so far. In your terminal window, run the following command:

```
~ $ python runner.py
```

Now point your browser to *http://localhost:8888*. It should look something like Figure 5-6.

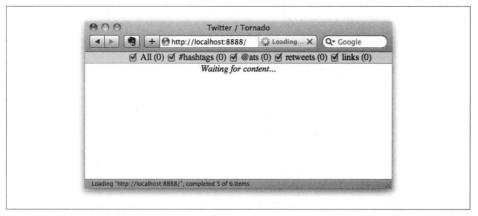

Figure 5-6. The updated, if still inactive, realtime Twitter interface

The JavaScript Parts

We've created our classes in Python and coded our templates in HTML, so now it's time for a bit of JavaScript. The template file that we created included a JavaScript file called *twitter.js* that was supposed to be served from the static directory. Let's create that file now. Create a new directory called *static* and create a file called *twitter.js* inside it. Set up the basics of that file with the following code:

```
google.load("jquery", "1");

google.setOnLoadCallback(
    function() {
        $(document).ready(function() { T.init(); T.poll(); });
    }
);

var T = {
    cursor: false,
    types: ['hashtags', 'retweets', 'ats', 'links']
};

T.init = function() {
    $('input[type=checkbox]').click(T.click);
};

T.click = function(ev) {
    if(ev.target.id == 'all') {
        for(i in T.types)
            $('#' + T.types[i]).attr('checked', $('#all').attr('checked'));
    }
    else
        $('#all').attr('checked', false);
};

T.poll = function () {
    var args = {};
    if(T.cursor) args.cursor = T.cursor;
    $.ajax({
            url: "/updates",
            type: "POST",
            dataType: "json",
            data: $.param(args),
            success: T.new_tweets
        });
};
```

This JavaScript sets up our application. Once again, we ask Google's Ajax APIs to load the jQuery library for us and wait for a callback from Google before we run any initialization functions. Once that callback arrives, we run the `init` and `poll` methods on an object called T.

We're going to build the entire client-side functionality of our Twitter application inside this T object. In constructing the object, we initialize two variables that we'll need in T's methods, cursor and types.

You probably remember that the logic that we built into the *runner.py* file relies on receiving a cursor parameter sent from the client. This variable is used to determine which tweets have already been seen by the client when it requests new updates. This variable is stored in the object's cursor field. We also create an array with the names of the possible types of tweets we'll be filtering, which will allow us to loop through them in various places in the code.

The first of T's methods that we define is the init method. This is used to set up anything before we actually get to requesting data from the server. It uses jQuery to bind a method to the onClick event of every checkbox on the page to the T.click method.

The T.click method is defined next. This method is called only as a callback from a JavaScript onClick event on one of our checkboxes. T.click is just to update the checkboxes in the user interface to behave as a user would expect. We're doing this because one of our checkboxes works a bit differently than the rest. A checkbox called "All" will enable the user to see all types of tweets as they come in. If users click on that, we want to set all of the other checkboxes to match it. So if a user checks the "All" checkbox, we want all of the other types to be checked as well. If the user unchecks the box, we want all checkboxes to become unchecked. We do that by looping through the array of T.types that we created earlier and checking or unchecking all of the matching checkboxes. If the user isn't clicking on the "All" checkbox, we mark it as unchecked.

We're also creating the poll method here. This is the method that actually makes the long polling request to our Tornado server. If our object has a cursor set, we'll pass that along as a parameter. We also specify T.new_tweets as a callback method for when the request is finished. The request is being made to the URL /updates, which has been mapped in Tornado to the UpdateHandler method in *runner.py*.

Now that we're polling for updates, let's create the method that will catch them as they are sent by the server. Append the following code to your *twitter.js* file:

```
T.new_tweets = function(response) {
    if(!T.cursor)
        $('#waiting').remove();

    T.cursor = response.tweets[response.tweets.length - 1].id;

    for(var i = 0; i < response.tweets.length; ++i) {
        if(T.should_show_tweet(response.tweets[i])) {
            var d = $(response.tweets[i].html);
            d.css('display', 'none');
            $('#content').prepend(d);
            d.slideDown();
        }
    }
}
```

```
        // clean up the DOM
        var limit = 100;
        var messages = $('.message');
        for(var x = messages.length-1; x > limit; --x)
            $(messages[x]).remove();

        T.poll();
    };
```

If we ran this code now, it would give us some JavaScript errors, but we've got everything in place to actually show the tweets on the page. The first thing we do is check
to see whether this is our first time through this function. We determine this by checking
for the existence of a cursor variable; if there isn't one, it's our first time through and
we remove the "Waiting for content…" message. After that, we save the id of the last
tweet to our cursor field. This is the field that is sent back in the poll method.

Next, we loop through all of the tweets we've just received, check to see whether we
should display them, and actually add them to the page. We've already built the HTML
string in *runner.py*, so all we need to do is add it to the DOM. We use jQuery to create
the DOM element, prepend it to our content DIV, and show it with the slideDown effect.

We'll be appending quite a few tweets to the page every second, so the DOM is going
to get quite large. To counter this, we're going to keep only the last 100 tweets on the
page. We use jQuery's CSS selector methods to grab all of the messages and remove all
but the latest 100 of them. Once we've cleaned up the DOM a bit, we call the poll
method and start the process over again.

You've probably noticed that we checked to see whether we should display the tweets
using the should_show_tweet method, but we haven't defined it yet. So let's create that
method now. Add the following code to your *twitter.js* file:

```
    T.should_show_tweet = function(tweet) {
        $('#all-count').text(parseInt($('#all-count').text())+1);

        var show_tweet = false;

        for(x in T.types) {
            var type = T.types[x];

            // does the tweet have the specified type?
            if(tweet.stats[type].length) {

                // does the user want to see it?
                if($("#" + type).attr('checked'))
                    show_tweet = true;

                var count_div = $('#' + type + '-count');
                count_div.text(parseInt(count_div.text())+1);

            }
        }
        return show_tweet;
    };
```

Although this method is called should_show_tweet, we actually do two different things. In the HTML template, we defined a space to keep track of the number of each type of tweet that we've received. So the first thing we do is increment the number of all tweets that have seen. On top of tracking the counts of each type of tweet, this will show how many total tweets have gone through the stream.

The tweet object that we're receiving is a JSON version of the object we built in *runner.py*. It has fields for the id, the html to display, and the dictionary of stats. This method only cares about that stats dictionary, which is nothing more than a key-value pair of the type of stat (hashtags, for example) and the result of our regular expression for that field. So to check whether a tweet has a hashtag or any of our filter criteria, we simply need to know if there are objects in the array for that array key. If we wanted to check for hashtags, we'd simply need to use the following code.

```
if(tweets.stats["hashtags"].length) {
    alert("Hurray! This tweet contains hashtags");
}
```

Since we're checking for several different types of filter criteria, we loop through the T.types array and check each type. If the tweet matches a specific part of our criteria, we then check to see whether the user has checked the corresponding checkbox in the HTML template. We're letting the users configure what types of tweets they want to see, and this check ensures that they only see those types. Initially the show_tweet variable is set to false, but if the user wants to see it, we set that variable to true and continue on with the method.

Since we're also counting the number of tweets we get for each type, we don't return immediately after determining whether we should show the tweet. That's because we're keeping track of several different types of tweets. Each time we get a match on one of those types, we increment the counter for that type; the next two lines of code do just that. This will ensure that we count the tweets even when we're not showing them.

We've finally finished writing the code, so let's start this up. In your terminal window, enter the following command:

```
~ $ python runner.py
```

Pointing your browser to *http://localhost:8888* should show quite a bit of data coming in. Figure 5-7 shows what it should look like.

The default settings for this application are pretty unusable. Unchecking some of the checkboxes should help a bit. It's easy to imagine setting up some extra filters to make the experience more compelling, but this is a good start to a realtime application with Twitter's data. Try changing the application to use the filter API with some keywords that interest you, or even track Twitter's trending topics. You could also let the user pick some keywords for filtering the data.

Figure 5-7. Data streaming through our Twitter application

If you look at the terminal window where you started the server, you'll notice tons of logging information is streaming by very quickly (see Figure 5-8). Because the data is coming in so fast and being served out in real time, this log moves very quickly.

If you point different browsers at the URL, you'll see even more logging information. When working with large amounts of data and concurrent users, you'll want to be careful with the amount of logging that your application does. If you were writing this log to a file, it could easily fill up a hard drive very quickly.

Figure 5-8. Watching the log messages from our application

## CHAPTER 6

Chat

One of the most compelling aspects of creating realtime web applications is the ability to create experiences that were previously available only on the desktop. The syndication example worked as a realtime experience from server to server, and the others have largely been from server to user. This chapter builds on those principles to create a realtime user-to-user experience. In this chapter, we're going to exploit JavaScript and Tornado to build a fully interactive realtime chat application reminiscent of AOL Instant Messenger.

Before moving onto the code, it's important to discuss what features a user expects to see when he logs into an instant messaging application. The obvious first expectation is that the application will deliver the messages instantly. Second, chat sessions happen between two specific users; this is not group chat. Finally, users of modern chat applications expect subtle realtime interactions, such as the ability to see that the user on the other end of the line is typing. This application will have those features while operating in a standard web browser.

Setting Up the Basic Code

The Basic HTML Frame

Building this application with Tornado means we can reuse the existing directory structure from our last application. We'll store our templates in the existing *templates* folder and our static JavaScript files in the *static* directory. To get started, open your *templates* directory and create a file called *chat-main.html*. Add the following code to that file:

```
<!DOCTYPE html>
<html>
  <head>
    <title>Realtime Chat</title>
    <style>.chat-content { max-height: 200px; overflow: auto; }</style>
  </head>
```

```
<body class="yui-skin-sam">
  <div id="container">

    <!-- a super basic login window -->
    <div id="login">
      <div class="hd">Enter a username</div><!-- login window titlebar -->
      <div class="bd"><!-- login window content -->
        <input type="text" id="username" />
        <input type="button" id="login-button" value="Log In" />
      </div>
      <div class="ft"></div><!-- login window footer -->
    </div>

  </div>

  <!-- Include a JavaScript file from Yahoo! -->
  <script type="text/javascript"
    src="http://yui.yahooapis.com/2.8.0r4/build/yuiloader/yuiloader-min.js">
  </script>

  <!-- Include our local JS file -->
  <script type="text/javascript" src="{{ static_url('chat.js') }}"></script>

</body>
</html>
```

This chat application is about demonstrating how realtime interfaces can make web applications behave with the same level of interactivity and responsiveness as desktop-based applications; it's not about building a complicated user interface. So our HTML for this application is just a shell of a page with the JavaScript includes that we'll need.

The most important thing to notice about this page is that we're including some JavaScript and stylesheets from Yahoo!. In this example, we'll be using some of the great (Yahoo User Interface Library (YUI) (*http://developer.yahoo.com/yui/*) JavaScript library. This library includes code for everything from Ajax convenience functions to interface elements called widgets. YUI allows you to mix and match components so that you can use only what you need. Because this application will use a few different parts of the YUI library, we're utilizing YUILoader to automatically calculate and include the JavaScript and CSS dependencies. Including the external files like this allows YUI to determine exactly what needs to be downloaded, and it can combine the JavaScript into one download. Fewer downloads means faster load times and a more thoroughly realtime experience.

One of the things that sticks out about the HTML shown earlier is the class names for the div and body tags. These classes are used by YUI to style the interface elements when it comes time to render the page. You're free to change or omit the class names, but you'll lose the benefit of the styles provided by the library.

The way we include the other JavaScript file should look familiar after reading the previous chapter. It's simply using Tornado's static_url function to include a file from our *static* directory. We'll add the *chat.js* file soon; it's important and does all of the client-side work in this example. However, let's set up the basic Tornado server file so that we can get this example running.

The Python Shell

Since this example also uses Tornado, there is no complicated server setup. We simply write a script using the right libraries and run it directly. Open up a file called *chat-server.py* and add the following code:

```python
import os, logging
import tornado.httpserver
import tornado.ioloop
import tornado.web
import uuid
import simplejson as json
from tornado.options import define, options

# Define options that can be changed as we run this via the command line
define("port", default=8888, help="Run server on a specific port", type=int)

# a convenience function to quickly build a notification object
def notification(_type, _data):
    return {'type': _type, 'data': _data}

# Declare the chat class. We'll fill it out later
class Chat(object):
    pass

# The Basic handler class
class BaseHandler(tornado.web.RequestHandler):
    @property
    def chat(self):
        return self.application.chat

# handle the main html request
class MainHandler(BaseHandler):
    def get(self):
        self.render("templates/chat-main.html")

# Extend tornado's web.Application module
class Application(tornado.web.Application):
    def __init__(self):
        # setup the URL handlers
        handlers = [
            (r"/", MainHandler),
        ]

        # setup the static path
        path = os.path.join(os.path.dirname(__file__), "static")
        settings = dict(static_path=path)

        tornado.web.Application.__init__(self, handlers, **settings)
```

```
            # Load the chat class
            self.chat = Chat()

    # actually start up the server
    if __name__ == "__main__":
        http_server = tornado.httpserver.HTTPServer(Application())
        tornado.options.parse_command_line()
        http_server.listen(options.port)
        tornado.ioloop.IOLoop.instance().start()
```

Much of this script will look familiar from the last chapter. We import a number of Python modules that this file requires and use Tornado's `define` function to define the port the server will actually run on. Once again, this can be changed at runtime.

The first thing in this file other than the standard pieces is a global function called `notification`. This is just a convenience function to help build the notification object that we send to the browser. While the realtime web is a largely being built on top of sending messages or notifications, each application needs to define what the messages look like. In this case they're going to have a type such as "login" and a data payload, such as information about the user that just came online.

Next, this script defines two new classes that are essentially empty. The `Chat` class will contain some of the basic functionality needed for this script, including keeping track of which users are connected and sending out new messages. This is an important class that will be filled in throughout the chapter.

The `BaseHandler` class extends Tornado's `web.RequestHandler` module. Each of our controller classes that actually respond to HTTP requests will extend this class, so any method we add to this class is available in those classes as well. This class defines the method `chat`, which simply returns the `chat` object from the main `application` object. Adding the `@property` decorator allows our code to access that method as we would access a read-only variable. This will help out in our controller functions by allowing us to reference `self.chat.`*`some_method`*`()` instead of `self.application.chat()` `.`*`some_method`*`()`. The Python `@property` decorator saves some typing and also allows developers to add logic into basic getter methods.

The `MainHandler` class also looks like a shell of a class, but that's actually all we need to serve the web page requests for this application. This class just accepts **get** requests and renders the *chat-main.html* file from our templates directory.

This example expands on the previous chapter by building an `Application` object that extends Tornado's `web.Application`. While the organization of this section has changed, the logic is just the same. We build a simple list that instructs Tornado which class is responsible for each URL. Next, we specify the settings, which in this case is nothing more than the location of the static files. Then, we pass those variables to the `tornado.web.Application` object when we initialize it.

The `Application` class also defines and loads a member variable called `self.chat`, which is an instance of the chat class that was defined earlier. Creating this object here, and only here, will ensure that we have only one server-side chat object for the entire lifetime of the server.

At the tail end of the script, we run the basic code to start the server. It parses the command-line options in case you want to override the default port or any other setting. Then, it instructs the Tornado's `http_server` to listen on that port. Finally, it starts up the loop that runs until the server is killed.

The JavaScript Base

Now that we have a runnable Python script and a serviceable HTML page, we just need to add some JavaScript to finish building the shell of our application. In the *static* directory, create a file called *chat.js*. This is the file that is included via the `static_url` function inside our *chat-main.html* template. In *chat.js*, add the following code:

```javascript
// Load the YUI JavaScript from Yahoo.
new YAHOO.util.YUILoader({
    require: ["connection","container","fonts",
              "json", "yahoo-dom-event", "dragdrop"],
    combine: true, // combine the files
    filter: "MIN", // minimize them
    // once the includes are loaded, initialize the chat code
    onSuccess: function() { chat.init(); }  // our callback function
}).insert();

// the basic object that we'll be using
var chat = {
    login_panel: false, //
    user_id: false,     // the current user (me)
    user_name: false,   // the current user name (me)
    users: [],          // all connected users
    user_count: 0       // the count of those users.
};

chat.init = function() {
    // Setup the onClick method
    YAHOO.util.Event.addListener("login-button",
                                 "click",
                                 chat.login);

    // turn the login div into a YUI panel
    chat.login_panel = new YAHOO.widget.Panel("login", { width:"230px",
                                                         visible:true,
                                                         close:false,
                                                         constraintoviewport:true
                                                       } );
    chat.login_panel.render();
};
```

This is just a shell of the JavaScript code that we're going to need, but it's enough to get started. To begin, we make a call using the YUI toolkit to load all of the JavaScript and CSS that we'll need for this application. YUI has truckloads of different features, but you're not required to download all of them every time. This allows you to mix and match and include only what is useful for each application. In this case, we're loading files related to Ajax commands, YUI interface widgets, font stylesheets, JSON encoding and decoding, basic DOM event wrappers, and drag-and-drop functionality. Aside from instructing YUI to minimize the JavaScript and combine it into one HTTP request, all we do is set up the callback function that gets called when all of the code has been loaded. We set that up to call `chat.init`, which will initialize our chat application.

The JavaScript side of the chat application will be built as one big JavaScript object. The next lines in the file start building that object, defining some variables that we'll use later. The variables `user_id` and `user_name` reference the current user, whereas the remaining variables are used to keep track of every other user using the application.

The `chat.init` method is what gets called as soon as YUI has loaded all of the required JavaScript and the page is ready to go. This method immediately adds an `onClick` event to the `login-button` input button. When clicked, this method will call a method on the `chat` object called `login`.

The next two statements simply tell YUI that the `div` we created in *chat-main.html* should be rendered as a YUI Panel and behave as one. In the options, we tell it to be visible, that it should not have a close button, and that it should stay in the viewport or the bounds of the browser window. A YUI Panel is a `div` that is rendered to look and act like a separate window. It's just a `div` on the page, but it has the appearance of a window, complete with a title bar, and can be moved around by the user.

Checking the Progress

At this point, we have a shell of JavaScript, Python, and even some HTML. Running the script now will give us a good look at what users will see when they first come to this application. Open your terminal window and start up the server:

```
~ $ python chat-server.py
```

If you open your browser to *http://localhost:8888*, it should look something like Figure 6-1.

The first thing to notice is that YUI really added a lot of functionality right out of the box. First, it styled the simple `div` from our HTML and made it look like a window. It also added drag and drop functionality, allowing users to move the `div` around their browser windows. At this point, it looks like an application that may do something, but it isn't able to do anything at all. It's time to start plugging in some real functionality.

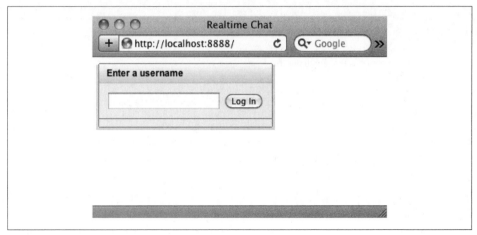

Figure 6-1. The login window

Logging In

The first thing we'll need to add to this script is the ability for users to sign in. This won't be a complicated login process; it will only require users to select a username in order to access the system. Using Tornado's authentication functionality, it would be fairly easy to implement a much more robust login scheme, but that's overkill for this example.

On the Server Side

To accommodate users logging into the chat application, the Python script is going to need to accept login requests for the form we created before. To do that, we'll need to expand the list of URL handlers from the main application class. In the *chat-server .py* file, locate the `Application` class and make the following highlighted change:

```
class Application(tornado.web.Application):
    def __init__(self):
    # setup the URL handlers
        handlers = [
            (r"/", MainHandler),
            (r"/login/?", LoginHandler),
            (r"/updates/?", UpdateHandler),
            ]
```

This addition tells Tornado to accept requests for */login* and direct them to a class called `LoginHandler`. That class is illustrated next; add it to the *chat-server.py* file:

```
class LoginHandler(BaseHandler):
    def post(self):
        # generate a unique ID for each user
        user_id = str(uuid.uuid4())
```

```
# get the user_name submitted from the form
user_name = self.get_argument('username')

# Add this user to the chat class
self.chat.add_user(user_id, user_name)

# We're done, notify the client.
self.finish(dict(user_id=user_id, user_name=user_name, users=self.chat.users))
```

This login handler class just does a couple of things before handing the real work off to the chat class to process the request. Any time it receives a post request, it generates a unique enough identifier using Python's uuid. This user_id field will be used internally by the server and client side of this application to identify users.

This controller function also collects the username field from the text input field on the HTML form and sets it to user_name. Our call to self.get_argument doesn't specify a default value if none is specified by the client. If it's not included in the HTTP request, Tornado will automatically reject it with a 404 error, so we don't have to do any checking to see whether it exists. Other than an empty field, this code accepts any value it receives for a username. If you were building this for a production environment, you would probably want to check for duplicate usernames, invalid characters, and anything else your application would require.

The user_id and user_name are then passed off to a method called add_user in the chat object. That's the code that is going to do the heavy lifting for the login process, and we'll get to that next. But at the end of this method, we call Tornado's finish method to print out a JSON response. This response includes the user_id, and the accepted user_name, as well as a list of all of the connected users. To generate that list of users, the Chat class needs to be expanded.

The current Chat class has nothing more than a pass statement inside it. The pass statement is Python's way of having an empty block, or empty class in this case. We're going to want to replace the current Chat with the following code:

```
class Chat(object):
    listeners = []  # connected clients waiting for a callback
    users = []      # the list of currently logged in users

    def add_listener(self, callback, user_id=None):
        data = {}
        data['user_id'] = user_id
        data['callback'] = callback
        self.listeners.append(data)

    def add_user(self, user_id, user_name):
        # assemble the user data into an object
        user_data = dict(user_id=user_id, user_name=user_name)

        # store the user data in the users list
        self.users.append(user_data)
```

```
# let the other users know about this new user
note = notification('login', user_data)
self.send_notification(note)
```

This code introduces two variables that are used to store information about the current chat session. The `users` variable is a list that will contain all of the users currently logged in. The `listeners` variable is a list of the web clients that are currently awaiting a callback. The two methods defined here are designed to populate those lists with data.

The `add_listener` method simply appends the supplied information onto the `listeners` list. The listeners list is exactly the same as the `waiters` list from the previous chapter. Because this application works using Tornado's long polling framework, any client that connects hits an asynchronous method. Before that method returns, it sets up a callback method that should be called when new data becomes available. In this script, all of that is handled by this `Chat` class, and `add_listener` method queues up all of the clients waiting for new messages. When new data is available, after an `add_user` calls for example, the listeners on this list are notified by calling their callback methods.

You may remember the next method, `add_user`, because we actually wrote code that uses it already. In the `LoginHandler` controller, we call `self.chat.add_user` and supply it with the user information; that is this method. It takes those user variables and appends them to the `users` list defined earlier. The next thing this method does is create a notification object called `note` with the `notification` global function defined earlier. This is the object that is sent to clients to let them know something has happened. In this case, the server will inform the clients that a user has logged in and give them the user's information. This `note` object will be sent to all of the connected clients via the `send_notification` method, which we'll define next.

This chat class needs only one final thing: the ability to run the callback methods for each of the listeners when new data arrives. This is done through the `send_notification` method. When a client logs in, we send a notification to all of the connected clients. When one user wants to send a message to another user, we need to send a notification to that user. To get this functionality, add the following code to the `Chat` class:

```
def send_notification(self, message, user_id=None):
    # create a copy of the listeners list and clear the original
    tmp_listeners = self.listeners
    self.listeners = []

    # loop through the list of listeners
    for data in tmp_listeners:

        # if we're not sending it to all users,
        if user_id != None:
            # and we're not sending it to this user
            if user_id != data['user_id']:
                # keep listening, but don't send any messages
                self.listeners.append(data)
```

```
        continue

    # run the callback function
    callback = data['callback']
    try:
        callback(message)
    except:
        logging.error("Error in listeners callback", exc_info=True)
```

At a very high level, this method loops through all of the clients currently listening for
a callback and sends each of them a message. This implementation is a bit more complicated than that because we may or may not be sending the notification to all of the
connected clients. This method has to account for several things. First, if it sends a
message to a specific user, it must remove that user from the listeners list, as she will
be receiving a notification and will need to reconnect. It also needs to know whether
it's sending a notification to a specific user or to every user who is currently connected.
Finally, it needs to run the actual callback method. The flow of the method looks
something like Figure 6-2.

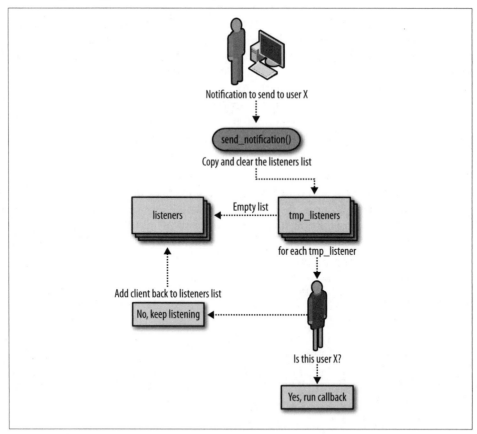

Figure 6-2. The flow of send_notification

The first thing this method does is create a copy of the `listeners` list called `tmp_listen ers` and then clear the original list. We clear out the list because every listener whose callback we actually run no longer needs to be in the listeners list. If the callback is called, we'll end up closing the HTTP connection to the client, and they'll have to reconnect and add themselves to the listeners list again. So instead of looping through `listeners`, we clear it out and loop through `tmp_listeners` instead.

If no `user_id` is supplied to this method, we simply run the callback on every single listener and never add any back to the original listeners list. However, if a `user_id` has been supplied, we need to check each listener and send it only to the correct user. As we loop through the list and find users that are not matches, we add them back to the main `listeners` array and `continue` on with the loop. Each time we actually run the callback, we supply the `message` as the parameter, catching any errors and logging them.

Several of our methods thus far have dealt with callbacks and responding to them, but this script hasn't actually added the ability to request them. So that's the next thing to add. Although requesting callbacks isn't needed to actually log in, it is needed to find out when other users have logged in. So let's add that before we move on to the Java-Script portion. In your *chat-server.py* file, add the following code, but be sure to add it after the `BaseHandler` definition.

```
class UpdateHandler(BaseHandler):

    @tornado.web.asynchronous
    def post(self):
        user_id = self.get_argument('user_id')

        # add a listener, specifying the handle_updates callback
        self.chat.add_listener(self.async_callback(self.handle_updates),
                               user_id=user_id)

    # when we get a callback, send it to the client
    def handle_updates(self, update):
        if not self.request.connection.stream.closed():
            self.finish(update)
```

According to the URL mapping that we specified, this `UpdateHandler` class handles all the requests that come into the */updates* URL. This class has two main jobs, which are handled by the two methods defined here. When a web client requests updates from the server, whether the updates are login notifications or chat messages, it does so by making a long polling request to the */updates* URL. That request is handled by the `post` method. The only work to be done is to add the client as a listener of the chat object. The call to `add_listener` tells the chat object to call the `handle_updates` method when new data arrives for the supplied `user_id`. Because this is an asynchronous method, that callback method is wrapped in Tornado's `async_callback` functionality.

Once the chat class has data available for a specific client, it will call that client's callback function. That function is `handle_updates`, which has one job: send the data to the client. This method handles that by checking to ensure the client is still connected and then calling Tornado's `finish` method with the supplied Python dictionary. Tornado will automatically convert this dictionary to a JSON object, and finally close the connection to the client. At that point, it's the responsibility of the JavaScript client to reconnect and start the process over.

JavaScript

On the server side of things, we built a couple of URL endpoints that were designed to be used by the JavaScript side of the application. The `/updates` URL will be used to subscribe to notifications as they're sent from the server, and we designed the `/login` URL to help a user log in. We now need to hook up the JavaScript side of the application to interact with those URLs.

We've already built some of the JavaScript required for the application. The YUI code should be loading and the basic chat object has been configured, but as of yet, nothing is talking with the server. In the code we've already written, an event listener has been configured so that when the user clicks on the login button, we're expecting to get a callback to a method called `chat.login`. That method needs to make an Ajax request to the `/login` URL. Open your *chat.js* file and add the following code:

```
chat.login = function() {
    var username = document.getElementById('username').value;

    if(!username.length) {
        chat.login_panel.setFooter("Please specify a username");
        return false;
    }

    // Give the user feedback about what's happening
    chat.login_panel.setFooter("Logging in...");

    // setup the callback function and HTTP parameters
    var callback = { success: chat.login_success };


    // Make the Ajax request
    YAHOO.util.Connect.asyncRequest('POST',
                                    '/login',
                                    callback,
                                    'username=' + username);
};
```

Applications built on the realtime web must be responsive to every user interaction, so the first thing this code does is give the user some immediate feedback. If the user has neglected to supply a username, we politely ask her to provide one and return without going any further. Otherwise, we inform the user that the application has received the request and is working on getting her signed in.

To notify the user of these types of status messages, we update part of the login window that we created in HTML and then rendered as a YUI Panel in the `chat.init` method. These Panel interface widgets have a footer `div` that was designed to give the user this type of feedback. We simply call the `setFooter` method and YUI takes care of the rest.

The rest of the method is dedicated to the actual Ajax request. Since this request is an asynchronous HTTP request, we specify a callback method named `chat.login_success`. This will be called by YUI's Connect class as soon as the Ajax call returns successfully. The `/login` URL takes only one parameter, the `username` to associate with the user who is logging in. Once we make that request, we exit this method and wait for a response in our callback method. It should happen almost instantly. Open your *chat.js* file and add that callback method:

```
chat.login_success = function(ev) {
    // Tell the user we got a response
    chat.login_panel.setFooter("Success!");

    // Wait a moment and then close the login window
    setTimeout(function() { chat.login_panel.destroy(); }, 500);

    // parse the response data and setup the chat object
    data = YAHOO.lang.JSON.parse(ev.responseText);
    chat.user_id = data.user_id;
    chat.user_name = data.user_name;

    // loop through the list of other users
    for(var x in data.users) {
        var user = data.users[x];
        if(user.user_id != chat.user_id)
            chat.add_user(user);
    }

    // begin (long) polling the server for updates
    chat.poll();
};
```

Once again, the first step of this method is to give the user some feedback. In this case, we tell her that the login was successful by updating the footer of the login window. After that's displayed, we're not actually going to use that window anymore, so we wait for half a second and close that with the YUI Panel's **destroy** method. Beyond that, we know the response we receive from the server is a JSON object, so we parse that and set up the variables in the chat object with the proper `user_id` and `user_name` values.

The response we get from the call to `/login` provides the `user_id` and `user_name` of the user who just logged in, but it also provides a list of all the other connected users. We loop through that list, and each time through, as long as we're not looking at the current user, we call the method `chat.add_user`. This method generates chat windows for each of the connected users. This is what that method would look like:

```
chat.add_user = function(user) {
    chat.user_count++; // keep track of the # of connected users
```

```
        var u = {}; // build the user object
        u.user_name = user.user_name;
        u.user_id = user.user_id;
        // setup the window
        u.panel = new YAHOO.widget.Panel("user-" + user.user_id,
                                { width:"300px",
                                  constraintoviewport:true,
                                  x: chat.user_count * 50,
                                  y: chat.user_count * 50
                                } );

        // set the title of the window
        u.panel.setHeader("Chatting with " + user.user_name);

        // add content div, where we'll display the chat
        var content = document.createElement('div');
        content.setAttribute('id', 'chat-' + user.user_id);
        u.panel.appendToBody(content);

        // the textarea we'll use to send messages to this user
        var textarea = document.createElement('textarea');
        textarea.setAttribute('cols', 36);
        textarea.setAttribute('id', 'text-' + user.user_id);
        u.panel.appendToBody(textarea);

        // show the online status and hide it after half a second
        u.panel.setFooter("Online...");
        setTimeout(function() { u.panel.setFooter(''); }, 500);

        // keep track of all of the connected users.
        chat.users[user.user_id] = u;
        // render the window
        u.panel.render("container");
    };
```

There is quite a bit of code in this method, but most of it is geared toward creating the HTML elements that are needed in the actual chat window. The first thing it does is increment the user_count variable. There are ways that we could dynamically figure out how many users are connected each time we need to know, but keeping it calculated in advance will save some computation and lead to a faster experience on browsers with slow JavaScript implementations.

 The speed of JavaScript is another factor in truly realtime web experiences. For more information on this topic, I highly recommend the book *High Performance JavaScript* by Nicholas C. Zakas (O'Reilly).

In addition to creating and showing some HTML elements that represent the user on the screen, we also want to build a JavaScript object that represents the user in the code. That object contains the user_name and user_id fields as well as the actual YUI Panel object. The login panel is created with an ID that is unique to the user being added.

The x and y coordinates are set dynamically to ensure that this window doesn't completely cover any of the other windows that have already been displayed.

Next, we set the title of the Panel window and create the HTML elements within it. The first element created is the `div` that will actually be used as the content area of the chat. When a user sends a message, it will be rendered in the content `div`. Since the `chat` object will add the content to this `div` from other functions, we set the `id` attribute of the `div` to a value that is unique to the user it represents. The `textarea` is then rendered in the same fashion. This `textarea` will be the input field for sending new messages in the chat window.

Now, we've built the contents of the chat window, we want to give the user some feedback about what just happened. So, in the footer of the newly created window, the next line shows that the user is "Online." Rather than keep that as a permanent status message for the user, we set up a function to clear the message after half a second. It may seem like a superfluous action, but it's these types of small details that create a well-rounded experience for the user.

At this point, we're done building the internal representation of the user, so we add it to the `chat.users` array. This object is used in other methods to help keep track of users as they perform different actions. After that, we simply need to render the chat window to the screen.

The final bit of code needed to tie the whole login process together is the ability to poll the server to receive notifications. As shown earlier, the `login_success` method looped through all of the connected users and added them to the screen. Once it finished displaying the users, it ran a method called `chat.poll` to start polling the server for new updates. It's a simple little method to add to the *chat.js* file:

```
chat.poll = function() {
    var callback = { success: chat.handle_updates };
    YAHOO.util.Connect.asyncRequest('POST',
                                    '/updates',
                                    callback,
                                    'user_id=' + chat.user_id);
};
```

After seeing how the Ajax request worked in the login method, this code should look pretty familiar. All this does is make a request to the `/updates` URL and specify a callback for when it successfully returns. In the Python code, the class `UpdateHandler` responds to the `/updates` URL, it's designed to be general enough to handle responses for all types of events. So we've specified a general `handle_updates` as the callback method for those requests. We'll be expanding this method a bit, but to handle login requests, it's fairly straightforward:

```
chat.handle_updates = function(ev) {
    // parse the JSON
    var message = YAHOO.lang.JSON.parse(ev.responseText);
```

```
        // if it's a login request, add the user to the screen
        if(message.type == 'login') {
            chat.add_user(message.data);
            chat.poll(); // keep polling
        }
    };
```

This method gets called as a result of a successful Ajax request. It receives a parameter that is a JavaScript object containing information about the request. There are fields that include the response headers and status messages, but the only field we're concerned with is `responseText`. This field contains a text representation of the output of our `UpdateHandler` server method. That object is a JSON string, so we parse that into a native JavaScript object and inspect the message's `type` field. If it's a `login` message, we pass the data part of the object up to the `add_user` method, which will show the window on the screen. After that, we run the `poll` method to keep polling the server in order to receive more updates as they happen.

At this point we're logging in successfully, adding users to the screen, and polling for updates from the server. We're really getting somewhere. Figure 6-3 shows what it should look like if you start the server and log in different usernames in a few different browser windows.

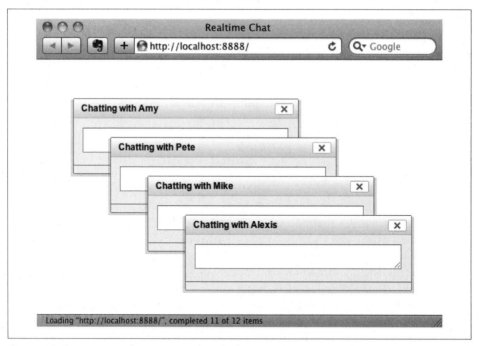

Figure 6-3. Starting up a chat session with multiple users

Basic Chatting

It looks like a chat application and it allows multiple users to log in, but it has one fatal flaw: users cannot actually send or receive any chat messages. To allow users to send messages, we need to make a couple of changes. The server-side Python code has almost everything needed to support this feature; now it just needs to accept the messages from the web client and funnel them to the other users. Luckily, much of that code is already written.

Chatting on the Server Side

The Python code already has the ability to send generic messages to users via the `send_notification` method. So the only thing we need to handle basic chatting is to catch messages from the user and funnel them through that method. To do that, we need to add one more URL handler to the array. In the `Application.__init__` method of *chat-server.py*, make the following addition:

```
class Application(tornado.web.Application):
    def __init__(self):
    # setup the URL handlers
        handlers = [
            (r"/", MainHandler),
            (r"/login/?", LoginHandler),
            (r"/updates/?", UpdateHandler),
            (r"/send/?", SendHandler),
            ]
```

This code just sets up another URL handler so that Tornado knows which class should respond to requests to the /send URL. That class, `SendHandler`, will be responsible for accepting the user input, building a message, and sending it to the receiving user. In *chat-server.py*, add the following code above the `Application` class:

```
class SendHandler(BaseHandler):
    def post(self):

        # who is the message to and from?
        to_user_id = self.get_argument('to_user_id')
        from_user_id = self.get_argument('from_user_id')

        # setup the message object that is sent to the user
        data = dict(from_user_id=from_user_id,
                    to_user_id=to_user_id,
                    text=self.get_argument('text'))

        # build and send the notification
        msg = notification('message', data)
        self.chat.send_notification(msg, user_id=to_user_id)

        # send a response to the user sending the message
        msg['type'] = 'sent'
        self.finish(msg)
```

Although we haven't built the JavaScript side of this method yet, it's not hard to imagine what should go into a request to send a chat message. That call would need to know who the message was being sent from, who is receiving it, and the actual text of the message. The first part of this method collects the to and from parameters and puts them into a dictionary with the text of the message itself. That `data` object is populated with both the `to_user_id` and the `from_user_id`, which will be used by the JavaScript side of the application to determine who sent the message.

Next, we build the notification object using the `notification` function, which builds a Python dictionary in the format expected by the `send_notification` method. Once that is built, we send the message to the user through that `send_notification` method.

Finally, it's probably a good idea to let the sending user know the message has been sent successfully. To do that, we just update the `type` field of the `msg` object to reflect that the message has been sent instead of received.

Sending Messages

Now that the server is expecting us to send messages, let's get it set up on the client side. For each connected user, the chat window has an HTML `textarea` input field designed for writing messages; however, there is no way to submit them. Rather than forcing the user to type a message and then click a "send" button, this application is going to automatically send messages when the user presses the Enter key. To do this, we need to make modifications to the *chat.js* file. First, we need to listen for keyboard events on that text area. The best place to do that is inside the `chat.add_user` method that already exists. At the end of that method, add the following code:

```
    // render the window
    u.panel.render("container");

    // listen for keypresses
    YAHOO.util.Event.addListener("text-" + user.user_id, "keypress", chat.keypress);
};
```

That line of code sets up an event listener to catch all the keypresses that occur in the `textarea` field. Any time a user types into that text field, we'll immediately get a callback to the `chat.keypress` method. Let's add that next:

```
chat.keypress = function(ev) {
    // the ev.target is the textarea field
    var textarea = ev.target;

    // parse the user_id from the textarea id
    var to_user_id = textarea.id.replace("text-", "");

    // setup the basic Ajax HTTP parameters (to and from)
    var params = "from_user_id=" + chat.user_id;
    params += "&to_user_id=" + to_user_id;
```

```
// Did they press the enter key?
if(ev.keyCode && (ev.keyCode == 13)) {

    // add the message text to the parameters
    params += "&text=" + textarea.value;

    // reuse the handle_updates method and run the Ajax
    var callback = { success: chat.handle_updates };
    YAHOO.util.Connect.asyncRequest('POST',
                                    '/send',
                                    callback,
                                    params);
}
};
```

The main job of this code is to listen for every keystroke until it detects that the Enter key has been pressed. Once that happens, it will make an Ajax request to the server.

The first thing this method does is figure out which user is supposed to be on the receiving end of this message. When we added each textfield to the page, we gave them all predictable id attributes. Each id is the string text- followed by the user_id. So to figure out the user, we simply parse out everything after text- in that id field. That value becomes the to_user_id, which is the user who should receive this message.

We know it's time to send the message if the user has hit the Enter key. To detect this, we simply inspect the ev object, which is the event object that arrives as the only parameter to this callback method. In JavaScript, the Enter key is represented by the number 13. If the keyCode is 13, the user is pressing the Enter key; otherwise, she's just typing the rest of the message.

Once we've detected that the user is pressing the Enter key, it's time to send the message via a standard Ajax request. The textarea contains the text of the message, so we just need to append that to the existing parameter string contained in the params variable. Then, we specify that we want a callback to our existing chat.handle_updates method upon a successful request. Next, we fire off that request and wait for the callback to tell us that everything worked.

Right now, that message will be sent to the server and the server will attempt to send it to the other user, but nothing happens on this end. We're going to want to respond a bit to a successful request. To do that, make the following changes to the chat.handle_updates method:

```
    chat.poll(); // keep polling
}
else if(message.type == 'sent') {
    // clear the textarea
    var input = document.getElementById("text-" + message.data.to_user_id);
    input.value = "";
    input.focus();
    // show the message
    chat.append_message(message.data);
```

```
        }
    };
```

Having built a generic `chat.handle_updates` method, we can easily add new functionality by catching all notifications in this one method. This particular bit of code checks
the type of the notification message to see whether it's `sent`. If it is, it does two different
things. First, it clears out the text box and focuses it. This will ensure that the user
can just keep typing and sending messages without using the mouse or any other
interaction. The second and most important part of this code is that it calls
`chat.append_message` to show the message to the user. It's important that we display it
to the user on the receiving side, but we also have to show it to the user who is sending
it. Add the `chat.append_message` method to your *chat.js* file:

```
    chat.append_message = function(data) {

        // the user that sent the message
        var user_id = data.from_user_id;

        // the display name of who sent the message
        var from_user_name = "";

        // if it's from the current user, append it to the "to" user box.
        if(user_id == chat.user_id) {
            user_id = data.to_user_id;
            from_user_name = "You"; // it's from You, not them
        }
        else
            from_user_name = chat.users[user_id].user_name;

        var doc = document;
        var div = doc.createElement('div'); // create the HTML element

        // insert the message text into the message div
        div.appendChild(doc.createTextNode(from_user_name + ": " + data.text));

        // get the content div
        var contentDiv = doc.getElementById("chat-" + user_id);

        // append the content
        contentDiv.appendChild(div);

        // ensure the window is scrolled down to the newest message
        contentDiv.scrollTop = contentDiv.scrollHeight;
    };
```

The `chat.append_message` method is used for displaying messages both sent and received by the current user. So the first thing we do is figure out who sent us this message
and store it as `user_id`. This `user_id` variable will eventually be used by this method to
determine which chat window we should use to display this message. If we're receiving
this message from another user, we're going to append the message to that user's window and display it as coming from that particular username. However, if the message
is from us to another user, we'll display it in the window as sent by "You."

Next, we create a DIV element and append the message to it. Once we have the final div text that we'll be using, we append it to the actual chat window. Then, we grab the contentDiv, onto which we'll actually be appending the content. This is either the window of the user who sent the message or the window of the user who is receiving it. After appending the content, we scroll the contentDiv to ensure the newest message is still on the screen.

Receiving Messages

Since our methods are fairly generic, most of them are already working double duty for sending and receiving messages. We can send messages from the client, and the server already handles directing those messages back to the correct receiving client, so all we need to do is watch for those messages. To receive those messages, update the chat.handle_updates method and add the following code:

```
    else if(message.type == 'sent') {
        ...
    }
    else if(message.type == 'message') {
        chat.append_message(message.data);
        chat.poll(); // keep polling
    }
};
```

This code has a fairly easy job to do, so it does it quickly and gets out of the way. First, it calls the existing chat.append_message method to append this message to the correct window. Then, it continues polling the server for updates. When this code gets into the chat.append_message method, the only difference is that it will display the message as coming from the user who sent it instead of coming from "You."

We now have a pretty functional chat application. We can log in and send and receive messages in realtime. With YUI we can even drag windows around the screen and more or less act like a desktop application. Start up the server, launch a couple of browser windows, and test out what we've got so far.

```
~ $ python chat-server.py
```

Now open your browser window to *http://localhost:8888*. After logging in with a couple of different browser windows and chatting for a bit, you should see something like Figure 6-4.

Acting Natural

At this point we have a reasonably full-featured chat application. You can log in and chat with as many users as you like, and messages are sent around in realtime, but the experience is not quite complete. After a user sends a message to another user, there isn't a lot of feedback about what is happening. Users of modern chat applications expect to be informed about what the other user is doing. Is the user typing? Did the user start typing and stop? Is this person still online? These are the types of features that change a standard chat script into a living, breathing realtime application. Luckily, with the code that's already written, these features are easy to implement.

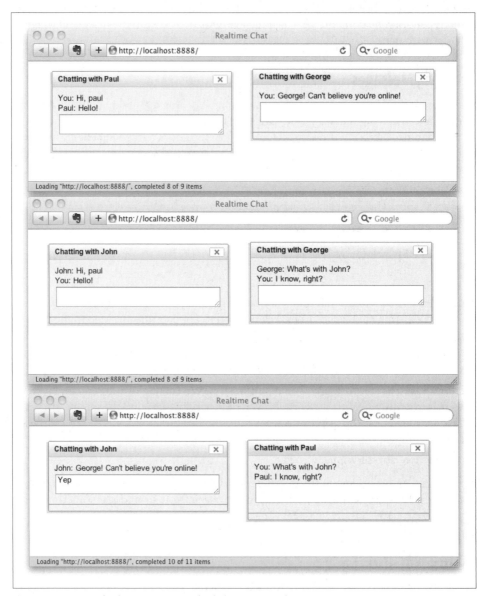

Figure 6-4. A sample chat session in multiple browser windows

When the ability to see that a user is typing was introduced into chat applications, it seemed like a little thing. But after using this feature for even a short amount of time, it became hard to remember how chatting worked without it. To enable it in this application, it's going to take a mixture of both Python and JavaScript. In the *chat-server.py* file, add a new URL handler to deal with typing messages:

```
class Application(tornado.web.Application):
        handlers = [
            (r"/", MainHandler),
            (r"/login/?", LoginHandler),
            (r"/updates/?", UpdateHandler),
            (r"/send/?", SendHandler),
            (r"/typing/?", TypingHandler),
        ]
```

This will route any requests for the URL **/typing** to a new class called **TypingHandler**. Moving right along, add the following code somewhere above the **Application** declaration:

```
class TypingHandler(BaseHandler):
    def post(self):
        # Who is typing to who?
        to_user_id = self.get_argument('to_user_id')
        from_user_id = self.get_argument('from_user_id')

        # build and send the notification
    data = dict(from_user_id=from_user_id, to_user_id=to_user_id)
    msg = notification('typing', data)
        self.chat.send_notification(msg, user_id=to_user_id)

        # respond to the sending user
        msg['type'] = 'recv'
        self.finish(msg)
```

This code actually looks quite similar to the **SendHandler** class. The first thing it does is gather the variables that were included as parameters to the HTTP request. Next, it builds a simple dictionary of those variables and creates the notification object. At this point, the only difference between this and the **SendHandler** class is that this class doesn't include any **text** parameter in the notification object. We're not actually sending the chat message at this point, just a notification informing the receiving user that someone is typing. After the notification is sent, we respond to the user who is actually doing the typing to indicate that the message was received.

That's all the server-side code needed for this feature. All that's left is to hook up the client-side code. In this case, the JavaScript code has two different jobs to do. First, when a user starts typing, it needs to make a request to the **/typing** URL to inform the other user. Then, on the receiving end, the JavaScript needs to update the UI to show that it's happening.

Luckily, we're already monitoring keystrokes on the client side while waiting for the user to press the Enter key. This code can easily go in that method as well. However, we don't want to send an update to the server with every single keystroke. We just want to determine whether a user is typing and ensure we send the notification once every couple of seconds. So first we want to keep track of every keystroke. To do that, let's add another variable to the main chat object. In the *chat.js* file, modify it to include the following variable:

```
var chat = {
    // initialize variables
    login_panel: false,
    user_id: false,     // the current user (me)
    ...
    previous_typing_ping: 0,
    timeouts: {};
};
```

We're going to ping the server every couple of seconds to let it know that the current user is typing a message to another user, and previous_typing_ping will hold the last time that we actually sent that message. When the user types a key, we'll be able to check whether enough time has elapsed between "now" and previous_typing_ping to warrant a new ping. Now that we have a place to store the amount of elapsed time, we need to actually monitor the typing and make the HTTP request. To do that, add the following code to chat.keypress:

```
// setup the Ajax params
var params = "from_user_id=" + chat.user_id;
params += "&to_user_id=" + to_user_id;
if(ev.keyCode && (ev.keyCode == 13)) {
    ...
}
else {
    // the current time, in milliseconds since 1970
    var now = new Date().getTime();

    // ping every 1.5 seconds (1500 milliseconds)
    if((now - chat.previous_typing_ping) > 1500) {
        // update the "previous" time
        chat.previous_typing_ping = now;
        // notification the server
        YAHOO.util.Connect.asyncRequest('POST', '/typing', false, params);
    }
}
```

This code monitors every keystroke that a user makes inside a textarea, except for the Enter key, which is caught by the if statement. When we get any other keystroke, we check to see how long ago we last submitted a request to the server. The first time a user starts typing, the previous_typing_ping variable is zero, which means the time difference between now and then is easily greater than one and a half seconds. So the first time a user types a key, we'll immediately send an HTTP request to /send. If the user types two keys in a row, chances are good that it'll be within that 1.5 second window, and we won't send a notification to the server.

We're not sending a request with every keystroke, because that would be a ton of keystrokes and thus a lot of HTTP requests. We can easily determine whether a user is typing and still conserve HTTP requests by giving it a reasonable timeout between keystrokes. Figure 6-5 shows this process.

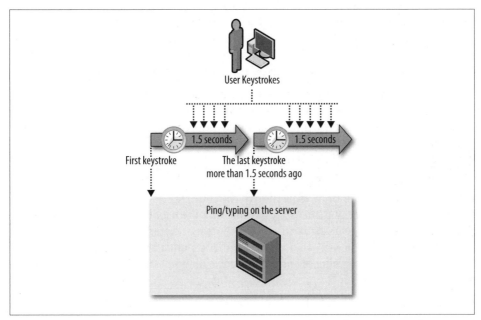

Figure 6-5. Waiting 1.5 seconds between requests to report new keystrokes

We're effectively queueing up and sending notifications when one user starts typing to another user. All that's left is to inform the user on the receiving end. Add the following code into the chat.handle_updates method of *chat.js*:

```
if(message.type == 'login') {
    ...
}
else if(message.type == 'typing') {
    // get the user
    var u = chat.users[message.data.from_user_id];
    u.panel.setFooter(u.user_name + ' is typing...');
    // clear any existing timeouts
    clearTimeout(chat.timeouts[u.user_id]);
    // setup a new timeout
    chat.timeouts[u.user_id] = setTimeout(function() {
                                   u.panel.setFooter(u.user_name + ' typed...');
                               }, 3000);
    chat.poll(); // keep polling
}
```

```
    else if(message.type == 'message') {
        chat.append_message(message.data);
        chat.poll(); // keep polling
        // clear the typing timeout
        var u = chat.users[message.data.from_user_id];
        clearTimeout(chat.timeouts[u.user_id]);
        // clear the footer status
        u.panel.setFooter('');
}
```

All of the notifications sent from the server go through this one function. So we simply add a new condition to the if statement and put our logic in there. We saved a reference to the user window along with each user object in the form of u.panel. We use that object and set the footer to inform the user that the other user has started typing.

We know that if the user continues to type, we'll get another message in 1.5 seconds, so we can actually inform the local user when the remote user has stopped typing. If we don't receive another typing message in the next three seconds, change the footer status message to say "typed" instead of "is typing." This will let the user know that the other party has started typing and stopped for some reason. If that user starts up again, we'll get another typing ping, and the status will be changed back to "is typing."

Finally, we make one minor modification to the code that handles receiving a message. When we get a message, we can safely assume that the user has stopped typing, so we clear the footer message along with any timeouts associated with it. When you set a timeout in JavaScript, it will call a callback function after a set period of time. If you keep track of the return value of the setTimeout call, you can clear it later if you want to cancel the timeout.

Restart the server, open a couple of browser windows, and try this out. It should look similar to Figure 6-6.

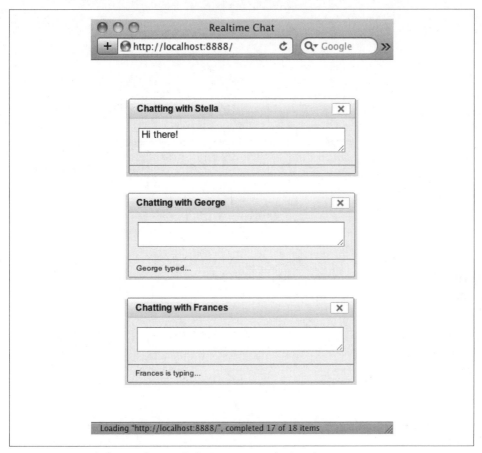

Figure 6-6. Several chat windows with the typing status displayed

## CHAPTER 7

Instant Messaging

We've already built an example of a fully featured chat application that functions entirely in a browser window, but realtime experiences are increasingly happening outside of the browser. Users expect to be able to input data and get it back out not only from an unending array of mobile devices, but also from inside applications that they currently use. This chapter shows an example of integrating a web-based application with standard instant messaging protocols and programs.

There are many different instant messaging protocols that are in wide use today. Skype, Windows Messenger, AOL Instant Messenger, and Yahoo! Instant Messenger all have their own clients and their own protocols. Those are all proprietary protocols that are not technically open to interoperability, but there is a popular open protocol called XMPP (*http://xmpp.org/*). Being an open technology, it's supported by many instant messaging clients, including Apple's iChat, Digsby (*http://www.digsby.com/*), and Pidgin (*http://www.pidgin.im/*). Basically, whatever the platform, there is an application that supports XMPP.

The easy availability of client applications is a good reason for us to use this technology, but the size of the userbase is another consideration. Thankfully, XMPP has a huge built-in userbase due to Google using it in their Google Talk service, which is linked to their Gmail service. Google also offers nearly seamless XMPP integration for developers on their cloud computing platform, Google App Engine (*http://appengine.google.com*).

Getting Started with Google App Engine

Google App Engine is Google's cloud computing offering, allowing developers to build applications on their infrastructure. It's even free to get started and entirely free for most applications. However, if you reach a certain threshold, you are charged for your usage. Applications can use up to 500 MB of storage and enough CPU and bandwidth to serve about 5 million page views per month before a developer is charged anything.

This example will build an application using Python, but applications can also be built using Java or any language that can be interpreted inside the Java Virtual Machine. It's fairly easy to build these applications once you understand the basic differences between how App Engine works and how standard development works outside of the cloud. MySQL and other relational databases are not available inside App Engine; instead, applications save data using the built-in key-value-based datastore API. Another difference is that web requests must be served within 30 seconds, so the long polling that we used in previous examples doesn't work in App Engine. However, any limitations imposed by the service can easily be overcome by using App Engine for its good parts and other solutions for their good parts. The very last example in this book demonstrates how to integrate all of these technologies.

Setting Up an Account

Getting started in App Engine requires a standard Google Account and a phone capable of receiving SMS messages to verify your account. Navigate to the Google App Engine website (*http://appengine.google.com*) and, if you're logged in, you'll be greeted with the button shown in Figure 7-1 inviting you to "Create an Application."

Figure 7-1. Creating your first application

After clicking that button to create an application, you're first asked to provide a phone number to verify that you're a person. Google will send an SMS message containing a short verification code and take you to another page where you can enter that code.

Once you have been verified, your App Engine account is ready to go. At this point you can start setting up your application. From Google's perspective, they only need to know two things about your application. First, pick an Application Identifier that you'd like to use. This ID will be used as part of the URL when users access your application on the Web. These identifiers must be unique across all of App Engine, so check the availability and pick something suitable. If you want to write a new application in the future, you can always create a second application and give it a new identifier. You're also asked to provide a title for the application. This title will be used for the screen shown to users when they're trying to sign into your service. Figure 7-2 shows my attempt at filling out this form.

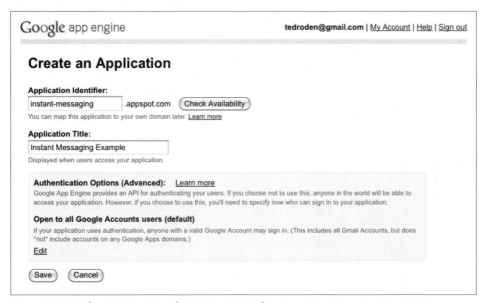

Figure 7-2. Configuring your Google App Engine application

Creating an Application with the SDK

To develop applications on Google's cloud, you must first install the Google App Engine SDK for Python. It's available for Mac OSX, Windows, and Linux from the App Engine project on Google Code (*http://code.google.com/appengine/downloads.html*). Download the appropriate package and install it for your platform. Both the Mac and Windows versions have a graphical interface for creating projects, launching the development server, and deploying the code to Google's servers.

After installing the SDK, you have a program called Google App Engine Launcher. Using that application, create a "New Application" from the File menu. It prompts you for an "Application Name" and a directory to house it in. The Application Name should match the Application Identifier that you selected when creating your application on the Google website. Figure 7-3 should resemble what you see.

Figure 7-3. Setting up your application in Google App Engine Launcher

Inspecting the default application

The launcher program creates a basic shell of an application inside the directory specified earlier. It creates three files that are needed for the most basic application. The files that are created by default are even populated with a simple "Hello World" application. The basic application consists of the following files:

app.yaml
> A configuration file giving App Engine the most basic information about an application. It specifies whether to use the Java or Python runtime, the version of the application, and the version of the App Engine API being used. If different URLs are handled by different physical files, you can specify that in this file as well. Certain features of the App Engine framework can also be configured or requested by making modifications to this file.

index.yaml
> This file is used by App Engine's Datastore API to instruct it how to best index the data inside your application. App Engine is clever enough to automatically update this file based on your code, so you won't need to update this until you have specific indexing requirements.

main.py
> The main Python file that handles all of the HTTP requests by default. This is where the application code to your application gets started. This filename can be changed

as long as the *app.yaml* file is updated as well. Applications are not limited to one Python file; this is just the single file created by the launcher application.

The application created by the launcher program is actually complete and ready to run. From the launcher interface, click the button called "Run," which will start up the development server on your local machine. Assuming your project was also set up to run on port 8080, you can point your browser at *http://localhost:8080* to see something like Figure 7-4.

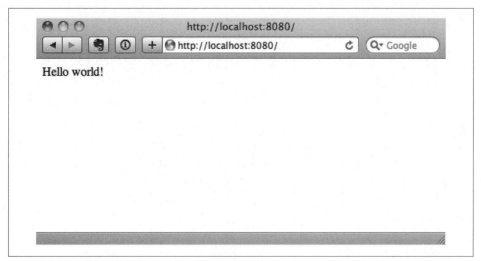

Figure 7-4. "Hello World" without touching a line of code

Taking Advantage of Google

Writing applications on App Engine gives the developer access to Google's web-serving infrastructure as well as some other useful services. One of the most immediately useful features is the ability to get some user information for free through Google Accounts. It takes only one line of code to force a user to log in, and knowing they're logged in, you can easily make use of some of their user information.

The Python part of a Google App Engine application, as specified in *main.py*, is very similar to the way Tornado works. In `main()`, the actual application object is created by defining which classes respond to which URL requests. If a request comes into a specified variable via an HTTP `get` request, the `get` method of the class is called; the same logic applies for `post` requests.

Starting with the shell of the application created by the launcher application, let's modify it slightly to force users to log in and prepare for the instant messaging part of our application. When you open the *main.py* file, it should look like the following code below. Expand it by adding the highlighted:

```
import wsgiref.handlers

# App Engine supports standard logging, use it.
import os, logging

from google.appengine.ext import webapp, db

# import some more app engine module
from google.appengine.api import xmpp, users, urlfetch
from google.appengine.ext.webapp.util import login_required

class BaseHandler(webapp.RequestHandler):
    # the jabber id of the server
    server_jid = os.environ['APPLICATION_ID'] + '@appspot.com'
    # the server URL
    server_url = "http://%s.appspot.com" % os.environ['APPLICATION_ID']

class MainHandler(BaseHandler):
    # force the user to log in to see this page.
    @login_required
    def get(self):
        user = users.get_current_user()
        logging.info("Got request for MainHandler")
        self.response.out.write('Hello, %s!' % user.nickname())

def main():
    application = webapp.WSGIApplication([('/', MainHandler)],
                                          debug=True)
    wsgiref.handlers.CGIHandler().run(application)

if __name__ == '__main__':
    main()
```

This code is still essentially a "Hello World" application, but it has been expanded in a couple of key ways. We added a couple of new import statements to pull in modules supplied by `google.appengine` as well as from Python's standard library, all of which is available in the App Engine environment.

Another modification is the creation of a `BaseHandler` class to use in place of App Engine's `webapp.Request` module. This class serves exactly the same purpose as the `BaseHandler` class introduced in the chat application created with Tornado, which is to offer some convenience functionality during web requests that are specific to our application. In this case, we're setting up some variables that can be accessed later. These variables make it easy for our application to refer to both its URL address and its XMPP address.

We've also added a `@login_required` decorator to the `MainHandler` class. This one line of code tells Google that any user who views this page must be authenticated using their Google Account credentials. If a user hits this page without first authenticating, Google will automatically take them to a special login page, redirecting them here once that is complete. The `get` method still serves the same purpose, but this time it logs some information and responds with the logged-in user's nickname instead of saying hello to the entire "World."

Keeping Track of the User

Getting to this application from a web browser now requires that the user is authenticated with his Google account. However, the main point of this application is to accept content outside the web browser, so we're going to have to keep track of which users have signed up and check against that list in the future. Thankfully, App Engine provides a simple Datastore API that will allow us to create objects, save them, and load them again later. One of the nice side effects of using this Datastore API is that we are not required to create and manage the database structure. The Datastore API looks at your object definitions and does everything you need to start using the data. To get started, let's set up a basic model class that represents the user. Add the following class to *main.py* after the `BaseHandler` class:

```
class IMUser(db.Model):
    account = db.UserProperty()
    email = db.EmailProperty()
```

This defines a class called `IMUser` that is a subclass of App Engine's `db.Model` class. That's all the setup we need to actually start using it as if we had already built database tables and set up the server. Having defined our object, let's start saving which users have successfully authenticated. Update the `MainHandler` class:

```
class MainHandler(BaseHandler):
    # force the user to log in to see this page.
    @login_required
    def get(self):
        user = users.get_current_user()
        logging.info("Got request for MainHandler")

        # get the IMUser if they've been here before
        u = IMUser.gql('WHERE email = :1', user.email()).get()
        if not u:
            # if it's their first time here, store it in the cloud
            u = IMUser(email=user.email(), account=user)
            u.put()

        self.response.out.write('Hello, %s!' % user.nickname())
```

This code checks to see whether a user has logged in before and, if not, saves them to the cloud. To do this, we use Google's SQL-like query language called GQL. The GQL language lets us search the datastore as if it were a local database table. In this case we're saving the email address and the actual Google user account object. This allows us to query the datastore for existing users with nothing more than an email address.

The Deploy Button

The actual process of getting an application up and running in the cloud is very complicated. Files need to be copied to data servers all over the world, server software needs to be restarted, indexes must be updated and created to reflect the new code, and certainly countless other thankless activities. However, you don't actually have to worry about any of that. Deploying an application here is as basic as running a simple command-line script, and the Google App Engine Launcher program makes it even easier with a big button called "Deploy."

With our code updated to log users in and show them their names, let's try it out on Google's servers. Pressing that big "Deploy" button should open up a log window with output similar to this:

```
*** Running appfg.py with the following flags:
    --no_cookies --passin update
google_appengine/appcfg.py:41: DeprecationWarning: ...
    os.path.join(DIR_PATH, 'lib', 'antlr3'),
Application: instant-messaging; version: 1.
Server: appengine.google.com.
Scanning files on local disk.
Initiating update.
Cloning 3 application files.
Uploading 3 files and blobs.
Uploaded 3 files and blobs
Deploying new version.
Checking if new version is ready to serve.
Will check again in 1 seconds.
Checking if new version is ready to serve.
Closing update: new version is ready to start serving.
Uploading index definitions.
If deploy fails you might need to 'rollback' manually.
*** appcfg.py has finished with exit code 0 ***
```

There's not a whole lot of useful information there, but unless you got a big error message, you can safely assume that your application is now running on App Engine. To test it out, open your browser to *http://application-id.appspot.com/*. The `application-id` should match the one you set up with Google; mine is *instant-messaging*. When you load that page, you should be immediately redirected to a Google login page similar to the one shown in Figure 7-5.

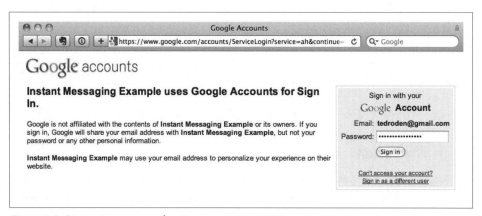

Figure 7-5. Signing into your application

This is where Google uses the title you picked when creating your application. When forcing a user to sign in, it redirects her to a Google-branded page to let her know exactly what type of data will be shared between Google and our application. Once the user signs in, she is redirected back to the application, and the new and improved Hello World message appears. After logging in, you should see something similar to Figure 7-6.

Figure 7-6. An authenticated and personalized greeting

The Dashboard

In `MainHandler`, we use `logging.info` to log some data announcing that the `get` method has been called. In Google App Engine, these messages are stored in and available from the App Engine dashboard (*http://appengine.google.com*). The dashboard website shows all the stats about your application, including HTTP requests, CPU usage, bandwidth consumed, the data stored, and of course all of the log messages your application has created.

At the moment, we're only interested in viewing the logs and the data that has been stored. To view logs, click on the "Logs" tab on the left side of the screen, and you'll see a list of errors that have occurred. You can filter that view with a select box that will let you limit the page to different types of logging messages. If you change it to "Info," you should see something resembling Figure 7-7. This is the list of log messages that have been emitted by our application each time the `MainHandler.get` method was called.

To view the data stored with the application, click on "Data View" under the "Datastore" heading. If there are no options, type "SELECT * FROM IMUser" and run it as a query. This shows a list all the users that have logged into the application. If you ever have an issue with data not matching up with what you expect, you can always come to this page and inspect each object. Figure 7-8 shows an example of the datastore data viewer.

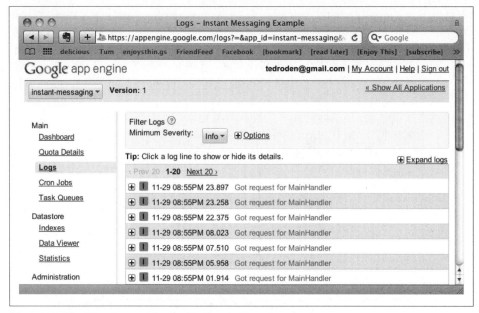

Figure 7-7. The "Logs" tab of the App Engine dashboard

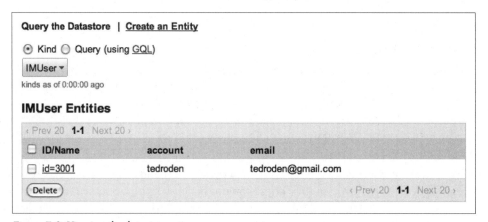

Figure 7-8. Viewing the datastore

Receiving Instant Messages

So far, we've written some code, signed up for services, and launched applications, but nothing we've done involves sending or receiving instant messages from our users. However, getting all that set up will make those two actions much easier. Since we're forcing people to log in with their Google accounts, we know that all of the users have an XMPP account that can send and receive messages from the application. In this case, we're starting with accepting incoming instant messages from users. Accepting messages via XMPP opens up the door to very interesting ways of interacting with users. Building in accepting messages before sending them also helps us get around a security and usability issue without much effort.

The XMPP protocol does not allow users to send messages to other users unless the receiving user has allowed it to happen. This is generally done through an "invitation." In practice, one user would request a chat session, or invitation, and if the other user accepted it, the chat session would begin. Within our application, we don't want to be sending chat messages or requests to any unsuspecting users, so to prevent that, we're going to ensure they send us a message first. Once they do that, our application can send messages freely to the user.

To deal with XMPP in App Engine, we must first announce that we're going to use XMPP services. This is one of the services that is configured by editing the *app.yaml* file. Open that file and add the following lines:

```
inbound_services:
- xmpp_message
```

This tells App Engine that our application would like to send and receive XMPP messages. If App Engine gets an XMPP message addressed to our domain, it will convert it to an HTTP request and post it to a specific URL in our application. So in the application side, the only thing we need to do to listen for these requests is listen to a special URL. Update the main function to accept the special XMPP URL:

```
def main():
    application = webapp.WSGIApplication([('/', MainHandler),
                                          ('/_ah/xmpp/message/chat/', XMPPHandler),
                                          ],
                                         debug=True)
    wsgiref.handlers.CGIHandler().run(application)
```

App Engine posts any XMPP messages addressed to our application to /_ah/xmpp/message/chat/. We simply set up our application to use the XMPPHandler class when it receives such a request. XMPPHandler handler will then be used for every XMPP message that is received.

To get started receiving messages, let's just accept the messages and log them to the console. In *main.py*, add the following class:

```
class XMPPHandler(BaseHandler):
    def post(self):
        # Parse the XMPP request
        message = xmpp.Message(self.request.POST)
        # Log it to the console
        logging.info("XMMP sender: %s - body: %s" % (message.sender, message.body))
```

The internals of accepting an XMPP request work exactly like receiving any other request in App Engine. In this case, the payload of the POST request is the raw XML of the XMPP message. We use the xmpp module to parse that message and turn it into an object that we can easily manipulate. Once we have it, we log the important fields to the console.

Everything is now in place to accept and parse XMPP requests in this application, so let's try it out and send some messages. Testing an application in App Engine is normally as easy as pressing the Run button and viewing the code locally on your machine. However, there is currently no way to send XMPP messages to the local version of App Engine, so we're going to have to redeploy the code when we make changes. Press the Deploy button again to send the code to the server.

Once the code has been successfully deployed, we can start sending messages to the server. To send a message, you need to open your instant messaging client and initiate a chat. To send a message to the server, you'll have to specify the recipient as *applica tion-id@appspot.com*, where *application-id* is the identifier that you picked earlier. Most instant messaging programs should have a similar interface for initiating a chat with another user. In iChat, it will look like Figure 7-9.

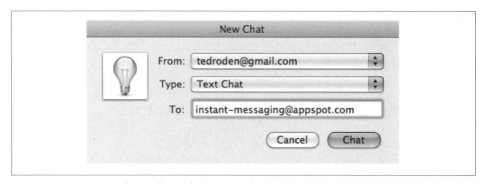

Figure 7-9. Initiating a chat to the application in iChat

This should bring up a chat window where you can start chatting. Send some messages to the server; you won't receive any responses at the moment, but they are getting to the server. To verify this fact, check the "Info" logs in the App Engine dashboard. The result should look like Figure 7-10.

A message being sent from an instant messaging window has to take a pretty long journey before it reaches the "Logs" tab in the App Engine dashboard. When it leaves your instant messaging application, it is sent to the Google Talk servers, which pass it on to the XMPP servers in the App Engine cloud. App Engine then takes the message data, which is entirely XML, and posts it to `/_ah/xmpp/message/chat` on your application. That URL is mapped to the `XMPPHandler` method, which then parses the message and logs it. Figure 7-11 illustrates this whole process.

Figure 7-10. The instant messages as received by the server

Sending Instant Messages

Receiving messages that originated from an instant messenger client is nice to have, and certainly opens up a lot of possibilities for collecting data in realtime. But the true realtime power of this technology comes from the ability to both send and receive these messages.

Let's expand on our existing application by taking the message that we received and just printing it back to the client. In the *main.py* file, make the following addition to the XMPPHandler class:

```
class XMPPHandler(BaseHandler):
    def post(self):
        # Parse the XMPP request
        message = xmpp.Message(self.request.POST)
        # Log it to the console
        logging.info("XMPP sender: %s - body: %s" % (message.sender, message.body))
        message.reply(message.body)
```

That additional line of code takes the message that was received and calls the `reply` method to send the body right back to the sender. If you'd like to test this out on the server, go ahead and deploy the code as it is now. Figure 7-12 shows a typical chat session with the server after adding this functionality.

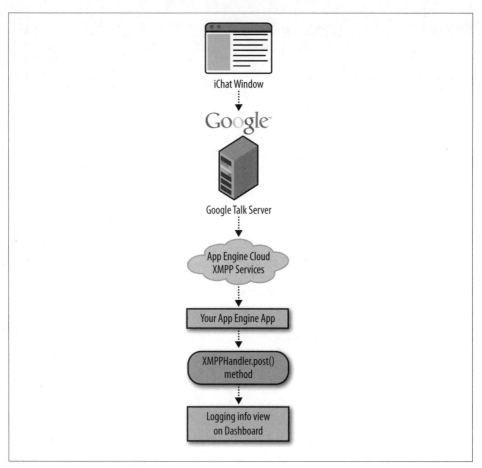

Figure 7-11. The lifetime of the instant message

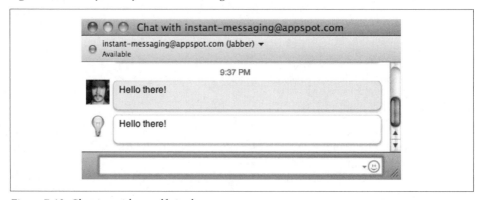

Figure 7-12. Chatting with myself via the server

Responding Intelligently

At this point, we're receiving messages and sending back simple output. Let's take some time to examine the data as it comes in and respond to it. We'll allow the user to enter simple commands to our application and respond appropriately to the request.

The Basic Commands

We're going to expand this application to accept basic commands and respond with the appropriate response. To do this, we must first understand the command format. To keep it simple, we'll assume that any instant message that we receive is a command. The first word of that message is the command itself, and the rest of string represents any additional parameters for the command.

Let's start by parsing out the command itself from the rest of the message. Add the following code to your XMPPHandler class:

```
class XMPPHandler(BaseHandler):
    def post(self):
        message = xmpp.Message(self.request.POST)
        logging.info("XMPP sender: %s - body: %s" % (message.sender, message.body))
        # The command from the user
        cmd = message.body.split(' ')[0].lower()
        # the rest of the message
        body = message.body[len(cmd) + 1:]
```

Because the format is **command** and the rest of the string, to parse out the command, we simply need to grab anything before the first space character. We then convert it to lowercase to make it easier to match in the next step, which determines what we do with each command. Keep adding to that method:

```
        # echo the data back to the client
        if cmd == 'echo':
            message.reply(body)

        # convert string to rot13 and repeat it back to them
        elif cmd == 'rot13':
            message.reply(body.encode('rot13'))

        # add up all the numbers
        elif cmd == 'sum':
            numbers = body.split(" ")
            total = 0
            # try to add the numbers together
            try:
                for x in numbers:
                    total += int(x)
                text = "%s = %d" % (" + ".join(numbers), total)
            except:
                text = "Couldn't add these up. Invalid numbers?"
```

```
        message.reply(text)
    else:
        message.reply("I don't understand '%s'" % cmd)
```

This gives the user several different options for interacting with the application. First off, by typing `echo Hello World`, this would reply to the client with the string `Hello World`.

If the user sends the `rot13` command, we'll respond by replacing each character in the **body** with the character thirteen places away in alphabetical order. The Python standard library provides this functionality in the same library that can encode strings in base64 and compress them with zlib.

When we receive the `sum` command, we'll assume the rest of the string is a series of number separated by spaces. We'll take each of those numbers and add them together, returning the final sum. We'll also take the each of the numbers and join them with a plus character to display the entire equation. If we have trouble adding them, we've most likely received something that isn't a number, so we just complain back to the user in this case.

If the user either sends a command that we do not understand or doesn't send one at all, we just respond and tell him that we don't understand. Figure 7-13 shows a chat session using all of these commands.

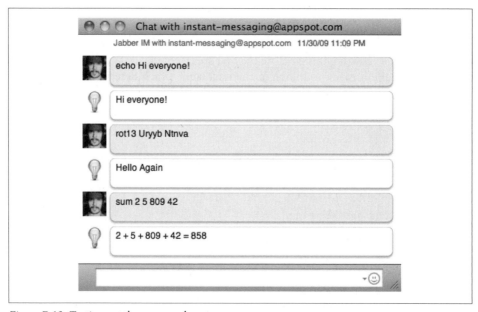

Figure 7-13. Testing out the commands

Checking Authentication via Instant Messenger

Sending and receiving instant messages is a somewhat personal matter. When an instant message arrives to an end user, it generally interrupts him by opening a window. So we don't want to be sending messages to users who have not authenticated with the application.

Forcing a user to be authenticated during a web request is as simple as adding the `@login_required` decorator. However, deep inside the XMPP response, we're not able to seamlessly redirect a user to a web page and expect him to be sent right back. So adding a decorator to this method wouldn't have the same effect. This is why we started saving the `IMUser` objects in `MainHandler` for each user who did visit the site.

When we receive an XMPP request, we may not have access to the `get_current_user` method, but we do have access to the user's email address. We can easily check that email address against any of the users who have authenticated. To do a super basic authentication check, update your `IMUser` class with the following:

```python
class IMUser(db.Model):
    account = db.UserProperty()
    email = db.EmailProperty()

    def is_authenticated(self, email):
        # remove the "resource" string to reveal the email address by itself
        if email.find('/') != -1:
            email = email[:email.find('/')]
        im_user = IMUser.gql('WHERE email = :1', email).get()
        if im_user:
            return True
        else:
            return False
```

When we receive an instant message from a user, the sender field contains the XMPP user identifier followed by a slash and a resource string. This slash and anything after it can be stripped away, resulting in the ID of the user, which for our purposes is an email address. To check to see whether a user has been authenticated, all we need to do is check that email address against the data store. If we locate the `im_user`, return `True`, and otherwise return `False`.

Now that we have the ability to check for authenticated users, let's check before we actually send out new messages. Update `XMPPHandler`:

```python
class XMPPHandler(BaseHandler):
    def post(self):
        message = xmpp.Message(self.request.POST)
        logging.info("XMMP sender: %s - body: %s" % (message.sender, message.body))

        ...

        # get the IMUser object
        if not IMUser.is_authenticated(message.sender):
            message.reply("Please register, it's painless: %s" % self.server_url)
```

```
        return

    # echo the data back to the client
    if cmd == 'echo':
        message.reply(body)

    ...
```

If the user isn't authenticated, we simply send him a message with a link to get authenticated and stop processing. If the user has been authenticated in the past, we simply continue on and respond to the request as we normally would. Although this is not exactly NSA-grade security, it's a pretty simple way of ensuring that we send messages only to users who want to receive them. Figure 7-14 shows a chat session with a user who has not authenticated.

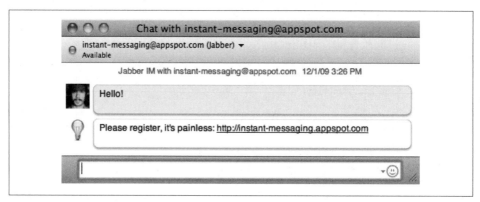

Figure 7-14. Forcing users to authenticate

Introducing a Third Party

So far, this example is fairly simple in its responses. It repeats text back to the sender, manipulates strings, and does basic arithmetic. However, we can easily add more sophisticated functionality using freely available APIs and start providing useful information through an instant message chat session. To get started, let's add the ability to look up weather information. When a user sends in the command weather and a zip code, we'll respond with the basic weather conditions at that location.

To get the weather information, we'll be using the Yahoo! Query Language (YQL) service (*http://developer.yahoo.com/yql/*). YQL provides a SQL-like language to various APIs around the Web. Using YQL and its SQL-like syntax, a developer can do everything from searching the archive of he *New York Times* to updating a Twitter status. We'll be using the service to load the current weather information.

YQL offers a couple of different response formats for each query. We'll be using the JSON format, but to handle that in App Engine, we need to import an external library. At the top of your *main.py* file, add the following import code:

```
from django.utils import simplejson as json
```

This line imports an easy to use JSON-parsing library called `simplejson`. App Engine offers this module as part of the code to include some compatibility with the Django project (*http://www.djangoproject.com/*). Normally you'd have to install this module separately, and even compile it to get the best performance, but including it this way saves several steps.

Loading the weather information from YQL is fairly straightforward. Add this function near the top of your *main.py* file:

```
def get_weather_for_zipcode(zipcode):
    # build the YQL statement
    yql = "select item from weather.forecast where location = %s" % zipcode

    # encode it for use in a web request
    yql = yql.replace(" ", "%20")
    url = "http://query.yahooapis.com/v1/public/yql?format=json&=%s" % yql

    # make the request and parse the json response
    response = urlfetch.fetch(url)
    data = json.loads(response.content)

    try:
        # return the current weather conditions
        return data['query']['results']['channel']['item']['condition']
    except:
        return None
```

This method takes a zip code as a parameter and builds a YQL statement with it. That statement gets encoded for use as a URL and is turned into the actual web request that we'll be using.

One of the limitations of App Engine is that you're not given direct access to the network. In order to make a web request, you have to use Google's `urlfetch` module. To make this YQL API request, we can just hand off the URL to `urlfetch.fetch` and it will synchronously handle the request and return a `response` object. The `content` of that object is the JSON response from the YQL request. This API actually returns a lot of data about the weather, including the forecast and links to images that represent the weather, but we're only concerned with the current conditions, so we parse that part out and return it.

To get the application to supply the weather information, we need to add a new command to the `XMPPHandler` class. In that class, make the following changes:

```
class XMPPHandler(BaseHandler):
    def post(self):
        ...

            # add up all the numbers
            elif cmd == 'sum':
                ...
            elif cmd == 'weather':
```

```
# assume body is a zipcode and get the weather report
weather = get_weather_for_zipcode(body)

# if we got a good response, respond with the weather report
if weather:
    text = "Currently \"%s\" - temp %s" % (weather['text'],
                                           weather['temp'])
# otherwise, ask the user to try again
else:
    text = "Couldn't load weather? Invalid Location? Try again."

# finally, send the message
message.reply(text)

# we didn't get a command that we understand... complain
else:
    message.reply("I don't understand '%s'" % cmd)
```

This code adds a new command to the application called weather. When a user sends the weather command during an instant message session, we'll use the newly created get_weather_for_zipcode function. If we get a valid response, we'll pass it back to the user in the form of a simple list of weather conditions. If not, we'll tell the user that we couldn't load the weather data and ask him to try again.

After making this change, you'll need to redeploy the code to see it on the server. Once it's loaded on App Engine, send a couple of weather requests to see the response. Figure 7-15 shows an example of what it should look like.

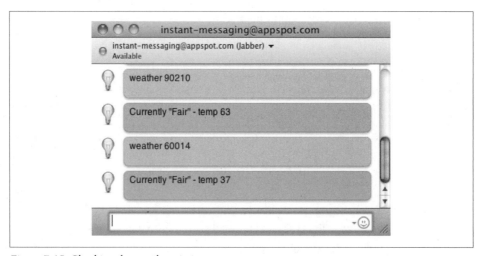

Figure 7-15. Checking the weather via instant message

Setting Up an API

Due to the nature of App Engine, you may or may not be able to build your entire application using the service. However, just because it has certain limitations that make it ill-suited for all aspects of realtime web development, this doesn't mean you should ditch it all together.

For the sake of discussion, let's say that we wanted to expand our Twitter application to send instant messages when it encountered certain words as they came through the stream. Perhaps a user could set up the ability to track his own username in realtime. This would be a perfect use of App Engine if it weren't for the fact that you can't run the code that connects to Twitter and monitors the updates. The 30-second execution limit would get in the way and make it unsuitable for that part of the application.

However, since we've already built the Twitter application using the Tornado framework, there is no need to build it on App Engine. We could simply add some API functionality to this instant message code and then modify the Twitter application to use that API.

To accept the API requests, we need to add a handler when we create the main application object. In the `main` function of *main.py*, make the following modifications:

```
def main():
    application = webapp.WSGIApplication([('/', MainHandler),
                                          ('/_ah/xmpp/message/chat/', XMPPHandler),
                                          ('/api/send', APISendHandler)
                                          ],
                                          debug=True)
```

That just tells App Engine to use the `APISendHandler`, when it receives a request to `/api/send`. Above the `main` function, add that class to the file:

```
class APISendHandler(BaseHandler):
    def post(self):
        # pull out who the message is to, and what they want to say
        to = self.request.get('to')
        body = self.request.get('body')

        if not IMUser().is_authenticated(to):
            self.response.out.write(json.dumps({'status': 'fail',
                                                'mesg': 'User not authenticated.'}))
            return

        # check to see if the "password" matches
        if self.request.get('secret') == 's3cret-c0de':
            # if so, send the message and write a response
            xmpp.send_message(to, body)
            logging.info("to: %s, body: %s" % (to, body))
            self.response.out.write(json.dumps({'status': 'ok', 'mesg': 'Sent.'}))
```

```
# if the password is wrong, don't send any instant message
else:
    self.response.out.write(json.dumps({'status': 'fail',
                                        'mesg': 'Wrong secret code.'}))
```

This API expects three HTTP parameters when it's called. It expects to receive a to parameter, which is the account of the user on the receiving end of this message. It also expects body, which will be used as the content of the message. Finally, because this API call will respond when anyone on the Internet hits the URL, we're forcing every request to know a secret code. This acts like a password, and if this is not correct, we don't send anything at all.

The first thing we do is check to see whether the user is authenticated, because we don't want to send instant messages via the API that we wouldn't send through the web interface. If the user is not authenticated, respond to the request and return from this method. In a production environment, it would probably be wise to respond with a different message that does not identify the exact problem. As it stands, spammers could easily hit this API looking for valid email addresses.

Next, we move on and check the password, or secret. Assuming it is correct, we use the xmpp module to send the message and print out a JSON-formatted object that can be easily parsed by the caller of the API. If the secret is incorrect, we don't bother sending out the message, but we do inform whoever contacted the API that they used the wrong secret code.

Redeploy this application, and let's test it out. From the command line, you can simply use curl or any other command-line-based HTTP client. Using curl, the command would be similar to the following:

```
~ $ curl -d "secret=s3cret-cOde&body=Hi+You&to=you@gmail.com" \
http://application-id.appspot.com/api/send
{"status": "ok", "mesg": "Sent."}
```

Immediately after calling this method, you should receive an instant message from the application. If you do, you now have a fully functioning API that can send instant messages to your users. If not, check the logs in the App Engine dashboard; chances are the fix is easy.

 According to the XMPP specification, a user can send messages only to someone who has added them to their contact list. If you're going to launch an application with this API, ensure that the user first sends a message to your application-id@appspot.com account. Once they send you a message, you'll be able to send them messages whenever you like. This is XMPP's way of allowing an opt-in mechanism.

Adding this instant messaging functionality—which opens an instantaneous communication channel with a user, regardless of whether they're using your site in the web browser—opens up a lot of doors. Part of building a truly realtime experience is allowing users to get data in and take it out from whatever method is most readily available. Instant messaging provides a paradigm that is familiar to most users and allows for communication in places not available via the standard web browser.

## CHAPTER 8

SMS

Previous chapters have focused on communicating with users in realtime while they are sitting in front of their computer. In this chapter, we step back from the desktop and venture out into the real world.

A big part of creating realtime user experiences means delivering messages to a user, whether she is on the website, in a chat window, or via text messages sent to her phone. Users increasingly expect that the applications they use online can notify them of updates long after they have stepped away from the computer. But sending a message to a user is only half the battle; modern applications need to be able to receive messages that originate as SMS messages from any old mobile phone. Luckily, there are several ways to accomplish this.

The SMS Landscape

There are several different methods of sending or receiving an SMS message sent to or from a user. Most wireless providers offer an email address that can be used to send an SMS message to a user. There are also several different providers of that offer varying degrees of SMS integration, including the ability to send and receive messages to specific mobile phones through a simple API. The most complete option wold be to connect a GSM/GPRS modem to a computer and send and receive messages just like you're reading from and writing to a local landline-based modem. Sadly, that's outside the scope of this chapter.

Email to SMS

The easiest way to send an SMS to a user is simply by sending an email. If your application has the ability to send out updates via email, SMS messaging can be implemented quite easily. Although there are some drawbacks to this method, it's a very quick way of getting this functionality added into your application, and it's currently being used by sites such as Google and Facebook.

To send one of these SMS messages, you need to send an email to a specially formatted address provided by the wireless carrier. Most of the addresses are in the format of phonenumber@wirelesscarrier.net. When you send an email to one of these addresses, the wireless carrier converts it to an SMS message and forwards it on to the user. These messages are free for the developer sending the message (aside from bandwidth costs associated with sending an email), but standard text messaging rates do apply to the user receiving the messages. The following table is an incomplete list of the email formats needed to send an SMS at several carriers:

Provider	Email format
Alltel	phonenumber@message.alltel.com
AT&T	phonenumber@txt.att.net
Cingular	phonenumber@cingularme.com
Metro PCS	phonenumber@MyMetroPcs.com
Nextel	phonenumber@messaging.nextel.com
Powertel	phonenumber@ptel.net
Sprint	phonenumber@messaging.sprintpcs.com
SunCom	phonenumber@tms.suncom.com
T-Mobile	phonenumber@tmomail.net
US Cellular	phonenumber@email.uscc.net
Verizon	phonenumber@vtext.com
Virgin Mobile	phonenumber@vmobl.com

Considering that most web applications support sending email messages in some form, the difficult part of supporting this type of SMS service is determining the relationship between phone numbers and their wireless carriers. The most common way to handle this mapping is simply to ask the user which carrier she uses when asking for her phone number. Figure 8-1 shows how this process is handled on Facebook.

Actually sending a message with this method is simple: in the functionality of your application that sends an email, just replace the user's email address with the formatted SMS email address. Rather than write code to demonstrate how this works, it's clearly illustrated by sending an SMS message from the command line of a Unix-like operating system. On your Mac or Linux computer, try the following command:

```
troden@nelson ~$ echo "SMS from the command line" | mail -s "Greetings" \
myphonenumber@txt.att.net
```

This command just pipes a simple string into the standard mail command, which will send it off to AT&T's servers. Once there, the message will get converted into an SMS message and delivered directly to my phone. Figure 8-2 shows what this message looked like when it finally arrived at my phone. Try substituting my email address and wireless carrier for yours, and you should receive a text message after a few moments.

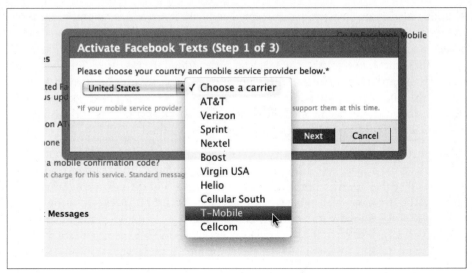

Figure 8-1. Entering your wireless carrier on Facebook

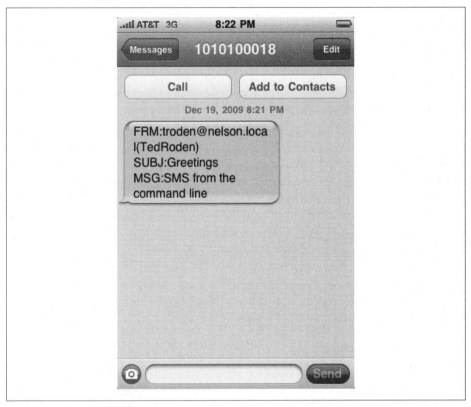

Figure 8-2. The emailed message on a phone

Although it's certainly easy to send an email and have it arrive as a text message to the end user, it's not the best experience for a number of reasons. First of all, you can see from the screenshot that the formatting of the message is not great, and this is totally out of our control. In this case, the wireless carrier added the FRM: field, but there is no real set standard as to what that message will look like. If you sent it from another carrier, the message may look different and include different additional text. Messages are also slow to arrive at the end user's device; what takes a few seconds through a traditional SMS service takes much longer using this method.

So this method isn't great. It can't be formatted and the speed is too slow, but it also fails the user experience test using another important metric: users cannot respond to messages that they receive. In this case, the message is sent directly from the carrier's servers rather than an answerable wireless account. If a user responds to the message, the carrier will respond with an error, and the message certainly won't be delivered your server. As a developer, if you're giving users access to SMS messages sent from the server, it only makes sense that you let them respond in some way.

SMS APIs

There are several services that offer the ability to send and receive messages via a web-based API. From full-featured XML-RPC or REST-based APIs to webhooks and callback URLs, these APIs make it possible to integrate SMS into your application at a much deeper level than a simple email-to-SMS gateway. To send a message, the developer hits a URL with some fairly obvious parameters, and the service does the work of actually translating that message to an SMS message and sending it to the user.

Most of these providers offer a version that is totally free, but each message includes a short advertisement in any outgoing message. So if you were to send an SMS message to a user, you'd have around 120 characters to work with, and the service would append a short advertisement to the end. Almost universally, these services offer a paid version that removes the advertisements from the messages. For a certain price per month and per message, you can send messages without the advertisements appended to the end.

The major benefit of using these services is that you're given relatively cheap access to a shortcode—a short phone number used primarily for SMS messaging—that your users can use. However, because this shortcode is shared among any number of other web applications, your users must preface every message with a reserved keyword. Each application registers a specific keyword and then, in order to send a message to the service, the user must start each SMS with that keyword.

For example, if you had a service that provided movie showtimes, you may register the keyword `movietimes`. When a user wanted to request showtimes for a certain movie, she would have to text `movietimes` *movie title* to the shortcode provided by the service. If the user sends the wrong keyword to the shortcode, your application will never be notified. Even when the user is replying to a message sent from your server, the user will have to prepend the keyword to the message. Figure 8-3 shows the flow of a message from the user to the server.

In this case, when a user sends an SMS message using the keyword `realtime`, the API provider directs the request to a third-party server called `realtime-apps.com`. Despite all of the different services sharing the same short code number, each service is notified only if the message has the proper keyword at the start of the message. When a message is sent to a specific keyword, the message is routed to a specific service, and none of the other servers are notified.

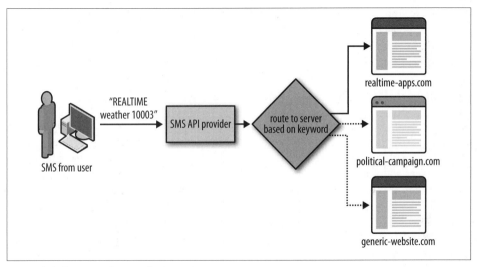

Figure 8-3. Routing a keyword to a server

SMS API providers

There are a number of service providers that offer the ability to send and receive SMS messages. The following table shows some of the major players in this space, most of which have free options that are perfect for development and suitable for production use. In the sections that follow, we'll build an application that uses a few of these services. In the event that this book does not cover the service that you would like to use, check the service's website; most of these providers have fully featured API classes to help developers as they get started.

Provider	Free version with advertisements	Ad-free version	Ability to send messages	Ability to receive messages
Email to SMS	-	-	Yes	No
ZeepMobile (*http://www.zeepmobile.com*)	Yes	Yes	Yes	Yes
Textmarks (*http://www.textmarks.com*)	Yes	Yes	Yes	Yes
Clickatell (*http://www.clickatell.com*)	No	Yes	Yes	Yes

Building the Basic Application

To demonstrate some basic SMS functionality, we're going to build an application that can handle sending and receiving SMS messages from two different SMS API providers. This application will look and feel very similar to the instant messaging application from the previous chapter, with the main differences lying in how the user interacts with the application and how our code sends and receives the messages.

Extending the Instant Messaging Application

This type of application is another perfect candidate to run on Google's App Engine platform. However, rather than register and create a new application, we'll just extend the existing application to send and receive SMS messages in addition to its existing functionality to handle instant messages via XMPP. At the moment, any URL request that comes into the instant messaging application is handled by the *main.py* file, as we specified in our configuration. To handle the SMS requests, we'll segment everything off into URLs that start with the /sms/ path. We can even create a new Python file to handle all of those requests. To set up this configuration, make the following change to your *app.yaml* file:

```
application: your-application-id
version: 1
runtime: python
api_version: 1

handlers:
- url: /sms/.*
  script: sms.py

- url: .*
  script: main.py

...
```

This change tells App Engine to send any request starting with /sms/ to the *sms.py* file. If the URL does not match that pattern, it will be picked up by the much more liberal *.* regular expression below and sent on to *main.py*. The SMS functionality is not provided by App Engine, so we do not need to add any new inbound_services to get the server to respond. Everything we do in this will actually be initiated via a standard HTTP request. From Google's point of view, this is a much more standard request than the XMPP request we used in the previous example.

To get this script started, let's add a lot of the housekeeping code that is needed just to get this thing set up. Create a file called *sms.py* and add the following code:

```
import wsgiref.handlers
import logging

import base64
import hmac
import sha
import time

import urllib
from google.appengine.api import urlfetch, users
from google.appengine.ext import webapp, db
from google.appengine.ext.webapp.util import login_required

from django.utils import simplejson as json

# the SMSUser data Model
class SMSUser(db.Model):
    # two properties... the google user account and the mobile phone number
    account = db.UserProperty()
    mobile_number = db.PhoneNumberProperty()

    # add a record for this mobile number
    def authenticate(self, mobile_number):
        u = SMSUser(mobile_number=mobile_number)
        u.put()

    # is a specific mobile_number already authenticated?
    def is_authenticated(self, mobile_number):
        sms_user = SMSUser.gql('WHERE mobile_number = :1', mobile_number).get()
        if sms_user:
            return True
        else:
            return False
```

Assuming you worked through the previous example, this code should look very familiar. It imports all of the different Python modules that this script will use. Then, it defines a simple db.Model module that will be used to store data about the SMS user as she interacts with this application.

Logic-wise, the biggest issue this code deals with is deciding whether a particular user is authenticated in one function and authenticating her in another. In this case, authentication is not meant to determine whether a user has entered the correct password, but to ensure that she wants to receive SMS messages from us. For the time being, sending and receiving SMS messages on an end user's mobile device is relatively expensive and can quite easily be considered an intrusion. Considering these facts, we want to be perfectly clear that any time this application sends an SMS message to a user, she has opted in to receive them.

To authenticate a user, we simply add her mobile number to the data store. Then, later on, to check whether she is authenticated, we just need to check to see whether her mobile number exists in the data store. This allows us to authenticate and verify a user without her hitting any web service; authentication can be done entirely through SMS messages.

An SMS Service Class

We're going to design this script to handle any number of different SMS APIs. The goal is not only to handle the SMS requests from the services that I've selected for this text, but to be able to easily extend it to use other services in the future. To do that, let's define a basic SMS message module that can be extended with methods that can be overridden for each new service. This way, the basic logic of the module doesn't have to change when adding new SMS providers in the future. This will just define a simple base class in Python; in a language such as Java, this would be considered defining an interface. However you want to classify it, add the following code to *sms.py*:

```python
# define the basic interface/base class
class SMSService(object):
    def __init__(self, short_code, keyword, api_key=None, api_secret=None):
        self._short_code = short_code
        self._keyword = keyword
        self._api_key = api_key
        self._api_secret = api_secret

    # easy programmatic access to the short code.
    @property
    def short_code(self):
        return self._short_code

    # each service will have a different way of sending a message to a user
    # they'll all have to override this method
    def send(self, number, body):
        # override this method
        logging.info("I should send a message to %s" % number)

    # Is the current user authenticated?
    def is_authenticated(self, mobile_number):
        # check with the user object
        return SMSUser().is_authenticated(mobile_number)
```

```
# should we authenticate a given mobile number?
def should_authenticate(self, mobile_number, event, body):
    if mobile_number:
        return True

# pass this up the chain
def authenticate(self, mobile_number):
    return SMSUser().authenticate(mobile_number)
```

This SMSService class sets up the basic behavior that the different SMS services will need to use. Since the basic interactions of each service are essentially the same, we can make a lot of safe assumptions with the base class. The __init__ method has the basic parameters that will be needed for every service, including the SMS short_code and keyword. Also, many services will require either an API key or secret, which can be defined by supplying the api_key and api_secret parameters.

Following that, there is a property method that will allow us safe access to the short_code variable by simple reference to self.short_code. Next is a method that will have to be overridden by every subclass of this one. The main difference between each of the SMS API interactions provided by the different services will be contained within the send method. Although we can safely assume that all APIs will have the same basic variables, such as keyword and short_code, we cannot assume how to construct the web service call needed by the final endpoint. So, we expect that this method will be overridden by each and every SMS class.

The next method determines whether the user is authenticated or not. In this case, we just pass all the logic up to the is_authenticated method on the SMSUser class. This method accepts a single mobile_number parameter, which is used to check against the data in the datastore.

After is_authenticated, we define a method called should_authenticate. This method gets called to find out whether a given user should be authenticated by the system. For example, if we check to see whether a user is already authenticated and find out that she is not, we would then call should_authenticate to see whether this is a good time to authenticate. In this example, we simply assume that if we have a mobile_number, we can allow authentication and return True.

The should_authenticate method also takes several parameters, even though they are ignored by this instance of the method. This is just to define the signature of the method that we're going to use in child classes. Many SMS providers signal that a user is authenticated when they provide the mobile number of the user, but other services have slightly more complicated logic. Providing the body and other parameters allows the child classes to take useful actions based on the contents of the message. This way, if a user sends an SMS saying, in effect, "authenticate me," the child class can inspect it and respond properly.

The Base Handler

This application sends and receives SMS messages by sending and receiving HTTP requests. When a message arrives, one of our controller classes is called. That class needs to do a number of jobs, no matter which controller is being called. With every HTTP request, at some point we need to determine which service should be used to interact with the user and respond differently depending on the service. Rather than handle all of that at the controller level, we can just override the base `RequestHandler` class to mask some of that complexity from the controller class.

```python
class SMSBaseHandler(webapp.RequestHandler):

    def __init__(self):
        self.user = SMSUser()
        # a dictionary filled with the supported services
        self._supported_services = {}
        # the service being used
        self._service = None

    # the controller will need to tell us which class to use
    def set_service_type(self, service_type):
        if service_type in self._supported_services:
            self._service = self._supported_services[service_type]()
        else:
            raise Exception('type', 'Invalid SMS Service Type')

    # a convenience property allowing easy access to the resulting class
    @property
    def service(self):
        if self._service:
            return self._service
        # no service is defined, throw an exception
        else:
            raise Exception('noservice', 'No service type set.')
```

In initializing this class with the `__init__` method, we just want to set up a few variables. First, `self.user` is initialized to ensure that we can access it throughout the entirety of the web request.

Next, we define an object called `self._supported_services` that will contain the services supported by this application. We'll fill in those services as we support each one, but this object is just a simple way to programmatically refer to a specific class by name. It's essentially a named list of classes so that we can easily equate `"service_name"` to an instance of a class called `SMS_Fancy_Service_Name`. This `self._supported_services` dictionary will be populated to look something like the following snippet:

```python
# No need to add this to your code, it's just an example
self._supported_services = {
    'some_service': Some_Service_Class,
    'another_service': Another_Service_Class
}
```

That variable is a dictionary of key/value pairs that specify the different classes that can be used by this script as an SMS service. This list of services will be used to map a plain-text service name to a class object that can be instantiated. The next block of code does exactly that: it takes the text name of a service, checks it against the `self._supported_services` list, and instantiates a class if it's a supported service.

That `set_service_type` method is called by each controller to inform the `SMSBaseHandler` which actual SMS API class we'll be using. For example, using the example `self._supported_services` dictionary defined earlier, the code would call `self.set_service_type('some_service')` to use the `Some_Service_Class` as the SMS provider. From then on, the controller class, and any code that it utilizes, does not need to know which service type is being used.

The next method defines the `self._service` variable and exposes it via the `service` property. This allows controllers to use `self.service` to access any of the SMS API functionality. Instead of constantly determining which class is being used with each web request, the controllers can make one call to `self.set_service_type` and then use the interface defined by `SMSService`. In practice, it would look very much like this:

```
# No need to add this to your code, it's just an example
self.set_service_type('some_service')
if not self.service.is_authenticated():
    raise Exception, "Not logged in!"
else:
    self.service.send(phone_number, "Greetings from SMS!")
```

Preparing to Accept Messages

Now that we have defined the basic interface for SMS services as well as a base class to handle the high-level functionality shared by each of the controller classes, let's look into responding to the SMS requests as they come in. Each of these requests will hit the server as either a POST or GET HTTP request, but the basic functionality will be the same, regardless of the request method. To start handling these requests, add the following class to your *sms.py* file:

```
class SMSIncomingHandler(SMSBaseHandler):
    # handle the GET requests
    def get(self, service_type):
        self.respond(service_type)

    # handle the POST requests
    def post(self, service_type):
        self.respond(service_type)

    # all of the HTTP requests end up handled by this method
    def respond(self, service_type):

        # setup the service type
        self.set_service_type(service_type)
```

```
# respond to the request
self.response.headers['Content-Type'] = 'text/plain'
self.response.out.write("Hello there via %s!" % self.service.short_code)
```

In Google's App Engine, when each request is made, the application automatically calls the get or post method on appropriate controller class. Since different SMS API providers use different methods of sending these request, we just forward each one to a single respond method. This gives us one method to work with, no matter which type of request is being made at the HTTP level. Both the get and post methods accept a service_type parameter and pass it along unchanged to the respond method.

At this point, the respond method has no real logic associated with it. The first thing to do is call set_service_type with the service_type variable. This variable contains the name of the service that is being used, and sending it as a parameter to set_service_type will ensure that it is available as an instantiated class when we need it.

Next, we respond with a basic bit of "hello world" text by simply printing it out as the response. Each API provider has a different way of sending a message to a user, but most of them will let you reply to an incoming message by simply returning anything when the service makes the HTTP request to our application. In this case, we simply set the content type to plain text and write out a quick message.

At this point we're more or less able to respond to any incoming SMS service that sends us a greeting, but with two major exceptions. We haven't yet set up any of the SMS API services, and although we've set up a controller to respond to HTTP requests, it's not mapped to any URL in our App Engine application.

Setting Up the Server

We've already built a few Python classes that are ready to respond to an SMS message as it comes in and have even defined the programmatic interface that we'll use to send messages and interact with the SMS APIs. However, at this point, the application is not responding to any HTTP requests. To do that, we simply need to set the URL parameters that we'll respond to when a provider pings our application.

Generally, when you set up a server to work with one of these SMS providers, you specify a callback URL that their service uses when a message is sent to your application. This means we can easily define a simple pattern and configure all of the providers to use it. That way, we can use one URL for any number of different providers and, although we'd need to add a small new class to handle a new provider, we can add it without modifying the controller itself. To get the application responding to these HTTP requests, append the following code to your *sms.py* file:

```
def main():
    application = webapp.WSGIApplication([(r'/sms/incoming/via/([a-z]+)/?',
                                           SMSIncomingHandler)],
                                          debug=True)
    wsgiref.handlers.CGIHandler().run(application)
```

```
if __name__ == '__main__':
    main()
```

Once again, this code should look familiar from building the instant messaging application in the previous chapter. This code simply sets up an application object and runs it. The single URL that we handle is routed to `SMSIncomingHandler` and is defined by the following regular expression:

```
r'/sms/incoming/via/([a-z]+)/?'
```

Anything that matches this regular expression will be passed along to the `SMSIncoming Handler` method. Anything that matches the `a-z` set will be passed along to the controller class as the first parameter, which is defined as `service_type`. This will allow us to set up a callback URL from "Acme SMS Service" to use the URL path `/sms/incoming/via/` **acme** while setting up "XYZ SMS Provider Incorporated" to use `/sms/incoming/via/` **xyz**. The only difference that our application will notice is that the first parameter of `SMSIncomingHandler` will be different.

Sending and Receiving the Messages

As it exists, the application we've built is fairly full-featured—except for the caveat that it doesn't actually do anything at all. We've built a lot of code that acts as a framework for the functionality that we still need to add. Without the ability to actually send and receive SMS messages, this application isn't very useful. So let's set up this application to interact with a couple of the more popular services in the SMS API service space.

TextMarks

Textmarks is a service that provides several different bits of functionality related to sending SMS messages. One of its core services is the ability to send and receive SMS messages via a simple HTTP-based API. The most basic service is also free, provided that you're willing to put up with advertisements attached to the end of each message. In this case you're given 120 characters to work with, and the rest may be used for an advertisement from a third-party company. You can pay for different levels of service that will allow you to remove this advertisement, but the free version is perfect for our purposes.

Reserving a keyword

To get started with this service, you must sign up for your keyword and configure your settings. Go to the TextMarks website (*http://www.textmarks.com/create*) and reserve a keyword to use for your application. You should see a form that looks like Figure 8-4.

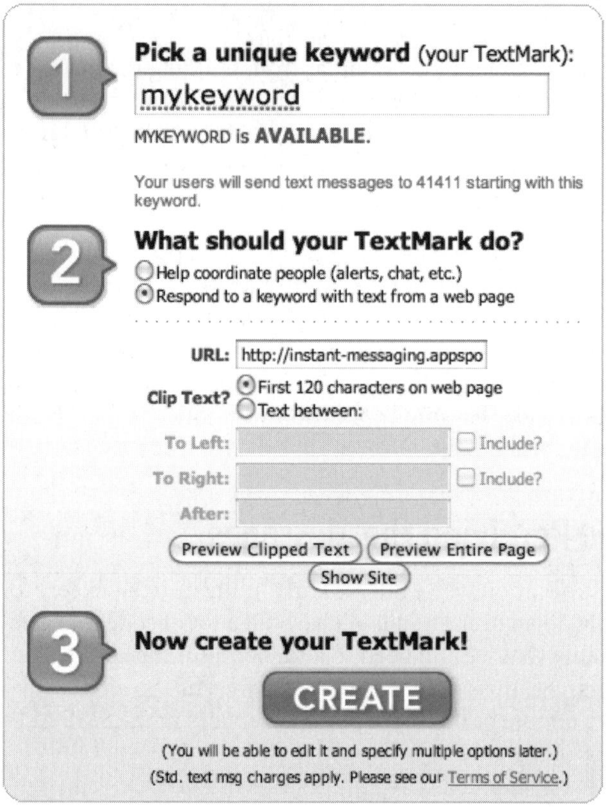

Pick a unique keyword (your TextMark):

mykeyword

MYKEYWORD is **AVAILABLE**.

Your users will send text messages to 41411 starting with this keyword.

What should your TextMark do?

○ Help coordinate people (alerts, chat, etc.)
⦿ Respond to a keyword with text from a web page

URL: http://instant-messaging.appspo

Clip Text? ⦿ First 120 characters on web page
○ Text between:

To Left: ☐ Include?
To Right: ☐ Include?
After:

(Preview Clipped Text) (Preview Entire Page)
(Show Site)

Now create your TextMark!

CREATE

(You will be able to edit it and specify multiple options later.)
(Std. text msg charges apply. Please see our Terms of Service.)

Figure 8-4. Reserving a keyword with the TextMarks service

For step one of the form, feel free to select any keyword that is available or makes sense with your intended application. Although any number of application developers can sign up for a keyword, the actual end users are all sending messages to the same short-code number. By asking your users to prepend a specific keyword when sending a message to that shortcode, TextMarks is able to know whether to send a message to our application or another application.

In the second step, instruct the service to "Respond to a keyword with text from a web page." This means that when a user sends a text message to a specific keyword, Text-Marks will request a URL of our choosing and respond with the text that appears in the response. To configure that URL, you'll want to use the same server that you used in the previous chapter. This is built using the `application-id` of your current App Engine application. In my case, the URL for this callback is `http://instant-messaging.appspot.com/sms/incoming/via/textmark?uid=\p&body=\0&action=\a`. Your URL should look identical with the exception that it uses your `application-id`.

If you didn't build the example in the previous chapter, you can flip back and follow the steps for creating an App Engine application. If you're integrating this into an existing App Engine application, just use your existing `application-id`.

While it should be clear that this application uses the URL pattern that we set up with our regular expression, it also appends some HTTP parameters to the request. We'll be using a few parameters to inform our application of what is happening with each request. These variables will be available to our controller classes by simply checking the HTTP request parameters. Each parameter is defined here:

`uid`
> This is the unique user ID that is sending the text message. In our case it will always be the mobile phone number of the user.

`body`
> The actual entire body of the text message sent from the user.

`action`
> The action identifier informing us what the user is trying to do. TextMarks will autosubscribe any user who sends a message to our service, so this is almost always "REQ." Other services may send actions such as "SUBSCRIBE."

Finally, click the "Create" button to reserve your account. After you click this button, the service will require that you link your account to an actual mobile phone number and will send you a message to confirm that you do have access to that number. Upon receiving this text message, enter the password into the form (which should look like Figure 8-5) and continue.

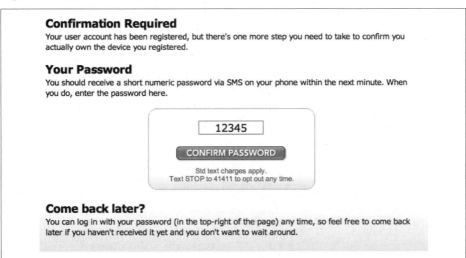

Figure 8-5. Confirming an account on TextMarks

After signing up for the service and registering a keyword, you'll still need to create an API key to use the API functions. This is a simple process initiated from the developer section on the TextMarks website (*http://www.textmarks.com/dev/api/reg/*). You'll be greeted with a form resembling Figure 8-6. After filling out this form, you should receive an email message from the service almost immediately with your API key. Save this key in a safe place; it'll be used when we start writing the messaging functionality.

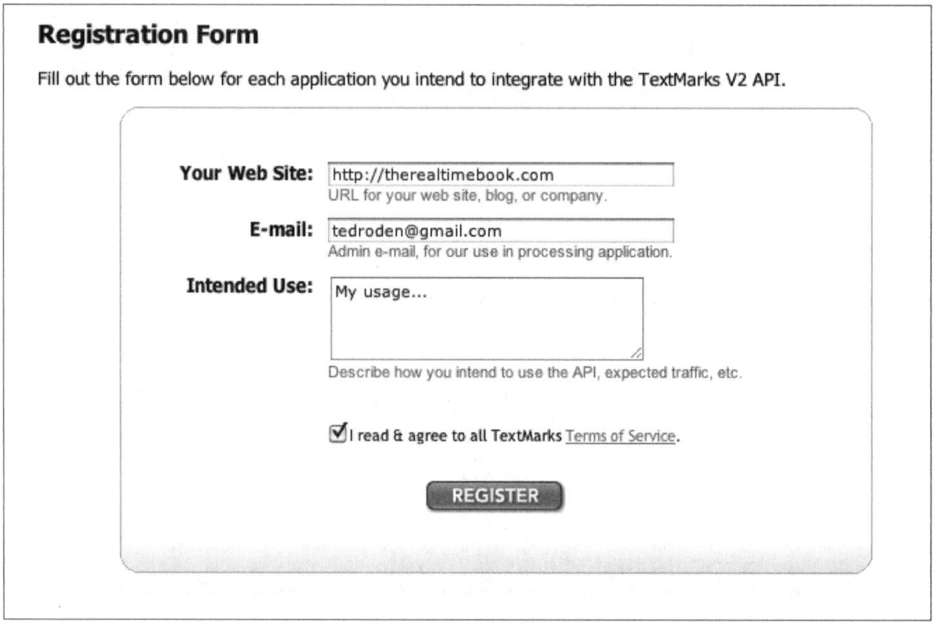

Registration Form

Fill out the form below for each application you intend to integrate with the TextMarks V2 API.

Your Web Site: `http://therealtimebook.com`
URL for your web site, blog, or company.

E-mail: `tedroden@gmail.com`
Admin e-mail, for our use in processing application.

Intended Use: `My usage...`
Describe how you intend to use the API, expected traffic, etc.

☑ I read & agree to all TextMarks Terms of Service.

REGISTER

Figure 8-6. Acquiring an API key on TextMarks

The Python class

Having built the `SMSService` interface class, we can start building the actual service classes by expanding on the class we have already defined. In this case, we'll create a class called `Textmark`. To handle sending messages from the TextMarks service, we only need to override two methods. Inside your *sms.py* file, add the following code:

```
class Textmark(SMSService):
    def __init__(self):
        # The authentication parameters supplied by textmarks
        self._auth_user = 'your-auth-user'
        self._auth_pass = 'your-auth-pass'

        # call the constructor of the parent class
        SMSService.__init__(self,
                    '41411',    # textmarks.com's short code
                    'your-keyword',
                    api_key='your-api-key',
                    )
```

```
            # override the send method from SMSService
            def send(self, number, body):

    # The Send URL
            url = "http://dev1.api2.textmarks.com/GroupLeader/send_one_message/"

            # setup the http arguments
            args = {}
            args['to'] = number
            args['msg'] = body
            args['tm'] = self._keyword
            args['api_key'] = self._api_key
            args['auth_user'] = self._auth_user
            args['auth_pass'] = self._auth_pass

            # make the HTTP API call to send the message
            result = urlfetch.fetch(url=url,
                                    payload=urllib.urlencode(args),
                                    method=urlfetch.POST)
            logging.info(result.content)
```

The first thing we need to do is override the __init__ method, which sets up the different variables such as the shortcode and API keys. While the SMSService class accepts and can handle variables such as the shortcode for the SMS service, the keyword that users will use to direct messages to our service, and the API key, we're going to need some extra variables.

The TextMarks API requires an API key as well as a username and password specified as auth_user and auth_pass. Populate these variables with the SMS number you used when signing up for the TextMarks service. Unless you've changed the password, the password field will be the one sent to you via text message to verify your account.

Having set up the special authentication variables that are unique to the TextMarks service, we simply call the constructor of the parent class to properly create the rest of the object. Because every service that uses TextMarks will share the same shortcode, the first parameter should be 41411. However, the shortcode is different for every service, so fill in the keyword that you reserved when signing up. The final parameter that we need to send to the constructor is the api_key parameter. This is the same API key that TextMarks should have emailed you when you signed up for an account. You can always locate your API keys, and sign up for more, on the TextMarks developer site (*http://www.textmarks.com/dev/api/reg/*).

With the main object initialized, we can rely on almost all of the default methods provided by the SMSService class. The main exception is that we need to override the send method. This method takes only two parameters, the mobile number that will receive the SMS message and the actual body of the message.

The TextMarks API has a number of what it calls API packages containing many functions. From the API, you can handle everything from unsubscribing users, sending bulk messages to every subscriber of your keyword, and even programmatically changing the callback URL and how to handle advertising on your keyword. Amongst the packages provided is one called `GroupLeader`, which contains a function called `send_one_message` that can be used to send one message to one user. To use this API function, we simply need to send an HTTP POST request to *http://dev1.api2.text-marks.com/GroupLeader/send_one_message/*.

The bulk of the code in this method sets up the arguments that get sent as the payload of that HTTP API call. After building a simple dictionary that contains all of the parameters, we run App Engine's `urlfetch.fetch` method, which actually makes the request. Whereas most of the parameters for this method are contained in variables that are handled by the `SMSService` class, the parameters required by this API call are outlined here:

`to`
> The mobile number that is the recipient of this message.

`msg`
> The body of the message itself, which should be no more than 120 characters when using the free account.

`tm`
> This is the keyword (or text mark) associated with your message.

`api_key`
> The TextMarks API key.

`auth_user`
> The username used to log in to the Text Marks website.

`auth_pass`
> The password used to log in to the Text Marks website.

Testing it out

At this point, our code may not do much, but it has the ability to respond to SMS messages. This is a good time to test it out to ensure that we're on the right track. Just like in the previous chapter, we can use the Google App Engine Launcher to deploy this application. Press the Deploy button to redeploy the instant messaging application.

Once this code has been pushed, there is nothing new to see by simply visiting the website. From your cell phone, send a text message to `41411` using your shortcode. You can send any message to the service that you want as long as it's preceded by the keyword that you registered with TextMarks. In my case, I would send a message along the lines of `realtime Hi There!` to `41411` and wait for a response. The transaction should look like Figure 8-7.

If you received an error message or no response at all, go to the App Engine dashboard and take a look at the logs. These logs generally provide a backtrace that is helpful in determining what went wrong.

Figure 8-7. Greetings sent via SMS

However, assuming that it did work, you will probably notice a couple of things about the transaction. First of all, the keyword is not case-sensitive, which is great for modern phones that tend to capitalize the first word of the sentence. Also, in addition to the expected response that greets the user with a friendly "Hello" message, there was also a slightly less friendly message sent. This second text message is sent directly from the TextMarks service, informing the user that they are now subscribed to the service and how to unsubscribe.

In the event that you want to keep testing the TextMarks functionality but want to save some money on your messaging plan, you can use the service's emulator. This is a small AJAX-based application that allows you to interact with your keyword without sending actual text messages. The application will send the proper POST messages to your server, but the response will be directed back to the web application. To access your emulator, go to *http://www.textmarks.com/your-keyword*. You will be able to send and receive messages through the interface pictured in Figure 8-8.

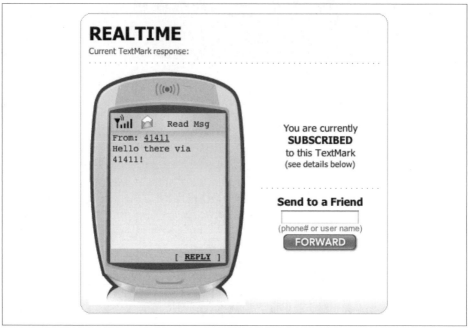

REALTIME

Current TextMark response:

((•))

📶 ✉ Read Msg
From: 41411
Hello there via
41411!

You are currently
SUBSCRIBED
to this TextMark
(see details below)

Send to a Friend

(phone# or user name)

FORWARD

[REPLY]

Figure 8-8. The TextMarks SMS phone emulator

Zeep Mobile

Now that we have this functionality up and running on one service, let's add in support for another. This will allow us to help keep costs down by taking advantage of the different pricing structures, and we can open our service up to more users in cases where one service supports a specific carrier and another does not.

Reserving a keyword

To sign up for a Zeep Mobile account, head over to the signup page (*https://www.zeep mobile.com/users/login*) and enter your email address. You will then receive an activation link to your email address that will enable you to set up your account.

Once you have an account, you need to reserve a keyword and generate your API keys. While you're logged in, click on the tab labeled "My Account," and then click on the button called "Generate New API Keys." Figure 8-9 demonstrates an example of this signup page.

In this example, I've selected the same keyword used in the TextMarks example; feel free to do the same. While most of the fields are administrative and help you remember which keys are for which purpose, it's important to specify the correct value callback URL field at the bottom of the form. This should be the same URL that was used in the Text Marks example, but with the word `textmarks` changed to `zeep`. This will direct all

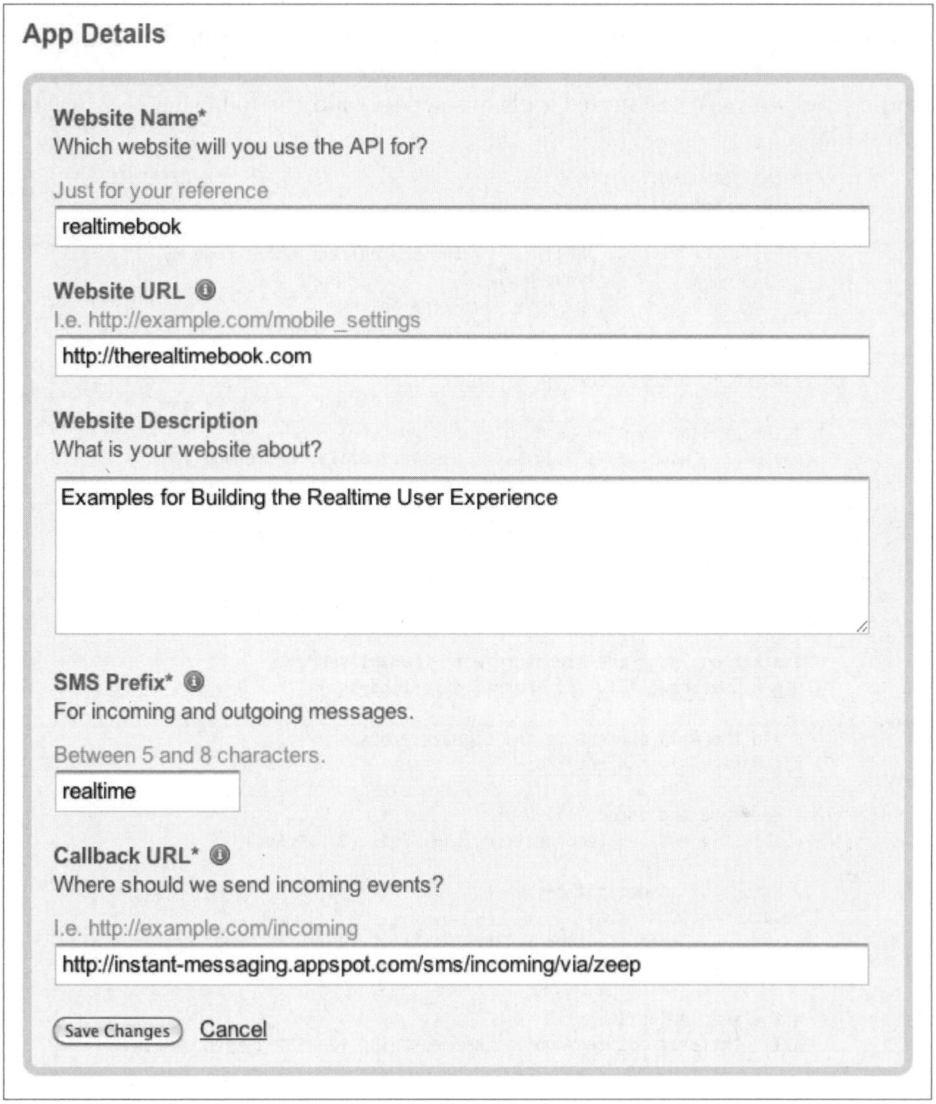

App Details

Website Name*
Which website will you use the API for?

Just for your reference

```
realtimebook
```

Website URL ⓘ
I.e. http://example.com/mobile_settings

```
http://therealtimebook.com
```

Website Description
What is your website about?

```
Examples for Building the Realtime User Experience
```

SMS Prefix* ⓘ
For incoming and outgoing messages.

Between 5 and 8 characters.

```
realtime
```

Callback URL* ⓘ
Where should we send incoming events?

I.e. http://example.com/incoming

```
http://instant-messaging.appspot.com/sms/incoming/via/zeep
```

(Save Changes) Cancel

Figure 8-9. Reserving a keyword with Zeep Mobile

of the callbacks from the service to the same `SMSIncomingHandler` controller that we created to handle all of the incoming messages. Changing the service name enables the code to quickly determine the source of each request.

After reserving your keyword, the Zeep Mobile website greets you with a newly created API key and secret. Keep these values handy, as we'll be using them in the code.

The Python class

Although there are similarities between the way the Zeep Mobile and TextMarks services act, the main differences come out in the way they handle authentication and sending messages. To get started with this service, add the following class to your *sms.py* file:

```python
class Zeep(SMSService):
    def __init__(self):
        SMSService.__init__(self,
                            '88147',    # the shared zeep short code
                            'your-keyword',
                            api_key='your-zeep-api-key',
                            api_secret='your-zeep-api-secret')

    def send(self, number, body):

        # the payload to send (and for the signature)
        payload = "user_id=%s&body=%s" % (number, urllib.quote(body))

        # the timestamp needed for the signature
        ts = time.strftime('%a, %d %b %Y %H:%M:%S GMT',time.gmtime())

        # the main part of the signature
        sig_content = "%s%s%s" % (self._api_key, ts, payload)

        # start building the signature with the api secret
        sig = hmac.new(self._api_secret, digestmod=sha)

        # add the main content to the signature hash
        sig.update(sig_content)

        # generate and encode the hash
        usable_sig = base64.encodestring(sig.digest()).strip()

        # setup the authorization headers
        headers = {'Date': ts,
                   'Authorization': 'Zeep %s:%s' % (self._api_key, usable_sig)
                   }

        # the send API url
        url = "https://api.zeepmobile.com/messaging/2008-07-14/send_message"

        # make the request
        result = urlfetch.fetch(url=url,
                                payload=payload,
                                method=urlfetch.POST,
                                headers=headers
                                )

        logging.info(headers)
        logging.info(result.content)
```

The first thing to notice about this class is that the __init__ method is very similar to the __init__ method of the Textmark class, even if it's a bit simpler. This method simply calls the parent constructor with the correct keyword and API parameters.

The bigger change comes from the send method. Whereas the Textmark class could simply make a simple web request with a username and password parameter, the Zeep Mobile service requires us to sign each request individually with our API information.

The signature is a fairly standard Hash-Based Message Authentication Code (HMAC) (*http://en.wikipedia.org/wiki/HMAC*) implementation. Generally, with these types of signatures, you build a string starting with your API secret, append several parameters, and encode using some predefined method. This is exactly how it works with the Zeep service. In this case, the parameters included in the signature are the api_key, the current timestamp, and the payload of the actual HTTP request. We take all those parameters, combine them into a single string, and create a hash using the API secret as the key. That is then encoded to the base64 encoding, which is then the actual request signature. Figure 8-10 shows the flow of creating this signature.

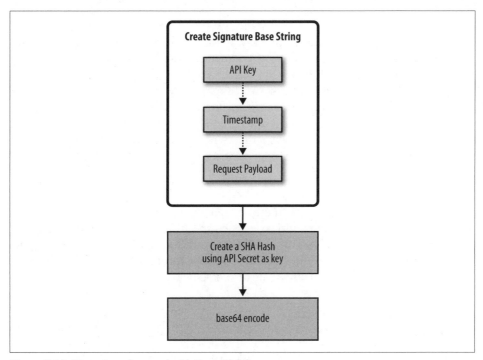

Figure 8-10. Reserving a keyword with Zeep Mobile

To make a request to the Zeep Mobile service, we just need to add our signature to the Authorization header in the HTTP request. This authorization header is in the following format: Zeep [*api-key*]:[*request-signature*]. So we simply build a string containing those two variables and add it to the headers array passed along in the request. In addition to the `Authorization` header, we also add a `Date` header. We need to make sure that the timestamp that we used when generating our signature matches this header exactly. When our request makes it to the Zeep Mobile servers, they'll use this `Date` header to validate our signature; if these values are different, our signature will not be verified.

Once we have all the parameters and headers set up, we simply make the HTTP request. This request includes all of the headers that we set up, and also includes the `payload` we created at the very start of this method. This payload contains a `user_id`, which is just the mobile number of the user on the receiving end of this message, and the `body` of message itself. To help with debugging, we're also going to log the headers and the result. If something goes wrong at some point, we can easily check the logs to see the root of the problem, and whether it's from the signature or the request itself.

Authenticating Users

The code we've built so far can accept SMS messages from users and respond with appropriate responses. However, as it stands, we're not saving any information about the users or authenticating them in any way. In this case, the main reason that we want to authenticate a user is so that we can send her messages that are more than simply responses to messages that she has sent to us. With a user who has been authenticated, we can send messages to our users who were not directly solicited. For example, if our application monitored the status of an airline flight, we would be able send a message to a user when our application notices the flight has been delayed. At the moment, we can provide that information only when the users asks for it; after she's authenticated, we can send her that information as soon as it's available.

The authentication process

Our application already has an interface defined to handle authentication. The `SMSService` class defines three methods designed specifically for this purpose. The flow between `is_authenticated`, `should_authenticate`, and `authenticate` is quite simple. First, we want to check whether the user is authenticated. If not, check to see if we should authenticate a user. If so, authenticate her. This logic flow is outlined in Figure 8-11.

The basic code

Having defined how this process will work, we need to decide where in the code it belongs. While most of the SMS service providers allow users to subscribe to a service through a web-based HTML form, our application is only going to allow users to authenticate themselves by sending an SMS message to the service. This means that we're able to check for and authenticate users easily from one spot, the `respond` method of the `SMSIncomingHandler` class. Because users can be authenticated only by sending us a

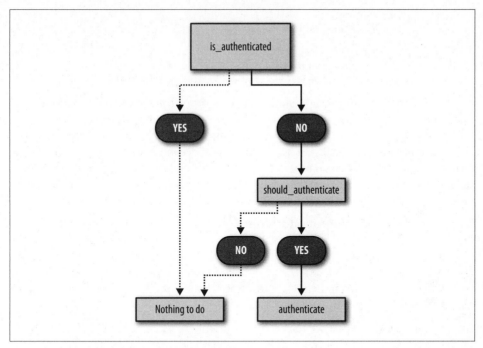

Figure 8-11. The flow of our authentication process

message, all requests, whether they are from authenticated users or unauthenticated users, funnel through this one method. If the user is trying to authenticate, we can easily honor that request from this one method. Update the `respond` method to reflect the following changes:

```
# all of the HTTP requests end up handled by this method
def respond(self, service_type):

    # setup the service type
    self.set_service_type(service_type)

    # prepare some HTTP parameters as variables
    uid = self.request.get('uid')
    event = self.request.get('event')
    body = self.request.get('body')

    # are we authenticated?
    if uid and not self.service.is_authenticated(uid):
        # should we authenticate?
        logging.info("Not authenticated, should we? (uid: %s)" % uid)
        if self.service.should_authenticate(uid, event, body):
            logging.info("Authenticating: %s " % uid)
            self.service.authenticate(uid)
        else:
            logging.info("No reason to authenticate uid: %s" % uid)
    elif len(uid):
        logging.info("Previously authenticated uid: %s" % uid)
```

```
    else:
        logging.info("No UID, not authenticating")

    # respond to the request
    self.response.headers['Content-Type'] = 'text/plain'
    self.response.out.write("Hello there via %s!" % self.service.short_code)
```

The first change to this method simply collects the various parameters that we may need during the authentication process. You'll remember that we set up the callback URLs of both services to send the exact same parameters. So we collect the uid, event, and body of the request. The uid is the mobile number of the user sending the message, although it may be empty. The event is the type of message being sent to the service, which can include a request to subscribe to this service. Finally, the body is the message text itself.

Before we can actually authenticate the user, we need to run a couple of sanity checks. First, we need to ensure that we actually have a uid, or mobile number. Without the uid, there is nothing to authenticate. If we have that, check to see whether that uid has already been authenticated with the is_authenticated method. Upon passing that first test, we log some text to indicate where we are in this process. This will help us if we need to debug the login process for a specific user.

At this point we know that we have a mobile number and that the user is not authenticated. Now we need to check whether the user should be authenticated. The different API providers handle this logic differently. On the TextMarks service, for example, the answer to this question is always a "Yes." The policy on TextMarks is that if a user sends an SMS to our service, they can be counted as subscribed. The default code written in the should_authenticate method of SMSService acts in this way. However, the Zeep Mobile policy is that a user is not subscribed until the user affirmatively requests to join the service by sending the message join *keyword* to their shortcode. Either way, the interface to the should_authenticate method is always the same.

Once we know that we have a mobile number, that the user is not authenticated, and that the user should be authenticated, the only thing left to do is actually authenticate the user. Using the authenticate method, we simply supply the mobile number, which is stored in the App Engine Datastore by our SMSUser class.

Authenticating with Zeep Mobile. The code is ready to run with SMS providers that have more liberal subscription policies, but authenticating while using Zeep Mobile service will require a bit more code. Using the existing interface, we can continue to use the is_authenticated and authenticate methods without changing anything. The only change comes in determining whether or not a specific user should be authenticated during the process. To add this functionality, modify your Zeep class and add the following method:

```
def should_authenticate(self, mobile_number, event, body):
    # the user is actually subscribing
    if event == 'SUBSCRIPTION_UPDATE':
        return True
```

This method follows the Zeep Mobile authentication logic and simply checks to see whether the user is requesting to subscribe to the service. When a user sends a message of `join keyword`, Zeep Mobile supplies the `event` parameter with a value of `SUBSCRIP TION_UPDATE`. So, to determine whether this user can be authenticated, we simply need to check to ensure that we have received a subscription event.

Testing the authentication process.   At this point, though we've sent a number of messages, we have not authenticated any users. We can easily test this out by sending SMS messages to the TextMarks shortcode, but let's try it using Zeep Mobile. Since Zeep has the additional logic, we'll be able to test the various states of authentication with the one service.

To save some money on text messages, head over to the Zeep Mobile website, create a virtual SMS device (*http://www.zeepmobile.com/account/test_devices*), and send the messages from there. You can create as many of these devices as you like, which is nice when testing out the various states of authentication. Open up your virtual device and send the following messages to your keyword. First, send a simple request such as `keyword Hi there`. Next, send a join request in the format `join keyword`. The result should resemble Figure 8-12.

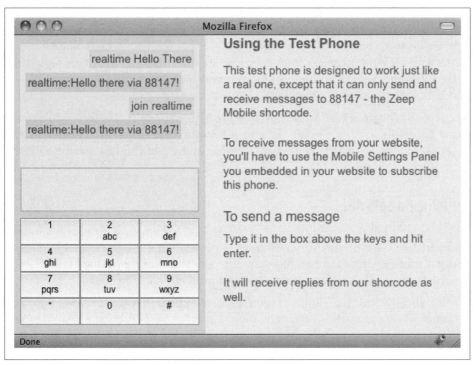

Figure 8-12. Authenticating via a Zeep Mobile virtual device

Because we have a standard response to any message that comes in to our application, the responses from the two requests that we send to the virtual device are identical, but the user is authenticated from one request to the next. Head over to the Google App Engine Dashboard and look at the logs by filtering on the "Info" severity. In reverse chronological order, the top log entires should be from the virtual device. While the uids are not valid mobile device numbers, we had no trouble with the authentication. Your log entries should resemble Figure 8-13.

Figure 8-13. Viewing the authentication logs on the Google App Engine Dashboard

Starting from the bottom of the logs, you can see that our first request made it to our server without a uid. Requests from Zeep that are not authenticated, or are requesting authentication, are sent without a uid. Without the uid, we don't bother trying to authenticate and simply respond to the request normally.

The second request, shown at the top of Figure 8-13, shows that our server did receive a uid. This request was the result of the join *keyword* command. This request was also accompanied by an event parameter, so when our code checked should_authenti cate, it returned True.

Building an SMS API

At this point we have an application that responds to SMS messages and authenticates users, but we have no way to send a user a message on our own timetable. A truly realtime user experience cannot just respond to messages as they come in from users; it needs to be able to send a user a message without any user interaction.

Having already built the authentication code, we know that we're allowed to send messages to certain users, so the only thing that is left to do is build an API that will allow us to send these messages. In your *sms.py* file, add another URL handler in the main function:

```
def main():
    application = webapp.WSGIApplication([(r'/sms/incoming/via/([a-z]+)/?',
                                          SMSIncomingHandler),
```

```
                            (r'/sms/send/via/([a-z]+)/?',
                            SMSSendHandler)
                        ],
                        debug=True)
    wsgiref.handlers.CGIHandler().run(application)
```

This just informs our application that if we get a request to a URL such as /sms/send/via/*xyz*, we should direct those requests to a class called SMSSendHandler. Any patterns that match the regular expression in this URL will be passed along as parameters to the get and post requests. In our case, we'll be using this URL to send messages via Zeep Mobile and TextMarks with URLs resembling /sms/send/via/zeep.

To add this functionality, add the following class to your *sms.py* file:

```
class SMSSendHandler(SMSBaseHandler):
    def get(self, service_type):
        self.respond(service_type)
    def post(self, service_type):
        self.respond(service_type)

    def respond(self, service_type):
        # set the service type
        self.set_service_type(service_type)

        # load the parameters
        mobile_number = self.request.get('mobile_number')
        body = self.request.get('body')

        # prepare our response variables
        response = ""
        status = ""

        # check to ensure the designated user is authenticated
        if self.service.is_authenticated(mobile_number):

            # send the message
            self.service.send(mobile_number, body)
            status = "success"
            response = "Sending request to %s" % mobile_number

        # not authenticated, don't send anything
        else:
            status = "fail"
            response = "Not Authenticated: %s" % mobile_number

        logging.info("API response: %s - %s" % (status, response))

        # send the JSON response object
        self.response.headers['Content-Type'] = 'text/plain'
        self.response.out.write(json.dumps({'status': status,
                                            'mesg': response}))
```

This code operates in a similar fashion to the `SMSIncomingHandler` class. It simply funnels the `get` and `post` requests through one method called `respond` and does all of its work in that method. This method accepts two HTTP parameters per request, the `mobile_number` that will receive this message and the `body` of the message itself.

Once we've collected the HTTP parameters and set up some variables that we'll use when responding to the request, the next thing to do is check to see whether the user is authenticated. If the user `is_authenticated`, we run the `send` method for this service and set the response variables accordingly. This is where our standard `SMSService` interface really shines. Although both Zeep Mobile and TextMarks have drastically different ways of sending messages, we can simply call this single method and it will get handled, regardless of which service is being used.

In the event that this user is not authenticated, we refrain from sending the message but still set the response variables. These variables are then logged, encoded to JSON, and sent back as the HTTP response. While any response that we provide in the `SMSIncomingHandler` sends an SMS message back to the user, responding to the HTTP request here just sends it back to the client making the API request. In this method, no message is being sent without calling `send`.

 This API method is intentionally simple. In production use, it should be secured to ensure that it can't be used to send unsolicited SMS messages to your users. It wouldn't hurt to add some error checking as well.

Testing the API

The idea behind building this API is that other parts of an application can use it to send messages to users when needed. So, to ensure that these messages can be sent, we need to test out sending messages from outside this application. To keep it simple, we'll use the command-line program called `curl` to make some requests and test it out. From the command line, enter the following command:

```
~ $ curl "http://your-app-id.appspot.com/sms/send/via/textmark?mobile_number=invalid-
number&body=Can+you+hear+me+now?"
{"status": "fail", "mesg": "Not Authenticated:
invalid-number"}
```

As expected, calling this method with a totally invalid number (in this case, **invalid-number**) fails miserably. But what happens if you use your personal phone number that you've been using to test? For sake of this example, let's assume that number is (555) 555-1212. Try that from the command line:

```
~ $ curl "http://your-app-id.appspot.com/sms/send/via/textmark?
mobile_number=5555551212&body=Can+you+hear+me+now?"
{"status": "fail", "mesg": "Not Authenticated: 5555551212"}
```

While that certainly looks like it should work, the number provided is not actually the number that we have on file. Each of these SMS services sends us the mobile number in E.164 (*http://en.wikipedia.org/wiki/E.164*), complete with the + prefix. So in this example, the number we have on file is actually +15555551212. To use that number in an HTTP request, we need to encode the + character to %2B. Try your phone number again in this format:

```
~ $ curl "http://your-app-id.appspot.com/sms/send/via/textmark?
mobile_number=%2B15555551212&body=Can+you+hear+me+now?"
{"status": "success", "mesg": "Sending request to +15555551212"}%
```

If you got the format right, you should see a similar response. You should also have received a text message from the TextMarks shortcode. Figure 8-14 shows an example of this.

Figure 8-14. Receiving a message sent via the API

## CHAPTER 9

Measuring User Engagement: Analytics on the Realtime Web

As a publisher on the Web or a website creator, there is nothing better than writing a new post or launching a new feature and then watching the traffic come rolling in. The problem is that the standard web analytics suites leave users waiting several hours, at best, before reporting on the traffic. Google Analytics provides a tremendous amount of depth and analytical capability, but the data that it collects from a website is not available immediately or even after a short delay. It could be hours before the data from a given website turns up on Google Analytics. The legacy analytics products allow you to see aggregate counts of hits, visitors, page views, and other statistics over a 24-hour period. However, they do very little to give a website creator a picture of what is happening on the site at any given moment.

If a website is interacting with users in realtime, providing constant updates and prompting for responses from the users on any number of different platforms, the analytics package had better be able to keep up. This chapter looks at a couple of new analytics packages that allow for monitoring your web traffic in realtime, and then we're going to dive in and create a small analytics application that can be deeply integrated with your site.

Realtime Analytics Services

Noticing the gap in time between the actual page view and the ability to analyze that traffic, several startups have launched paid services to give insight into the traffic much more quickly. Using included JavaScript files, these services monitor a website's traffic as it happens and then provide either an application or a website that enables users to view the stats in realtime.

Chartbeat

Chartbeat is a paid web service that enables users to monitor web traffic in realtime through a web-based user interface, an iPhone application, and SMS alerts. Installation onto a website is as simple as pasting in a bit of JavaScript code. Once installed, a user can start viewing stats through the web interface (*http://chartbeat.com/*); (see Figure 9-1) or by downloading the iPhone application.

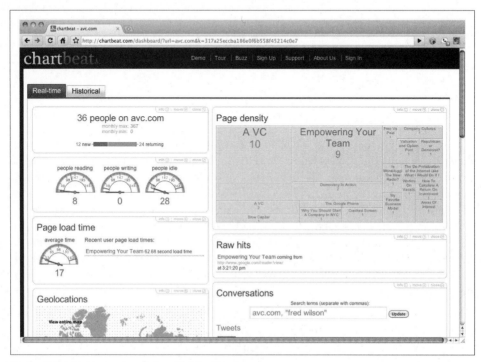

Figure 9-1. Monitoring a website with Chartbeat

On top of viewing standard analytics, such as the number of people looking at a site at a given time, Chartbeat also enables users to track who is talking about a certain website on services such as Twitter. It also offers fairly robust alerting tools. For example, Chartbeat serves as a simple uptime monitor, sending out SMS alerts if it notices that the site has stopped responding to HTTP requests. On the other hand, a user can configure Chartbeat to send out alerts via SMS or through push notification on the iPhone application if site activity goes beyond predetermined limits. Figure 9-2 shows the iPhone application.

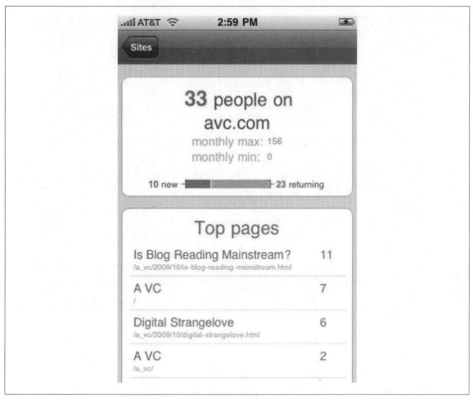

Figure 9-2. Monitoring a website with the Chartbeat iPhone application

Woopra

Another service providing realtime analytics tracking is called Woopra (*http://www.woopra.com/*). This service is also installed by adding some JavaScript code to a site and then watching the statistics as quickly as they are collected. However, one differentiating factor of Woopra is that it requires users to install a Java-based desktop application to monitor the traffic (see Figure 9-3).

Although Woopra lacks the alerting capability of Chartbeat, it does allow website owners to interact with their users on a very personal level. From the Woopra interface, a Woopra subscriber can initiate an instant message chat session with any user who is currently viewing the website (see Figure 9-4).

Figure 9-3. Monitoring a website through the Woopra desktop application

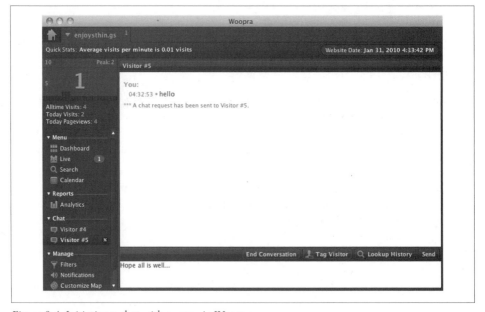

Figure 9-4. Initiating a chat with a user via Woopra

Customized Analytics

The paid realtime analytics services are useful to get an overview of what is happening on a website in realtime. However, the applications that we've been building so far have not been limited to the web browser. In order to properly figure out the current status of our applications, we're going to need to build a custom solution that can handle tracking the different types of actions our users take. In this section we'll build a simple analytics application that can track users as they navigate a website, but also tracks any other arbitrary action that happens outside of a web browser.

Sending Tracking Pings with JavaScript

For the web-browser-based part of collecting these analytics, we're going to use a simple JavaScript-based implementation. The JavaScript file that we build can be hosted either on the same machine as the main web application or somewhere else entirely. Once this JavaScript is ready, we'll include it from each page of the site and run a function to start tracking user actions. To get started, create a file called *realtime-analytics.js* and insert the following code:

```
var Analytics = {
    uid: 0,
    start_time: 0,
    last_activity: 0,
    ping_url: "{{ ping_url }}",

    start: function() {
        Analytics.start_time = new Date().getTime();
        Analytics.last_activity = Analytics.start_time;

        // ensure we have a user ID
        Analytics.setupUID();

        // setup the event listeners
        var updateLastActivity = function() {
            Analytics.last_activity = new Date().getTime();
        };
        window.addEventListener('click',     updateLastActivity, false);
        window.addEventListener('scroll',    updateLastActivity, false);
        window.addEventListener('mousemove', updateLastActivity, false);
        window.addEventListener('keypress',  updateLastActivity, false);

        // when we're unloading the page
        var beforeUnload = function() {
            // ping again, but note that we're exiting
            Analytics.ping('exit');
        };

        // ensure that we get one last ping in before we unload the page
        window.addEventListener('beforeunload', beforeUnload, false);
```

```
        // start pinging.
        Analytics.ping();
    }
};
```

This code doesn't do anything too complicated. We build the start of an object called Analytics, which will contain all of the client-side tracking functionality. First, we define a few variables that we'll be using throughout the object. The variable uid will be used to contain the unique identifier for each user who loads this page. The variables start_time and last_activity are used to contain the time of when the script first gets started and to monitor the time of the last user interaction, respectively. The final variable defined is called ping_url. This is used to inform the script which base URL to use when pinging the server. In this case, we'll be serving this code from our Tornado server, and the ping_url be determined by the server and populated into this field. This is a small convenience that will allow us to serve this up and copy the file to different servers. You could get some performance gains by serving this file from a content delivery network (CDN) and hard-coding this value in place.

The next bit of code here defines the start method, which is called from each web page to get the analytics process started. Inside this method we populate the timing variables start_time and last_activity. Next, we call the method setupUID, which will be defined next.

Once we have the basic variables set up and the UID has been either generated or loaded, the next job is to attach callback methods to any of the events that signal the user has been active. If the user moves a mouse, presses a key, clicks, or scrolls, we want to know and update the last_activity field. The only event that we want to track differently is the onbeforeunload event, which is the event that is called when a user navigates away from the page. When this happens, we want to not only log the time, but also ensure we get in one last ping to the server. The ping is defined next, but before we get to that, let's set up the uid field by writing the setupUID method. In your *realtime-analytics.js* file, add the following method:

```
Analytics.setupUID = function() {
    // check for a cookie
    var cookie_name = "realtime_analytics";
    var cookies = document.cookie.split(/\; ?/g);
    for(var i = 0; i < cookies.length; ++i) {
        var name = cookies[i].split("=")[0];
        if (name == cookie_name) {
            Analytics.uid = cookies[i].split("=")[1];
            return;
        }
    }

    // if we're here, we need to generate and store a UID
    // generate the UID
    Analytics.uid = new Date().getTime().toString();
    Analytics.uid += "-" + Math.floor(Math.random() * 100000);
```

```
        // save it as a cookie
        var expire = new Date();
        expire.setDate(expire.getDate()+60); // 60 days in the FUTURE
        var cookie_data = cookie_name + "=" + escape(Analytics.uid) +
            ";expires=" + expire.toGMTString();
        document.cookie = cookie_data;
};
```

This method has two jobs to do. First, this method must check the user's cookies to
see whether a cookie exists that stores the uid field. If that cookie exists, store it in the
Analytics.uid field and return. If it doesn't exist, simply create a unique identifier by
appending a random number onto the current time. This isn't the most scientific way
to generate a unique ID, but it is close enough for our purposes. Once created, we
simply store the uid in a cookie so that it sticks around for a while.

Now that we have the UID generated, we have everything ready that we're going to
need to ping the server. To add the ping method, add the following code to your
realtime-analytics.js file:

```
Analytics.ping = function(on_exit) {

    // was this method called because we were exiting the page?
    if ((typeof on_exit != 'undefined') && (on_exit == 'exit'))
        on_exit = 1;
    else
        on_exit = 0;

    var params =
        // send the UID
        "&u=" + Analytics.uid +
        // the X and Y coordinates where the user has currently scrolled to
        "&x=" + (typeof window.pageXOffset != 'undefined' ? window.pageXOffset : 0)  +
        "&y=" + (typeof window.pageYOffset != 'undefined' ? window.pageYOffset : 0)  +
        // The time since the last activity
        "&l=" + (new Date().getTime() - Analytics.last_activity)  +
        // The total time the user has been on this page
        "&t=" + (new Date().getTime() - Analytics.start_time) +
        // Is this ping the result of exiting the page?
        "&e=" + on_exit +
        // The title of this document
        "&dt=" + encodeURIComponent(document.title.slice(0, 50)) +
        // Where do the user come from?
        "&r=" + encodeURIComponent(document.referrer ? document.referrer : '-direct-') +
        // Append a random number to ensure the browser doesn't use the cache
        "&*=" + Math.random();

    // append the script to the page (make the actual ping)
    var scr = document.createElement('script');
    scr.setAttribute('type', 'text/javascript');
    scr.setAttribute('src', Analytics.ping_url + '?' + params);
    document.getElementsByTagName('head')[0].appendChild(scr);
```

```
    // setup a loop to ping again in 3 seconds
    window.setTimeout(Analytics.ping, 3000);
};
```

This method does the actual pinging to the server. The first thing we do here is figure out whether on_exit should be set. If this method is being called as a result of the onbeforeunload callback, the on_exit callback, as it's passed in as a parameter, will be set to "exit." Once that's figured out, we simply build the big list of parameters, shown next, that we'll pass to the server. These are variables that can help the server understand a bit about the current state of the page.

u

The unique identifier uid of the current user.

x

The x coordinate of the scroll position. This is how many pixels the user has scrolled along the X axis.

x

The y coordinate of the scroll position. This is how many pixels the user has scrolled along the Y axis.

l

This is the number of seconds since the last activity. Rather than submitting the timestamp of the last activity, we calculate the difference in time so that we don't have to synchronize clocks between the server and browser.

t

This is the amount of time that the user has been on the page.

e

This is the type of ping we're sending. If the value is 1, the ping is the result of a beforeunload event; otherwise, the value of this field is zero.

dt

This is the current title of the document.

r

The referrer value provided by the browser. This field tells us whether the user got to this page from clicking on a link or by direct access, which could also be from a desktop application such as an instant messaging window or a Twitter client.

*

A random number to ensure the browser makes a new web request rather than returning the data from cache.

At this point we've built a pretty big string of data that will get sent back to the server, so the next job is to actually send it. Since there is a good possibility that this script was loaded from a different domain, or at the very least a different port than the rest of the web page, we can't make a standard Ajax request. Ajax requests across domains and ports are, of course, blocked to ensure safety in a world of cross-site scripting and other concerns. To get around that, we'll simply supply these parameters onto the end of another included JavaScript file. To do that, we simply create the element and append it to the page. That officially sends the ping to the server. The only thing left to do in this method is to schedule the next ping. In this case, we call `setTimeout` and request another ping in three seconds.

Other than including this JavaScript file on an HTML page, this is all of the code needed to start pinging the server and measuring user traffic as it moves across a website. The purpose of this script is to be small, fast, ping the server, and get out of the way. The real analytics work is done on the server side.

Catching the Statistics on the Server

To keep this application totally portable, allowing it to be installed alongside just about any server implementation, we're going to use the Tornado framework to build this application. This will enable us to drop in the code and run it on any chosen port alongside any existing infrastructure. To get started, create a file called *server.py* and fill it with the following code:

```
# start with some standard imports that we'll be using
import os, logging
import tornado.httpserver
import tornado.ioloop
import tornado.web
import simplejson as json
import time
import re
from tornado.options import define, options
from tornado.escape import url_escape
import urllib

# Define options that can be changed as we run this via the command line
define("port", default=8888, help="Run server on a specific port", type=int)

class Analytics(object):
    users = {}
    pages = {}

    # Number of seconds for which a session is live.
    # After this time, they're considered idle.
    # the user must continue to ping
    live_session_time = 30

    # If the ping timeout passes, the user has left the page.
    ping_timeout_time = 30

    def user_ping(self, data):

        uid = data['uid']
        url = data['url']

        logging.info("Received ping from %s", uid)
```

```
if uid not in self.users:
    self.users[uid] = {}

# note the last time they actually pinged us (now)
data['last_ping'] = time.time()
# Assume the user is active
data['status'] = 'Active'

# add the data to the object
self.users[uid][url] = data
```

The first part of this should look familiar from the previous Tornado examples; we simply import the needed libraries and then define the default port. After that, we jump right in to creating our Analytics object. This object will keep track of all the analytics information that we'll be using during this application. To start with, we create two dictionaries called user and pages. These will hold the list of users and all the user information, as well as the list of web pages that are currently being accessed.

Next up, we set up some variables that will be used later in the program. The variable live_session_time is going to be used to determine how many seconds must pass before a user is considered "Idle" rather than "Active." If a user has loaded the page in his web browser but hasn't been moving the mouse or clicking around, we can start to assume that he is idle and not actively using the site. While a user is idle, the web page is still open in the browser and the script will continue to ping the server, letting us know that he's still around. The next variable, ping_timeout_time, is used to determine how long we're willing to wait between pings before we determine that the user has left the page entirely. If we don't receive a single ping in 30 seconds, we consider the user gone.

Then, we have the user_ping method. This method ends up being called as a result of the ping method from the JavaScript code. The only parameter is a data object that contains all of the fields that were passed in from the JavaScript client. We then update the self.users object to ensure that we're keeping track of this user. That users object will be populated with the different URLs currently loaded by a specific user. Because a user may have multiple tabs or browser windows open, we accept all of them while still understanding that it's just one user.

We then add a couple of extra fields to the data object. We want to save the server-side value for the most recent ping, which is saved into data['last_ping']. We also add a status field to the object. This field will be either "Active" or "Idle." For the time being, we'll assume that the user is active.

Although this code handles the logic of what happens when we receive a ping, it's not actually hooked up to the web server to accept the web request from the client. To add that functionality, add the following code to your *server.py* file:

```
class PingHandler(tornado.web.RequestHandler):
    def get(self):
```

```
# setup some local convenience variables for later
uid = self.get_argument('u')
url = self.request.headers['Referer']

# build the data object to pass to the user_ping method
data = {
    'uid': uid,
    'url': url,
    'user_agent': self.request.headers['User-Agent'],
    'referrer': self.get_argument('r', '-direct-'),
    'time_on_page': self.get_argument('t'),
    'last_activity': self.get_argument('l'),
    'x': self.get_argument('x'),
    'y': self.get_argument('y'),
    'title': self.get_argument('dt')
    };

self.application.analytics.user_ping(data)
```

PingHandler is the controller class that accepts requests from the ping JavaScript method. The first action is to set up some local variables, storing the uid and url variables for later use. The uid variable is passed along as the u parameter from the JavaScript file. The url variable can be collected by grabbing it out of the HTTP headers object. The Referrer page is the actual URL that the user is currently browsing, which is the URL we want to store.

The next thing we do is build the data object that gets passed to the user_ping method. This data is mostly a field-by-field copy of the parameters we received from the JavaScript file. We lengthen the field names a bit in order to make them easier to use as we inspect them in the future. The only field that we add to the object that hasn't already been collected is the User-Agent field. This field, like the 'Referrer' field, can be collected from the headers that get passed along with the HTTP request.

At this point, we're ready to respond to the ping requests from the JavaScript requests, but we're missing one key element: we cannot serve the actual JavaScript to the client. To do that, we're going to have to add another controller class. In your *server.py* file:

```
class JSHandler(tornado.web.RequestHandler):
    def get(self):
        # setup the ping URL that will be used
        ping_url = self.request.protocol + "://" + self.request.host + "/ping"

        # serve the file
        self.set_header("Content-Type", "text/javascript")
        self.render("realtime-analytics.js", ping_url=ping_url)
```

This method should be very straightforward. It simply looks at the request to determine which ping_url will be used in the JavaScript file. Then, it serves the file to the user. In practice, it would probably make more sense to hardcode this variable into the JavaScript file and serve it statically from a web server that specializes in serving static files or from a CDN.

Both of the controllers that allow for us to serve the JavaScript and accept pings from the server are ready to go. The next thing to do is set up the Tornado application object and start the server. Add the following code to your *server.py* file:

```
class Application(tornado.web.Application):
    def __init__(self):

        # create an application-wide version of the analytics object
        self.analytics = Analytics()

        # map the two controller classes to the URLs
        handlers = [
            (r"/ping/?", PingHandler),
            (r"/js/?", JSHandler),
        ]

        # define static file path that we'll be using
        settings = dict(
            static_path=os.path.join(os.path.dirname(__file__), "static-new"),
        )

        # start the application!
        tornado.web.Application.__init__(self, handlers, **settings)

# keep this at the bottom of the file
if __name__ == "__main__":
    tornado.options.parse_command_line()
    http_server = tornado.httpserver.HTTPServer(Application())
    http_server.listen(options.port)
    tornado.ioloop.IOLoop.instance().start()
```

Once again, this code should look fairly familiar if you've followed along with any of the other Tornado-based examples. The first thing we do is define an `Application` object that extends the `tornado.web.Application` class. In it, we instantiate an `Analytics` object that is used by the controller classes. Next, we define a couple of URL mappings from the actual URL to the controller class that handles the work. The rest of the code is essentially Tornado boilerplate code that gets the server up and running on the correct port.

Testing the pings

In order to test this out, the first thing you need to do is decide which server which is going to run it. This code was designed to be flexible in terms of where and how you run it. As such, you have a number of options with regard to running the server code. You can put it on a public-facing site, either on its own port or on the standard port 80, if that's available. If you just want to test it out yourself, you can easily start it locally and limit access to only your browser. Either way, once you've copied the code onto the correct server, launch it from the command line:

```
$ python server.py --port=8888
```

In my case, I decided to start the server on my local machine and run it on port **8888**, which is actually the default port for our script.

At this point, we're all set to install some tracking code and track some basic statistics. The tracking code is installed by copying a couple of lines of JavaScript onto any web page that should be tracked. Ideally, you'd want to cover your entire site by copying the code into the header, or preferably the footer, of your website. For page load performance reasons, it's probably best to install this code just before the closing **BODY** tag in your HTML page. To install the code, copy the following into the HTML of your website:

```
<script type="text/javascript" src="http://localhost:8888/js/"></script>
<script type="text/javascript" language="JavaScript">
    try { Analytics.start(); } catch(e) {}
</script>
```

The problem with this code is that it makes a web request to the server located at `localhost`. This is fine if the site you're testing on is located on your local machine, but it will never work for users who are not using your computer. If you want to run the analytics code locally but install the code on a public site, wrap the code in some logic to ensure that it shows up only for you. In my case, on a site developed with PHP, I added this code in the following way:

```
<? if($current_user_id == 1): ?> // if the user is "me," show the code
    <script type="text/javascript" src="http://localhost:8888/js/"></script>
    <script type="text/javascript" language="JavaScript">
        try { Analytics.start(); } catch(e) {}
    </script>
<? endif; ?> // if the user is not me, do nothing.
```

The downside to this is that the code will never run against any user other than me, but it allows us to develop the analytics code locally against the actual actions on a site that we're interested in tracking.

Now that the JavaScript is installed and the server is running, it's time to load the site and see what happens. Point your browser to a URL that will print out the code you've loaded, and watch the logging statements from the Tornado server. It should look something like this:

```
$ python server.py --port=8888
[I 100201 22:18:08 web:714] 200 GET /js/ (127.0.0.1) 4.68ms
[I 100201 22:18:08 server:35] Received ping from 1264985825771-73154
[I 100201 22:18:08 web:714] 200 GET /ping?&u=1264985825771-73154&x=0&y=0
    &l=1&t=1&e=0&dt=
    Everybody%20enjoys%20things%20%40%20enjoysthin.gs&r=-direct-&*=0.41045479103922844
    (127.0.0.1) 1.14ms
[I 100201 22:18:11 server:35] Received ping from 1264985825771-73154
[I 100201 22:18:11 web:714] 200 GET /ping?&u=1264985825771-73154&x=0&y=0
    &l=3001&t=3002&e=
    0&dt=Everybody%20enjoys%20things%20%40%20enjoysthin.gs&r=-direct-
    &*=0.6840199520811439
    (127.0.0.1) 0.62ms
```

```
[I 100201 22:18:14 server:35] Received ping from 1264985825771-73154
[I 100201 22:18:14 web:714] 200 GET /ping?&u=1264985825771-73154&x=0&y=0
    &l=6002&t=6002&e=
  0&dt=Everybody%20enjoys%20things%20%40%20enjoysthin.gs&r=-direct-
  &*=0.20731655228883028
  (127.0.0.1) 0.78ms
...
```

Obviously your logs will look slightly different than this, but the basics should be the same. Around every three seconds, you should see a logging message indicating that a ping was received. You'll also see the actual ping request as received by the server in another line. This repeats endlessly as long as your browser is on the server; when you navigate away from the page, the logging stops. We're on our way to being able to understand what exactly a user is doing when he visits a given website. But before we bother writing an interface to view this data, let's look at the data as it comes in, clean it up, and start to make sense of it.

Making Sense of the Traffic

At this point, we essentially have website that does some overactive logging. It logs hits as the users are on the site, but it doesn't tell us much that we can't learn from the standard server logs. This application is only going to hit the tip of the iceberg as far as analyzing the traffic, but we can really start to see how people are using a given site with just a bit of cleanup. We're going to do two main things. First, we're going separate users into groups of "Active" and "Idle" users. Then, we're going to figure out which pages are the most popular at any given moment.

At this point, after we receive a ping from a user, we add that to our users object, but then we never do anything with it. When tracking engagement in realtime, we're going to want to figure out exactly what the user is doing and, perhaps more importantly, if he is even still around. In order to do that, we'll inspect the list of users every time we receive a ping and ensure that everyone is still active, or at the very least, we'll make sure the users are all still on the site. To do this, amend the `Analytics` class of your *server.py* file with the following changes:

```
    def user_ping(self, data):
...

        # add the data to the object
        self.users[uid][url] = data

        # for every ping, let's cleanup the data...
        self.update_data()

    def update_data(self):

        # keep track of how many different pages are being viewed
        active_user_count = 0

        # clear the pages array, we'll recalculate it below
        self.pages = {}
```

```
# loop through all the users and the URLs they're looking at
for x in self.users.keys():
    for url in self.users[x].keys():

        # keep track of how many people are looking at a giving URL
        if url not in self.pages:
            self.pages[url] = 0
        self.pages[url] += 1

        # figure out the time of last ping and activity
        last_ping_in_seconds = int(self.users[x][url]['last_ping'])

        # get the time since last_activity and convert it to seconds
        last_activity = int(self.users[x][url]['last_activity']) / 1000

        # if the last_activity is less than session time,they're a live user
        if last_activity < Analytics.live_session_time:
            active_user_count += 1

        # otherwise, they're idle
        else:
            self.users[x][url]['status'] = 'Idle'

        # or, perhaps they've stopped pinging, remove them
        if last_ping_in_seconds <(time.time() - Analytics.ping_timeout_time):
            self.remove_user_url(x, url)

    # did we find a user that isn't looking at anything? delete them!
    if not len(self.users[x]):
        del self.users[x]
```

This appends a single call to the update_data method at the end of the user-ping method. Then, we define that method itself. In update_data, we initialize a variable to keep track of how many active users we have on the site and clear out the self.pages object.

After setting up the variables, we jump into a loop of each of the users by iterating over the key of the object. Because this object is built with the uid as a key, we can then use that key as the uid to reference the user going forward. In Python, it's possible to iterate over a dictionary object itself, but since we may be removing users from this object, we don't want to iterate over it in this case. If we do, Python would throw an error informing us that the size of the dictionary had changed during the loop.

Each entry in this users object contains an array of URLs that the user is currently browsing. We want to loop over this array as well. A count of the actual self.users object would give us the number of total unique visitors on the site, but we're interested in what they're actually doing. Looping over this array of URLs allows us to do just that.

Inside that loop, we start rebuilding the pages object. We count up the list of different users that are viewing each page on the site and store it in the self.pages object. After that, we set up last_ping_in_seconds and last_activity as integers. Respectively, these variables measure the time since the last actual HTTP ping from the client and the time since the user last moved his mouse or interacted with the page in some way.

If the `last_activity` variable is less than the `Analytics.live_session_time`, we know that we have an active user. Otherwise, we say that this user is "Idle" and update the `status` field of the object. We then check to see whether the `last_ping_in_seconds` happened outside the `ping_timeout_time`. If it did, we remove the user from the object by calling the `remove_user_url` method, which we'll define next. That method will remove just one of the URL entries for a given user. If, after running through the loop, we end up removing all of the entries for a given user, we remove the entire user from the `users` object.

The `update_data` method called a method to remove a URL entry from a specific user object in our big `users` dictionary. Let's define that method now. In your *server.py* file, add the following method to your `Analytics` object:

```
def remove_user_url(self, uid, url):
    # make sure we have a user here.
    if uid not in self.users:
        return

    # try to remove the user/url mapping
    try:
        del self.users[uid][url]
    except Exception, e:
        logging.error("Error remove user: %s, %url: %s", uid, url)
```

This method, `remove_user_url`, simply removes a specific URL mapping from a specific user inside our `Analytics.users` object. To do this, we just check to see if the entry exists and remove it. This means that we now have the ability to add and remove information about users and URLs as they come and go from the site.

While it's a good to ensure that we remove users after a predetermined amount of time, our JavaScript code actually sends a different type of ping when we know that the user is leaving the page. We have an event handler set up to track when the `beforeunload` event occurs, and when it does, the client will immediately ping the server to let us know that the user is leaving. Let's update our `PingHandler` class to remove the user when that happens. In your *server.py* file, add the highlighted code to the `PingHandler` class:

```
class PingHandler(tornado.web.RequestHandler):
    def get(self):

        # setup some local convenience variables for later
        uid = self.get_argument('u')
        url = self.request.headers['Referer']

        # remove the user if they're leaving the page
        ping_on_exit = self.get_argument('e')
        if ping_on_exit is not None and ping_on_exit == "1":
            self.application.analytics.remove_user_url(uid, url)
            return
```

```
# build the data object to pass to the user_ping method
data = {
...
```

This change simply checks to see whether the parameter designed to signal that the user is exiting the page, e, exists. If it does, we call the newly created `remove_user_url` method to remove this from the array. Once that happens, there is no sense in continuing on with the method, so we simply return right then and there.

Prior to adding the `Analytics.update_data` and `Analytics.remove_user_url` methods, we were collecting statistics that essentially created a running total of all the users who had viewed the site, which wasn't very useful. Now we're gleaning the tiniest bit of information about what users are doing, and we stop tracking them when they leave the page. With this information, it starts to become interesting to watch the users as they bounce around the site. Let's build a simple page to view the information we're currently gathering.

Viewing the Traffic

To view the information that we've collected thus far, we're going to build a simple HTML page that pings the server to get the latest stats. In order to set this up, we need to build a couple of things. We need to make an HTML template and tell Tornado to render it upon request. Then, we need to write a JavaScript file to ping and display the data, and finally a server-side method to prepare and return the results when asked. Let's start on the server side. In your *server.py* file, modify the `Application` object to respond to the following URLs:

```
class Application(tornado.web.Application):
    def __init__(self):

        # create an application-wide version of the analytics object
        self.analytics = Analytics()

        # map the two controller classes to the URLs
        handlers = [
            (r"/ping/?", PingHandler),
            (r"/js/?", JSHandler),
            (r"/", HomeHandler),
            (r"/get/stats/?", GetStatsHandler),
        ]
```

This just adds two new URL handlers and tells Tornado which controller classes to use when we receive requests on / and /get/stats. We'll use the first URL to host the HTML template and the second URL to host the methods needed when we ping the server through JavaScript. First, let's create the `HomeHandler` class. Also in your *server.py* file, add the following code:

```
class HomeHandler(tornado.web.RequestHandler):
    def get(self):
        self.render("home.html")
```

This method is about as simple as they come. When we receive a request, we simply serve out a static HTML page called *home.html*. Moving on from there, let's also add the `GetStatsHandler` class. This class is called from JavaScript to grab the latest user and pageview information. Add the following code to *server.py*:

```
class GetStatsHandler(tornado.web.RequestHandler):
    def post(self):
        # reference the main analytics object locally
        a = self.application.analytics

        # remove some stale users
        a.update_data()

        # convert the pages object into an array that's easily sortable
        sortable_pages = []
        for x in a.pages:
            sortable_pages.append({'url': x, 'count': a.pages[x]});

        # sort the pages so that we can show the most popular pages first
        def compare(a, b):
            return cmp(b['count'], a['count'])
        sortable_pages.sort(compare)

        # print the results
        self.write(dict(users=a.users, pages=sortable_pages[:5]))
```

When a request comes in for this URL, we have a couple of simple jobs. First, we want to clean up the data and ensure that everything is up to date. To do that, we call `Analytics.update_data`. The other piece of computation that we want to do is sort the pages into an array of descending popularity. The easiest way to do that is to convert it to a simple array and then run a basic sort based on the values of the keys. Once we have that calculated, we simply `write` back to the client as a dictionary object. Tornado automatically handles converting this object to JSON, which can be used by our client-side script without any effort.

Now let's build the HTML page that gets rendered when someone hits the root URL of our service. Create a file called *home.html* and add the following code.

```
<!DOCTYPE html>
  <head>
    <meta http-equiv="Content-Type" content="text/html; charset=utf-8">
    <title>Analytics</title>
    <script type="text/javascript" src="http://www.google.com/jsapi"></script>
    <script type="text/javascript" language="javascript"
     src="{{ static_url('viewer.js') }}"></script>
    <style>
      h1, h2 { font-family: sans-serif; }
      A { color: red; }
      #active_users A { font-weight: bold; }
      A.domain { font-size: small; color: #333; }
```

```
      .data SPAN { display: block; font-size: small; }
      .data .referrer A { font-weight: normal; color: #444; }
      ul li { padding-bottom: 1em; }
      TABLE TR TD { vertical-align: top; }
      UL  { list-style-type: none; padding-left: 1em;}
    </style>
  </head>

  <body>
    <table>
      <tr>
        <td>
          <h1>Active Users</h1>
          <ul id="active_users">
          </ul>
        </td>
        <td>
          <h1>Pages</h1>
          <ul id="pages">
          </ul>
        </td>
      </tr>
      <tr>
        <td>
          <h1>Idle Users</h1>
          <ul id="idle_users">
          </ul>
        </td>
        <td>
          <h1>Custom data</h1>
          <div id="custom_data">
          </div>
        </td>
      </tr>
    </table>

  </body>
</html>
```

This just creates a shell of a page with some fairly basic HTML. Everything inside the HEAD tag should look familiar from the previous Tornado examples in this book. Once again, we're using Google's Ajax API service to host part of our JavaScript and using Tornado's `static_url` function to link to our included JavaScript file. After some style information, which you can take or leave, we simply build an HTML table with some unordered list tags inside the cells. I apologize for using HTML tables for layout, but this is just a quick and dirty interface; in live practice, you can take only the parts you're interested in using.

 Although the style information associated with the HTML elements is optional, you should use the same element ID fields that are listed here. We'll be referring to these ID tags inside our JavaScript code.

Having created the HTML shell that we'll be populating through Ajax, let's create the JavaScript file that will do the client-side work. In the same folder that you've been working in, create a directory called *static* and add the following code into a file called *viewer.js*:

```
// ask google to load the jquery libraries
google.load("jquery", "1");

// when the library is loaded, get
google.setOnLoadCallback(
    function() {
        $(document).ready(A.poll);
    }
);

// create the main client side analytics object
var A = {
    poll: function() {
        // poll the server using ajax
        $.ajax({
            url: "/get/stats",
            type: "POST",
            dataType: "json",
            success: A.catch_new_data
        });
    }
};
```

After requesting the jQuery library from Google, we simply wait for a callback for the library to load and for the DOM to be ready. Once everything is read, we call the `run` method on the `A` object. In this object we're going to build all the functionality to populate the HTML template. To get started, we wait for the DOM and immediately start polling the server with the `poll` method. This method simply makes a request to our `/get/stats` URL. Once that method returns successfully, the jQuery library runs a callback method located at `A.catch_new_data`. Add that to your *viewer.js* file:

```
A.catch_new_data = function(response) {
    if(response) {
        A.display_users(response.users);
    }

    setTimeout(A.poll, 1000);
};
```

This method is called when we get a successful response from the `/get/stats` request. That request returns a JSON object with two fields: `users`, which is the object filled with the users currently using the site, and the `pages` object, which is nothing more than the most popular pages on the site. This method, `catch_new_data`, simply checks to see whether the response looks valid enough and runs another method to display the results. This method just takes the data received from the server and converts it into a viewable HTML format. Once it returns, this method schedules another `poll` request for one second in the future. Let's build the `display_users` method now:

```javascript
A.display_users = function(users) {

    // grab the HTML divs and clear them out
    var active_list = $('#active_users');
    var idle_list = $('#idle_users');
    idle_list.html('');
    active_list.html('');

    // loop through the users object
    for (var uid in users) {

        var user = users[uid];
        // each user can be looking at multiple URLs, loop through them
        for (var url in user) {
            u = user[url];

            // create a list item to add to the ul object
            var li = $('<li>');

            // create a link object to display the page the user is viewing
            var a = $('<A>');
            a.attr({href: u.url, title: u.user_agent});
            a.html(u.title);
            li.append(a);

            li.append($('<span>').html(' / '));

            // what domain/website is the user looking at
            var dom = $('<a>');
            dom.attr('href', 'http://' + u.domain);
            dom.attr('class', 'domain');
            dom.html(u.domain);
            li.append(dom);

            // create a DIV to hold some other data
            var data = $('<div>');
            data.attr('class', 'data');
            li.append(data);

            // display the referrer
            if(u.referrer) {
                var ref = $('<span>');
                ref.attr('class', 'referrer');
                ref.html('<a href="' + u.referrer + '">' + u.referrer.slice(0, 50)
                    + "</a>");
                data.append(ref);
            }

            // display the last activity and current scroll position
            var t = u.last_activity / 1000;
            if (t > 60) {
                t = Math.round(t / 60) + ' minute(s)';
            }
            else {
                t += " seconds";
```

```
    }
    var time = $('<span>');
    time.html('Idle Time: ' + t + ' | Scroll x: ' + u.x + ' y: ' + u.y);
    data.append(time);

    // if the user is idle, add them to the idle list
    if (u.status == 'Idle')
        idle_list.append(li);
    // otherwise to the active list
    else
        active_list.append(li);

            }
        }
    };
```

This is a big chunk of code, and it may look fairly intimidating, but it's actually very simple. For the most part, we're just taking the data we receive from the object and wrapping it in HTML tags. To get started, we use jQuery to grab the `active_users` and `idle_users` elements and promptly clear them out. Then, we loop through the list of the users that we've received. Much like the `Analytics.update_data` method on the server side, we loop through both the users themselves and the current list of URLs they are browsing.

Inside that loop, we create an LI element that is going to be used to house all the data about a particular session. The first thing we add to that is an anchor tag displaying the current page and linking off to that URL. We then append a slash, and after that the domain the user is currently viewing. Adding the domain is useful because, as a website creator, we can add our JavaScript code onto any number of sites and watch all of our web properties at the same time from the same URL.

Once we have displayed the current URL and domain that user is viewing, we build a DIV container in order to house the rest of the secondary data that we're going to view. The first field we add to that DIV is the referrer information. After that, we append the amount of time during which the user has been idle. If that number is more than 60 seconds, we convert it to minutes. Also, appended to that same HTML SPAN element is the x and y scroll position.

Once we've added all of the data to the LI element, we have to append it to one of the two lists. To do that, we check the `status` field as it was supplied by the server. If the status is "Idle," we add it to the `idle_users` listed; otherwise, it goes onto the `active_users` list.

With that one method, we're already populating two of the lists that we've created. Start up the server again and load up a couple of different tabs or windows in your web browser. Assuming that you started your server on port **8888** of your local machine, point one browser at *http://localhost:8888/*. Then, load up a few tabs full of the website onto which you've installed the JavaScript tracking code. Click around in some tabs and let other tabs rest. You should see the page views jump right onto the screen and move between the "Idle" and "Active" user lists as you click around. If you click away from one of the URLs, you should see it disappear from the page almost immediately. The end result should look similar to Figure 9-5.

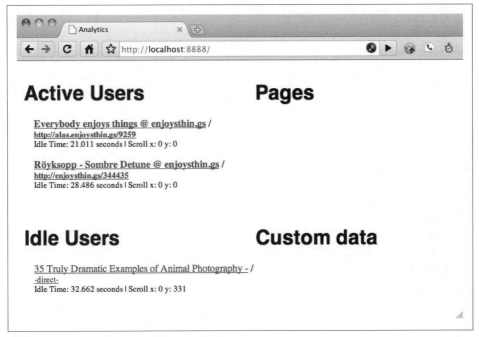

Figure 9-5. Viewing active and idle users on the site

We're populating two lists with that one method, but we're already receiving enough data to build three lists. The server-side **/get/stats/** API call returns two different objects, `users` and `pages`. We're displaying the users object already, but let's build a method to show the most popular pages on the site. Update the `A.catch_new_data` method to have an additional method call:

```
A.catch_new_data = function(response) {
    if(response) {
        A.display_users(response.users);
        A.display_pages(response.pages);
    }
    setTimeout(A.poll, 1000);
};
```

Now let's go ahead and add that method:

```
A.display_pages = function(data) {

    // grab the pages list and clear it
    var ul = $('#pages');
    ul.html('');
```

```
        // loop through the pages array
        for(var i = 0; i < data.length; ++i) {

            // pull out the URL and the number of hits from the object
            var url = data[i].url;
            var cnt = data[i].count;

            // create the LI and anchor objects.
            var li = $('<li>');
            var a =  $('<a>');
            a.attr('href', url);

            // remove the "http://" from the URL when displaying it
            a.html(url.slice(0, 50).replace(/^https?\:\/\//, ''));
            li.append(a);

            var s = $('<span>');
            s.html(" (" + cnt + ')');
            li.append(s);

            ul.append(li);
        }
    };
```

This method, `display_pages`, is an awful lot like the `display_users` method shown earlier. First, we grab the correct UL element and clear it out. Then, we loop through the data array, which just contains a list of the most popular pages. We build a simple LI element and append an anchor element onto it. The anchor element links the user off to the page that is currently popular and shows a slightly cleaned-up version of that URL. It also displays the actual hit count to that URL itself. After restarting the server, *http://localhost:8888/* should look something like Figure 9-6.

We've built a fairly nice little analytics application that shows the realtime picture of who is viewing the site. If someone is on one of the site's web pages, he will show up on this page. The moment he leaves the website, he'll be removed from this page. It's a good way to get an accurate, real feel for all of the users browser your site. The problem is that, as this book has discussed, many interactions on the realtime web take place outside of a web browser. As it stands, our application has no way of tracking users' actions when they interact with other components of our web application. To do that, we need to build some customized tracking options.

Tracking Backend Traffic and Custom Data

Watching users as they browse the site in realtime is quite interesting and useful, but it tells only part of the story. We need to ensure that this application can track arbitrary data collected from the backend traffic on the site. For example, using this custom feature, we can log the amount of traffic coming in and out through instant messenger or SMS. We can also use it to track newly launched features or keep an eye on signups in realtime.

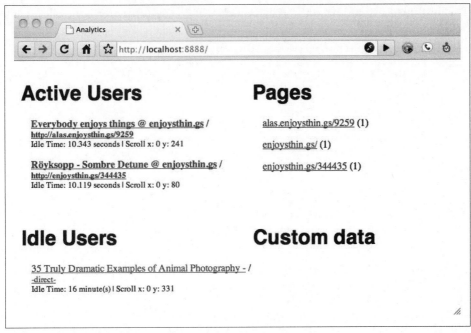

Figure 9-6. Viewing active and idle users plus the most popular pages

Let's build a super simple way to track custom data from any number of sources. We'll create an API method that can be called from anywhere with a few simple parameters. We'll collect the type of data that is being logged with a variable that will tell us if we're receiving an SMS event or a logout event or whatever else is useful to log and view in realtime. We'll also receive an arbitrary value for the data, which can be anything at all. Finally, we'll also collect a variable called expires_in_seconds, which tells us how long, in seconds, we should display this data. If the expires_in_seconds is set to 5, we display the value for 5 seconds and then get rid of it.

To get started with this functionality, we need to add another URL handler to the Application class. In your *server.py* file, make the following addition:

```
class Application(tornado.web.Application):
    def __init__(self):

        # create an application-wide version of the analytics object
        self.analytics = Analytics()

        # map the two controller classes to the URLs
        handlers = [
            (r"/ping/?", PingHandler),
            (r"/js/?", JSHandler),
            (r"/", HomeHandler),
            (r"/get/stats/?", GetStatsHandler),
            (r"/custom/?", CustomHandler),
            ]
```

This just directs traffic from the /custom URL to the `CustomHandler` controller. Let's define that next:

```
class CustomHandler(tornado.web.RequestHandler):
    # whether we receive a GET or POST request, respond
    def get(self):
        self.respond()
    def post(self):
        self.respond()

    def respond(self):
        # a local reference to the application's analytics object
        analytics = self.application.analytics

        # Grab the variables
        data_type = self.get_argument('type')
        value = self.get_argument('value')
        expires = self.get_argument('expires_in_seconds')

        # ping the analytics object
        analytics.data_ping(data_type, value, time.time() + int(expires))

        # assume everything worked...
        self.write("OK")
```

This controller class takes input from either GET or POST HTTP requests and passes them both along to a single method called **respond**. Inside that method we simply collect all of the parameters that we need and pass them along to a method in the `Analytics` object called `data_ping`. The `data_ping` method functions very similarly to the `user_ping` method. Let's create that now. In the `Analytics` object of your *server.py*, add the following code:

```
class Analytics(object):
    users = {}
    pages = {}
    data = {}

    # Number of seconds for which a session is live.
    # After this time, they're considered idle.
    # the user must continue to ping
    live_session_time = 30

    # If the ping timeout passes, the user has left the page.
    ping_timeout_time = 30

        def data_ping(self, data_type, value, expire_time):
        # ensure we have this this data type in the dictionary
        if not data_type in self.data:
            self.data[data_type] = []

                # append the new data to teh array
                self.data[data_type].append({'type': data_type,
                                             'value': value,
                                             'action_time':
```

```
                          time.strftime("%I:%M:%S %p",
                          time.localtime()),
                          'expire_time': expire_time})

    def user_ping(self, data):
        ...
```

This changes two parts of the `Analytics` object. First, we add a member variable called `data` that is available to our newly created `data_ping` method as well as throughout the object. This code also creates the `data_ping` method itself. Inside that method we simply build the `data` object. This object is a dictionary with any number of keys. The keys are strings supplied by the `data_type` variable. We create an entry using that key and initialize a variable if it's not already there. Knowing that we have an entry for this specific `data_type`, we can now append the data as a dictionary. The only modification that we make is to add another field that contains the current time so we can display it if needed.

At this point we can accept data from any source and store it internally in our object. We're also going to need to return it to the client when the request comes in for /get/ stats. Modify the `GetStatsHandler` class to return this new data object as well as the other objects:

```
class GetStatsHandler(tornado.web.RequestHandler):
    def post(self):
        ...
        # print the results
        self.write(dict(users=a.users, pages=sortable_pages[:5], data=a.data))
```

We're collecting data from an API URL and returning it to the web client through the /get/stats URL. However, we're still ignoring that expire time sent during the initial API request. We need to periodically look at the data that we receive and throw out any data that has expired. To do that, we can just append some code to the end of the `Analytics.update_data` method:

```
    def update_data(self):
        ...
        # loop through the data keys
        for x in self.data.keys():

            # for each key, clear out the data and keep only what we need
            tmp_data = self.data[x]
            self.data[x] = []

            for d in tmp_data:
                # if the expire_time has not yet passed, keep the data
                if time.time() < d['expire_time']:
                    self.data[x].append(d)
```

This new addition to the method simply looks at all of the data and determines which values are still valid. Looping through each key in the dictionary, this method makes a copy of the data for that entry and clears it out. Then, looping through each key in that array, we check to see whether the time has expired by comparing it to the current time.

If it hasn't expired, we append it back to the original array; otherwise, we simply ignore it.

Having added all the server-side code we need for this method, the next step is to update our JavaScript file to show this data. The first thing we need to do is update the method that is called whenever we get new data. In your *static/viewer.js* file, change A.catch_new_data to have this additional code:

```
A.catch_new_data = function(response) {
    if(response) {
        A.display_users(response.users);
        A.display_pages(response.pages);
        A.display_custom(response.data);
    }

    setTimeout(A.poll, 1000);
};
```

This new code looks a lot like the previous two lines. We're just calling a new method to handle the new data that we're receiving. To manage that data, let's add A.display_custom to the same file:

```
A.display_custom = function(data) {
    // grab the custom_data list and clear it
    var div = $('#custom_data');
    div.html(""); // clear it

    // if we have a data object
    if(typeof data == 'object') {

        // loop through each of the keys
        for (var data_type in data) {

            // add a new header for each key
            var h2 = $('<h2>');
            h2.html(data_type);
            div.append(h2);

            // create a list for each key
            var ul = $('<ul>');

            // add the data value and action_time to the list item
            for (var i = 0; i < data[data_type].length; ++i) {
                var d = data[data_type][i];
                var li = $('<li>');
                li.html(d.value + " (" + d.action_time + ')');
                ul.append(li);
            }
            div.append(ul);
        }
    }
};
```

This method is also very similar to the `display_users` method. The custom data is in a slightly different format, so we have a new method to handle it all. Once again, we grab the UL element and clear out any HTML that is already in it. Then, we loop through all of the keys in the object. Each of these keys is a new data point that we want to display. One might be "SMS Messages Sent," "New Logins," "Signups," or anything else worth tracking from the backend of the system. We display these keys as a header tag and then create a list to go underneath it. This list is then populated with the values stored inside the object. We display the value itself and the time the data was recorded.

Let's test this out. First off, restart your server and reload the main page. In my case, I can get there by navigating to *http://localhost:8888/*. You should continue to see the same sites pinging the server. While viewing those, let's make a few custom analytics requests. From your command line, let's run a few commands.

```
$ curl "http://localhost:8888/custom?type=Greetings&value=hello+earthling!&expires_
  in_seconds=60"
$ curl "http://localhost:8888/custom?type=Greetings&value=hello+again!&expires_in_
  seconds=60"
```

After running these commands, the data should have appeared in the log viewer almost instantly. Figure 9-7 shows an example of the custom data displayed on the screen.

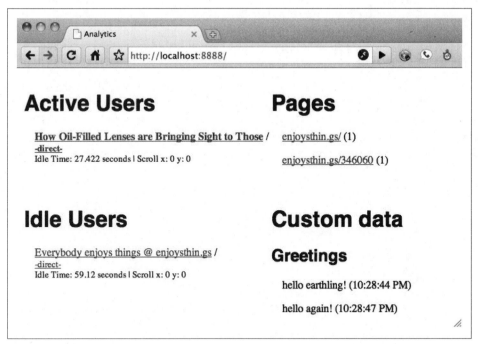

Figure 9-7. Viewing the web-based traffic plus our custom data

With this addition, we have the ability to track statistics and users in realtime as they trigger events on the backend side of a web application. This gives us the ability to collect the whole picture about what is happening in our application. In practice, using this functionality does not normally involve making `curl` requests from the command line but instead integrating this API call into significant events in the core functionality of an application. For example, a reasonable use case for this functionality would be to create a log entry for every user who signs up for a service. To do something like this in PHP, you'd add the following code to the same method that handles a successful signup:

```php
$data = array('type' => 'User Signup',
              'value' => 'Some User Name',
              'expires_in_seconds' => (60 * 60 * 24)); // keep this around for a day
$s = curl_init();
curl_setopt($s,CURLOPT_URL, "http://localhost:8888/custom");
curl_setopt($s,CURLOPT_POST,true);
curl_setopt($s,CURLOPT_POSTFIELDS,$data);
$return_value = curl_exec($s);
```

Sending Out Alerts

Having set up our application to monitor itself in realtime, one feature that is currently lacking in this application stands out as being particularly useful. It would be nice to get SMS alerts from our application in the event that the amount of users, or any other statistic, reaches a certain threshold. Let's add this functionality into this application.

To keep it simple, we'll send out an SMS alert when the number of currently active users goes above a predetermined number. This is going to be remarkably easy to build using the SMS functionality we built previously. To get started, let's update the *server.py* file to contain the basic SMS integration information:

```python
class Analytics(object):
    users = {}
    pages = {}
    data = {}

    # which number should we send a message to?
    SMS_alert_mobile_number = '+15555551212'

    # When should we send a message? after how many users?
    SMS_alert_current_users = 15

    # What's the URL of the SMS service you want to use?
    SMS_api_base_url = 'http://instant-messaging.appspot.com/sms/send/via/textmark'

    # how often do we send messages if the site stays busy?
    SMS_send_interval = 600 # send an SMS no more than every ten minutes

    # this is used internally to determine the last time we sent a message
    SMS_last_send = 0
    ...
```

These additions don't do anything other than configure some variables about how often to send out SMS alerts, which number to use when sending them, and the API to use in order to send them. Depending on the traffic you're expecting to get on your site, you'll probably want to configure the numbers to ensure that you're getting enough alert messages, but not too many.

To actually send the message, we're going to have to monitor the number of currently active users on the site. Once that number goes above our newly created `Analytics.SMS_alert_current_users`, we're going to send a message. We can easily add that to the `Analytics.update_data` method. At the bottom of `Analytics.update_data`, after you've counted the current number of active users and stored it in the `active_user_count` variable, add the following code to your *server.py* file:

```
def update_data(self):
    ...
            # did we find a user that isn't looking at anything? delete them!
            if not len(self.users[x]):
                del self.users[x]

        # if the active_user_count goes about the SMS threshold
        if active_user_count > Analytics.SMS_alert_current_users:
            # and we haven't recently sent a message
            if Analytics.SMS_last_send < (time.time() - Analytics.SMS_send_interval):
                logging.info("Sending an SMS Alert!")

                # note the current time
                Analytics.SMS_last_send = time.time()

                # build the URL
                url = Analytics.SMS_api_base_url
                url += '?mobile_number=' +
                        url_escape(Analytics.SMS_alert_mobile_number)
                url += '&body=' + url_escape("Currently %d users on the site!")
                    % (len(self.users)))

                # make the API request
                f = urllib.urlopen(url)
                f.read()
```

The `update_data` method was already counting the current number of active users, so the only addition we had to make was to check whether that number went above our predetermined limit. If it did, we check to see whether we've recently sent out a message, and if not, we simply make the API call to our SMS application. If you set the `SMS_alert_current_users` low enough, you'll be able to see the SMS message after opening a few tabs on your browser. If you hook it up to a live site, you should see a message like Figure 9-8.

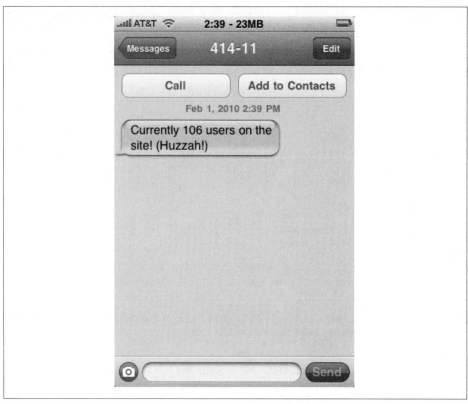

Figure 9-8. Receiving an SMS alert from the analytics application

When you have the realtime analytics that we've built in this chapter and add in this type of SMS alert mechanism to different parts of your website, it means that you can see your users move around your site in realtime and react in realtime. The ability to keep your finger on the pulse of your site with these technologies helps you understand much more quickly exactly how users are interacting with your application. If there is an issue, good or bad, you'll be able to confront it within minutes instead of days.

## CHAPTER 10

Putting It All Together

We've built a number of small applications that demonstrate a single aspect of the type of experiences that can be had on the realtime web. In this chapter we'll take the different technologies that we've started using and build a much larger, complete application.

In this chapter we'll build a game specifically designed to utilize many of the types of features that we've built. In the previous chapters, these features were designed to be applied to an already existing application. This chapter will explore an application that has these features integrated at a much deeper level as part of the core functionality of the application.

The Game

The game that we'll build in this chapter is a location-aware game designed to be played with a modern phone that supports geolocation JavaScript API calls. Like other location-based games, the purpose of this game is to encourage users to travel around their city and check in using a mobile phone. In this case, we're building a game called iPandemic, in which a user "coughs" to infect a new location rather than checking in and announcing her presence. If she turns up in a place where another user has already infected, this is considered a challenge, and both users have to take action within a set period of time or risk losing points and having their germs die off. Once a "germ" has infected a location, it will continue to grow until it reaches an enemy germ. When the two germs meet up, they fight and the strongest germ prevails.

Caveats

This game works best when it's played with a number of other people, so to test out different features, you can simply join in with the other users at *http://www.ipandemic .com*. Playing with the other users will help illustrate how the different parts of this game work much more easily than logging in with multiple mobile phones.

This game also requires a fair amount of Python code, plus HTML and CSS markup. All of this code is provided for download on this book's website (*http://therealtimebook.com*). It may be easier to download the code and follow along with the text rather than typing out each passage. Plus, I'll be omitting some of the CSS and nonessential code for brevity in the text, but it's all included on the website and in the working application at the iPandemic website.

Getting Set Up

The setup of this application involves signing up for different services and acquiring some API keys. We've already used several of these services this book. For services that you've already set up, you can either reconfigure the service to work with this new application or start fresh with each one.

We'll be using a number of different technologies to build this application and even hosting it on two different servers. To set up the environment, we're going to want to create a couple of directories. Assuming you're keeping this project in your home directory, open a terminal window and enter the following commands to create the basic directory structure of this project:

```
~ $ mkdir ~/ipandemic
~ $ mkdir ~/ipandemic/appengine
~ $ mkdir ~/ipandemic/appengine/static
~ $ mkdir ~/ipandemic/appengine/templates
~ $ mkdir ~/ipandemic/tornado
~ $ mkdir ~/ipandemic/tornado/templates
~ $ mkdir ~/ipandemic/tornado/static
```

Google App Engine

This application uses two different methods to host the code, the first of which is Google App Engine. Chapter 7 includes a complete explanation of how to sign up for and configure an App Engine account. You can easily reuse the account and application that you previously used. If you are going to set up a new application, you should configure it through the interface on the App Engine website (*http://appengine.google.com/*) and then set it up locally. Each App Engine application must have a unique application identifier, which are becoming increasingly hard to find. So, after you create the application on the App Engine website, create a file in *ipandemic/appengine* called *app.yaml* and add the following code:

```
application: your-application-id
version: 1
runtime: python
api_version: 1

handlers:
- url: /static
  static_dir: static/
```

```
 - url: .*
   script: main.py

inbound_services:
- xmpp_message
```

This file simply lays out the details of your application for both the actual App Engine service and the launcher application. Once you've created and saved that file, we can set up this application in GoogleAppEngineLauncher. From the File menu, select "Add an Existing Application," click the browse button, and select the directory containing the *app.yaml* file (see Figure 10-1).

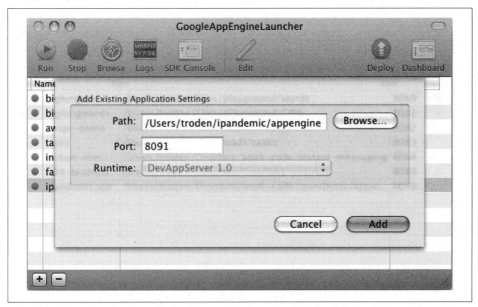

Figure 10-1. Importing our existing project with its unique App Engine ID

 Although the official App Engine application ID for the public iPandemic application is ipandemicapp, it's mapped to the *http://www.ipandemic.com* URL. Google App Engine allows you to map custom domains to your application. Throughout the rest of this of this chapter, you'll need to use the URL assigned to you in place of www.ipandemic.com.

Google Maps API Key

On the client side of this application, we're going to be using the Google Maps API to display the maps and draw the spread of each of the germs. Although this service is free to use, even for an unlimited amount of traffic, it does require an API key. To get one of these keys, head over to the Google Maps API site (*http://code.google.com/apis/maps/*

signup.html) to generate a new API key for this application. When the form asks for your URL, enter the App Engine URL created earlier. The next page will display your unique Google Maps API key; be sure to copy that URL and save it locally on your computer. We'll be using that key in this application, and there is no obvious way to get Google Maps to display the same key for you again.

EC2 or Other Hosted Server

Part of this application runs on Google's App Engine infrastructure, but another part is hosted on a standard web server. This server needs to have Python installed and you must have shell access, as we'll be running this application with the Tornado server, which must be started from the command line. Any public-facing server will work for this task as long as you have shell access and Python is either installed or installable. If you're using this server to host another application, you can easily host this right alongside it using a different port.

If you're using Amazon EC2 to host the part of the application that does not run on App Engine, you're going to want to open a new port for this application. To do that from your EC2 instance, you'll want to open the port with the following command:

```
~ $ ec2-authorize default -C ~/your-cert-file.pem -K ~/your-private-key-file.pem \
    -p 8088
```

Many of the community AMIs (Amazon Machine Instance) already have the `ec2-authorize` command installed. If you don't have it installed already, your package manager may have it under `ec2-api-tools`; otherwise, it can be downloaded directly from the Amazon Web Services developer website (*http://developer.amazonwebservices .com/connect/entry.jspa?externalID=351&categoryID=88*).

GeoModel

This application deals with geolocation in a number of different ways. As users cough and germs spread, we're going to need to determine how close one germ is to another. There are a couple of ways to do this, but a convenient method would be to ask our datastore to return a list of germs within a specified distance of a certain germ. While App Engine's data store does understand the concept of latitude and longitude coordinates through its `GeoPt` datatype, it has no built-in ability to return a list based on proximity. To get this functionality, we can use an open source third-party library called GeoModel (*http://code.google.com/p/geomodel/*). The easiest way to incorporate the source is to check out the latest version from Subversion directly into our project directory.

```
~/ipandemic/appengine $ svn co http://geomodel.googlecode.com/svn/trunk/geo
A    geo/geocell_test.py
A    geo/geocell.py
A    geo/geomodel.py
...
```

```
U   geo
Checked out revision 22.
```

The Basic Models

This game contains a fair bit more application logic than the previous examples and requires a decent number of model classes to define how everything behaves. To get these set up, we need to create a file to contain these models and set up the basics. In your *appengine* directory, create a file called *models.py* and fill it with the following code:

```python
from geo.geomodel import GeoModel
import geo.geotypes as geotypes

from google.appengine.api import xmpp, users, urlfetch, memcache
from google.appengine.ext import db
from django.utils import simplejson as json
import logging, os, string, random, urllib
from datetime import datetime, timedelta
import math

class Game(object):
    # setup some gameplay variables
    default_score = 5
    default_germ_spread = 0.03
    default_germ_speed = 0.0055
    default_germ_slowdown = 0.00015
    default_germ_strength = 0.03
    default_disease_strength = 0.5
    default_disease_strength_increment = 0.001

    # the color of the germs as they get displayed on the map
    default_color_friendly = "#577ff5"
    default_color_enemy = "#007b00"
    default_color_threat = "#ff0000"
```

This codes does all the imports that we're going to need for this file in the future. Then, we define a number of variables that we'll use to govern the gameplay of iPandemic. There is no real science behind these numbers, so feel free to modify them as much as you wish.

default_score

> Every user has a score, which is the number of points she has accumulated. When user join the game, we'll give them some points just for signing up.

default_germ_spread

> When a user first coughs and a germ is born, it takes up space on the map. This variable defines the default amount of space that the disease takes up. This is the spread of the disease.

default_germ_speed

> As time passes, each germ grows bigger and spreads across the map. This variable governs the default speed for how quickly the germ spreads.

default_germ_slowdown

While the germ spreads as time passes, the speed at which is grows slows down. This variable determines how quickly it slows down. Essentially, every time a germ grows, the speed as determined by the default_germ_speed decreases.

default_germ_strength

Each germ has a specific amount of strength. If a germ gets threatened by another user coughing or just due to the natural course of growing, the each germ's strength helps determine which will win.

default_disease_strength

Germs are part of a larger disease. As a user spreads germs, the disease itself gets stronger. This strength is also used to determine which germ wins when it's threatened.

default_disease_strength_increment

Throughout the course of the game, germs and diseases get stronger and weaker. This variable specifies the amount to change the strength as these events occur.

UserInfo

The next model to add to *models.py* is the UserInfo class. While Google provides the actual user object and even its authentication, we still want to store some data with each user and have some additional logic. Add the start of the UserInfo object to your *models.py* file:

```
class UserInfo(db.Model):
    # google's user object
    user = db.UserProperty()

    # save the date we created the user.
    timestamp = db.DateTimeProperty(auto_now_add=True)

    # the user's score in the game
    score = db.IntegerProperty(default=0)

    # when a new germ is created, what is the default strength?
    # as a user's score increases, this can increase as well
    default_germ_strength = db.FloatProperty(Game().default_germ_strength)

    # can we send IM and SMS to this user?
    allow_xmpp = db.BooleanProperty(default=True)
    allow_sms = db.BooleanProperty(default=False)
    mobile_key = db.IntegerProperty()
    mobile_number = db.PhoneNumberProperty()
```

This class adds the basic setup of our UserInfo object. Aside from the obvious member variables that we set up, we add some variables for functionality. The first of those is the default_germ_strength variable. This variable defines how strong a germ will be when created by this particular user. It defaults to the value defined in the Game class, but as the user progresses through the game, this variable can increase or decrease depending on outside factors, leaving more experienced users to create stronger germs from the start.

The other variables that we create will be used when we add the instant messaging and SMS functionality. The variables `allow_sms` and `allow_xmpp` define if we can send either type of message to the user. Because sending an XMPP message doesn't cost a user anything, we set up the `allow_xmpp` variable to default to `True`, meaning that we can send messages to that user.

Although it's free for the application and the user to receive XMPP messages, many users pay per SMS message. So we can't automatically send everyone SMS messages; each user will have to turn that on explicitly. Users will sign up for SMS functionality by sending a text message to the application. To sign someone up for this type of service, we're going to require that each send a text message that includes a unique `mobile_key`. This will allow us to identify which user is sending a message prior to storing her `mobile_number` and will allow us to ensure the user does want to receive SMS messages.

Let's move on to fleshing out the rest of the `UserInfo` class. Add the following methods to the class we've just defined:

```
def by_user(self, user):
    q = db.GqlQuery("SELECT * FROM UserInfo WHERE user = :1", user)
    return q.get()

def by_current_user(self):
    return self.by_user(users.get_current_user())

def by_mobile_number(self, mobile_number):
    q = db.GqlQuery("SELECT * FROM UserInfo WHERE mobile_number = :1",
                    mobile_number)
    return q.get()

def by_mobile_key(self, mobile_key):
    q = db.GqlQuery("SELECT * FROM UserInfo WHERE mobile_key = :1",
                    int(mobile_key))
    return q.get()

def sync(self, user):
    # if we have a user, ensure that we've logged them to our datastore
    if user:
        if not UserInfo().by_user(user):
            ui = UserInfo(user=user,
                          mobile_key=random.randint(1000, 9999),
                          score = Game().default_score)
            ui.put()
            xmpp.send_invite(user.email())
    else:
        raise Exception("No current user to sync")

def update_score(self, amount):
    self.score += amount
    self.put()
```

The first method, by_user, is a simple convenience method that allows us to quickly load a UserInfo by supplying one of App Engine's user objects. After that, by_current_user does the same thing, but it automatically loads the current user object. The next two methods are the same basic concept; the only difference is a unique value is used to load the UserInfo object.

The sync method is used after a user logs into this application. Every time a user logs in, we want to make sure that our application has a unique record for her. Using the sync method, we check to see whether the UserInfo already exists, and if not, we create a new one. Creating a new one means instantiating a new UserInfo object and supplying it with the user object as well as the mobile_key and the score. The mobile_key is the pseudo-unique number that a user will send in via SMS when signing up for SMS integration.

The final method in this class is the update_score method. This is used throughout the game to quickly adjust the score of a user when no other information needs to be updated.

Disease

The next model that we need to create is the Disease class. Each time a user "coughs," a Germ is created. Each Germ belongs to a certain user, but it is also part of a Disease. The class is fairly small, so let's just add the entire thing all at once:

```
class Disease(db.Model):
    # the time this disease was created
    timestamp = db.DateTimeProperty(auto_now_add=True)

    # the first patient with this disease
    patient_zero = db.UserProperty()

    # a fun name for the disease
    strain = db.StringProperty() # auto generated name

    # how strong is the disease?
    strength = db.FloatProperty(default=Game().default_disease_strength)

    def get_default_disease_for_user(self, user):
        q = Disease().gql("WHERE patient_zero = :1", user)
        disease = q.get()
        if not disease:
            disease = Disease().generate_disease(user)
            disease.put()
        return disease

    def generate_disease(self, user):
        disease = Disease()
        disease.patient_zero = user
        disease.strain = Disease().unique_strain_name()
        return disease
```

```
def unique_strain_name(self):
    while True:
        s = string.uppercase[random.randint(0, 25)] + \
            str(random.randint(1, 9)) + \
            string.uppercase[random.randint(0, 25)] + \
            str(random.randint(10, 99))
        q = db.GqlQuery("SELECT * FROM Disease WHERE strain = :1", s)
        if not q.count():
            break
    return s
```

The first couple of member variables defined in this class simply keep track of when this disease was created and by whom. The next variable, **strain**, is a shorter name that can be used to refer to this particular disease. The **strength** variable defaults to the value defined by the **Game** object but is adjusted throughout the game as germs are created and removed.

The methods for this class are all centered around doing one of two things, loading the disease and creating a new one if one doesn't exist for a particular user. The first method, `get_default_disease_for_user`, simply loads the disease if there already is one for the specified user. If one doesn't exist, it creates one by calling `generate_disease` and saving it to the datastore with `put`.

The method `generate_disease` simply instantiates a new **Disease** object, setting the `patient_zero` field to the supplied user and setting the name of the **strain** to the result of `unique_strain_name`. This method generates a unique strain name in the format of "A9A99." These strain names are meaningless, other than to look and sound vaguely like the name of a disease, so feel free to get creative with this name.

Germ

A large part of this game is spent "coughing" and spreading germs. These germs are the most fundamental part of this game. How often germs are created, how far they spread, and how often they defeat other germs are the basic metrics of success in this game. Let's put together the basic **Germ** model now and expand on it as needed. In *models.py*:

```
class Germ(GeoModel):
    user = db.UserProperty()
    timestamp = db.DateTimeProperty(auto_now_add=True)

    # every germ is part of a disease
    disease = db.ReferenceProperty(Disease)

    # how strong is the germ
    strength = db.FloatProperty(default=Game().default_germ_strength)

    # the current speed at which it's growing
    spread = db.FloatProperty(default=Game().default_germ_spread)
```

```
    # how fast does it increase its spread
    spread_speed = db.FloatProperty(default=Game().default_germ_speed)

    # grab a list of other germs near a certain lat/long
    def get_germs_near_point(self, lat, lon, max_distance_in_meters=100):
        center = geotypes.Point(lat, lon)
        base_query = Germ.all()
        data = Germ.proximity_fetch(
            base_query,
            center, max_results=10, max_distance=max_distance_in_meters)
        return data

    # would the current germ defeat another in a fight?
    def would_defeat(self, enemy):

        # determine the strength of each germ by
        # adding the current strength to the overall disease sterngth
        our_strength = self.disease.strength + self.strength
        enemy_strength = enemy.disease.strength + enemy.strength

        if our_strength >= enemy_strength:
            return True
        else:
            return False

    # We'll be outputting germs in the JSON format.
    # this method simply makes an germ object suitable for json encoding
    def format_for_json(self, current_user):
        return {
            'id': str(self.key()),
            'lat': self.location.lat,
            'lon': self.location.lon,
            'strength': self.strength,
            'spread': self.spread,
            'timestamp': GameUtils().date_rfcformat(self.timestamp),
            'threat': False,
            'disease': {
                'id': str(self.disease.key()),
                'strain': self.disease.strain,
                'name': self.disease.name,
                'host': self.disease.patient_zero.nickname(),
                'host_is_you': self.disease.patient_zero == current_user,
                }
            }
```

The first thing to notice about this class is that it extends the GeoModel class rather than the db.Model class that we've been using up until now. Extending the GeoModel class gives the germ some extra functionality to help with the geolocation logic that we'll be using. Extending this class means this object contains a location member variable and another variable called location_geocells. We'll be using the location field directly to save the specific location of each germ, and the GeoModel class will update the location_geocells field and use that during location-based queries on this datatype.

This is a shell of the final germ class that we'll end up using, but it's enough to get started without complicating things too much. The first couple of member variables spell out who created this particular germ and when they did it. After that, we keep track of the disease to which this germ belongs. Then we set up the strength, spread, and spread_speed of this germ.

The first member function in this class is called get_germs_near_point. This method searches the datastore for other Germ objects within a certain number of meters of the specified latitude and longitude parameters. This allows us to figure out the user's location and query the datastore to find out which germs are in the immediate vicinity. The proximity_fetch search is provided by the GeoModel from which the Germ class extends.

The next method, would_defeat, takes in one germ as a parameter, which it then compares against itself to determine who would win if they were to fight one another. To calculate this, we look at the strength of each germ and add it to the strength of each disease. Whichever disease has the most overall strength would win this fight. It's a pretty simple, and fast, way to determine the strongest germ.

Finally, the last method that we add to the Germ class at this point is the format_for_json method. This application sends the germ information to the browser and other clients encoded in the JSON format. Encoding the entire class into JSON would leave us with a lot more data than is necessary, so we build a simple Python dictionary that can translate directly to the JSON format for the browser.

We'll be adding more functionality to this class as we continue building this application, but this is enough to get the game started.

CommandCenter

The next class that we're going to define is called CommandCenter. This class contains functionality similar to what we created in Chapter 9. Any time a germ gets created, changes, or gets deleted, we'll notify this class. This class can then run all sorts of analytics based on the data. We'll actually use this data to generate a command center view that allows users to monitor all of the germs as they spread around the planet on top of some other realtime functionality. We'll get to all of that in a bit, but first we want to create the basic logging methods so that we can start keeping track of these changes from the start. Update your *models.py* file and add the following class:

```
class CommandCenter(object):
    cc_memcache_key = 'cc-germs'

    def get_germs(self):
        # grab the germs from memcache
        germs = memcache.get(self.cc_memcache_key)
        if germs is None:
            germs = {}
        return germs
```

```
        # this will update if it's already in there
        def add_germ(self, germ):
            # grab the germs from memcache
            germs = self.get_germs()

            # add or update this germ
            k = str(germ.key())
            germs[k] = germ.format_for_json(False)

            # This germ has not been deleted
            germs[k]['deleted'] = False

            # mark this as updated and store everything back in the cache
            germs[k]['updated'] = GameUtils().date_rfcformat(datetime.now())
            memcache.set(self.cc_memcache_key, germs)

        def delete_germ(self, germ):
            # grab the germs from memcache
            germs = self.get_germs()
            k = str(germ.key())

            # if this germ exists, mark it as deleted and updated
            if k in germs:
                germs[k]['deleted'] = True
                germs[k]['updated'] = GameUtils().date_rfcformat(datetime.now())

            # put them back in memcache
            memcache.set(self.cc_memcache_key, germs)

        # notify everyone of the changes
        def update(self):
            # we'll fill this in later
            pass
```

This is a very simple class that we can use throughout the code to keep track of the germs that are currently in play. We keep the list of germs in memcache, formatted in JSON encoding, and even keep track of the deleted germs after they've left the datastore. This allows us to build pages that show the activity of the germs as they happen without hitting the datastore each time we want to load it. The way we're going to use this will also allow us to publish these updates across the Web in realtime.

This is the first class that we've built that uses the App Engine implementation of memcache. For the uninitiated, memcache is a key/value store that allows us to store data in memory for simple and fast access. Memcache is very simple to use, and the App Engine implementation stays true to that form. You simply define a key and get and set data using that key. The only member variable in this class is that cache key. In this case it is stored in the cc_memcache_key variable and will be used to store the list of germs that the CommandCenter knows about.

The first method in this class, get_germs, simply loads all of the germs out of memcache and returns them. If there isn't anything in the datastore, it returns an empty dictionary.

The `add_germ` method takes in a germ as the parameter and either adds it to the cache if it doesn't exist or simply updates it if the germ is already in the cache. Each germ is stored using the unique key as the dictionary key, which allows us to update it easily in the future. Rather than storing the entire germ, we simply store the JSON encoding version, which is all we'll need in the future. We also want to keep track of whether or not this particular germ was `deleted`. Since we're adding the germ now, we can safely assume that it hasn't been deleted. We'll also use this method to update existing germs, but we won't be updating germs that have been deleted, so we can affirmatively say that this particular germ hasn't been deleted.

However, when we do want to delete a germ, we need to call `delete_germ`. This method is a lot like the `add_germ` method. The main difference between the two methods is that this time we simply check to see whether the germ is in the cache; if it is, we mark it as `deleted`, update the `updated` timestamp, and leave it alone. In applications that want to use this data, we want to affirmatively tell them that this germ has been deleted and not expect them to rely on noticing the absence of data from one update to the next.

Finally, we have the method that will actually tell any interested parties that the data has been updated. There are a couple of steps between where this application is now and when it makes sense to notify third parties, so let's just leave this method blank for the time being. We'll get back to it once we have updates to send around.

Textmark

This application interacts with users in realtime through a number of different methods. One of those methods is via SMS. This application sends out SMS messages if a user earns points while she isn't interacting with the system and even allows users to "threaten" and respond to threats via SMS. To do that, we need to include some simple SMS functionality.

In Chapter 8, we built out some SMS functionality that allowed an application to send and receive SMS messages from a couple of different services. This application also needs to send out SMS messages. Rather than supporting more than one service in this application, I've just picked one. If you'd prefer to use another service, just swap it out for that one; the code should be almost identical to that in Chapter 8. If you elect to use the TextMark service as well, add the following code to your *models.py* file:

```
class Textmark(object):
    auth_user = 'your-textmarks-username'
    auth_pass = 'your-textmarks-password'
    short_code = '41411'
    keyword = 'your-textmarks-keyword'
    api_key = 'your-textmarks-api-key'

    # override the send method from SMSService
    def send(self, number, body):
```

```
# The Send URL
url = "http://dev1.api2.textmarks.com/GroupLeader/send_one_message/"

# setup the http arguments
args = {}
args['to'] = number
args['msg'] = body
args['tm'] = self.keyword
args['api_key'] = self.api_key
args['auth_user'] = self.auth_user
args['auth_pass'] = self.auth_pass

# make the HTTP API call to send the message
result = urlfetch.fetch(url=url,
                        payload=urllib.urlencode(args),
                        method=urlfetch.POST)
logging.info(result.content)
```

This code should look very similar to the code from Chapter 8. It's a fair bit simpler because we don't need to support more than one service, but the base logic is the same. We set up the basic API information as the member variables of the class and then provide a single member function.

That single member function is the **send** method, which is used to actually send the message. As parameters, it takes in the mobile **number** of the recipient and the **body** of the message. We assemble the simple API parameters into a dictionary and post them to the TextMarks service using the App Engine **urlfetch** class. In case there are issues, we log the response, but other than that, we're done with the SMS class.

Messenger

We've already added a class to send SMS messages, but we're only part of the way to our message-sending goals. We want to be able to send both SMS and XMPP-based instant messages from the same interface. To do that, we'll wrap the functionality up into a class called **Messenger** and use that class to send a message. To add this class, add the following code to your *models.py* file:

```
class Messenger(object):

    # to send an message via SMS, simply pass this on to the Textmark class
    def send_via_sms(self, mobile_number, body):
        sms = Textmark()
        sms.send(mobile_number, body)

    # simply call the xmpp send_message method to send xmpp messages
    def send_via_xmpp(self, to, body):
        xmpp_response = xmpp.send_message(to, body)
        logging.info(xmpp_response)
```

```
# send a message
def send(self, from_user, to_user, body, response_key=False):
    if from_user:
        body = from_user.nickname() + ": " + body

    # load the UserInfo to figure out which methods we can use to send a message
    ui = UserInfo().by_user(to_user)

    # are we allowed to send xmpp messages?
    if ui.allow_xmpp:
        im_body = body
        if response_key:
            im_body += " Respond with @%d [message here]" % int(response_key)

        self.send_via_xmpp(to_user.email(), im_body)

    # are we allowed to send sms messages?
    if ui.mobile_number and ui.allow_sms:
        sms_body = body
        if response_key:
            sms_body += " Respond with \"%s @%d [message here]\"" %
            (Textmark.keyword, int(response_key))
        self.send_via_sms(ui.mobile_number, sms_body)
```

This model gets right down to the business of sending messages; there are no member variables for this class. The first method defined is the **send_via_sms** method, and because we've already defined all the logic to send an SMS message in the TextMark class, we simply pass along the parameters we receive in **send_via_sms** to the send method of the TextMark class.

The next method, **send_via_xmpp**, is similarly simple. All of the work for sending an XMPP message is handled inside Google App Engine's **xmpp** class. We simply call the **send_message** method and log the response. Unlike sending an SMS message, where we're limited to a small number of characters in every message, we don't have the same restraints in sending XMPP messages, so we append a short message to the end of every outgoing message. This additional message just instructs the user how to opt out of receiving XMPP messages from this application.

Throughout this application, we don't want to have to repeatedly check to see which type of messages we're allowed to send to each user and then send each of them. Instead, we'll simply wrap up that functionality into a single **send** method. From that method we can also prepare the message with any other content that is needed. First off, we want to announce which user is sending a message if it's coming from a specific user. If user "jondoe" sends a message, we want to prepend "jondoe: " onto that message. We also may want to append information about how to respond to this particular message. If there is a **response_key**, we want to instruct the user to prepend that key onto the message in his response. We simply check to see whether we can send each type of message to the user and send the same message via any and all available methods. This way, if a user sees a message arrive as an SMS, she can respond via her instant messenger program for the same result. It also allows her to receive the message on her phone after she's stepped away from her computer.

UserThreats

As germs are created and die, they interact with other germs. If one user, Thom, opens up the application inside an area that has been infected by a user named Jane, Thom is threatened by that germ. Thom is then required to take some sort of action because he is "threatened" by the germ. In this case, he faces a threat simply by being in the area of an existing germ. Thom has some options. He can challenge Jane by sending her a message that is delivered to her in realtime through a number of different methods. At this point, two different UserThreats objects have been created. One threat was directed at Thom because he turned up in hostile territory. Another threat was created by Thom, who directed a challenge directly at Jane. One way or another, these threats need to be dealt with by the users, and the class UserThreats stores these threats in the datastore until then. Let's build the basic parts of this class. Add the following to *models.py*:

```
class UserThreats(db.Model):
    # who needs to respond to this threat?
    user = db.UserProperty()

    # what type of threat is this?
    threat_type = db.StringProperty()

    # some threats can be addressed via IM/SMS usign a specific key
    response_key = db.IntegerProperty()

    # when does this threat expire?
    expire_time = db.DateTimeProperty()

    # does this threat involve a specific germ?
    germ_threat = db.ReferenceProperty(Germ)

    # did a specific user initiate this challenge?
    challenge_user = db.UserProperty()


    def create(self, user, germ_threat, expires_in_minutes=5, challenge_user=None,
            threat_type="natural"):
        # because failing to respond to threats affects score and strength
        # we want to make sure not to create the same threat multiple times
        q = UserThreats.all()
        q.filter('user =', user)
        q.filter('challenge_user =', challenge_user)
        q.filter('germ_threat = ', germ_threat)
        q.filter('threat_type =', threat_type)

        # if this threat doesn't exist
        if not q.count():
```

```
# turn the number of minutes into a specific timestamp
expire_time = (timedelta(minutes=expires_in_minutes) + datetime.now())

ut = UserThreats(user = user,
                 challenge_user = challenge_user,
                 threat_type = threat_type,
                 germ_threat = germ_threat,
                 expire_time = expire_time)

# if this is a challenge threat, setup a new response key
if threat_type == 'challenge':
    # get the biggest response key
    cq = UserThreats.all()
    cq.filter('user = ', user)
    cq.filter('threat_type = ', 'challenge')
    cq.order('-response_key')
    biggest = cq.get()
    if biggest and biggest.response_key:
        ut.response_key = biggest.response_key + 1
    else:
        ut.response_key = 1

# save and return this threat
ut.put()
return ut
```

To start, we extend the db.Model class and give it the expected user property. We also want to keep track of the threat_type. This can be set to either "natural," which occurs when a user loads the application in an infected area, or it could be "challenge," which is the threat that occurs when one user challenges another. The response_key is used during challenge threats. This is the key that allows the user to respond directly, in realtime, to threats as they happen. The expire_time variable is the time at which this threat expires. If a user does not respond to a threat before this time, bad things will happen. Also, most threats reference a specific germ, which is stored in the germ_threat variable. Finally, if the threat is a challenge threat, we store the user who issued the challenge in challenge_user.

Creating a challenge threat involves a small bit of logic to ensure that everything goes smoothly. The first thing we need to do is check to see whether this particular challenge has already been created. Because failing to properly address a challenge results in losses and gains of points for different users, we want to ensure that we have a unique challenge. If we do have a new challenge, we convert the parameter expires_in_minutes to an actual datetime object that can be stored in the datastore. We then take all of the parameters that we received and pass them on to the UserThreats object.

If this is a "natural" threat type, we're done and all we have to do is save and return the newly created object. However, if this is a challenge threat, we want to add an additional field to the object. We want to generate and store the response_key field. When one user receives a challenge threat from another user, we notify the threatened user with an XMPP-based instant message and optionally an SMS message. We want the user to be able to respond to the threat directly from whichever form of communication is fastest.

To ensure that we always know which threat a user is responding to, we save a numeric response_key with each challenge threat. The user can then reply to the threat by prefacing @response_key before any message. If the response key is 1, the user would reply with "@1 response_key [message to user]." To determine this number, we simply look at all of the open challenge threats and determine the next available response_key. Because this application functions in realtime and users are constantly addressing threats, this number is almost always one, but we want to make sure that each response is directed to the proper challenge_user.

GameUtils

Another model that needs to be created is the GameUtils class. This class contains two functions that are needed for various parts of the game but are much more general than the other models. Add this class to your *models.py* file:

```python
class GameUtils(object):
    def distance_in_miles(self, lat1, lon1, lat2, lon2):

        r = 3963 # "radius of the earth" (in miles)

        lat1 = float(lat1)
        lon1 = float(lon1)
        lat2 = float(lat2)
        lon2 = float(lon2)

        dLat = math.radians(lat2-lat1)
        dLon = math.radians(lon2-lon1)
        a = math.sin(dLat/2) * math.sin(dLat/2) + \
            math.cos(math.radians(lat1)) * math.cos(math.radians(lat2)) * \
            math.sin(dLon/2) * math.sin(dLon/2)
        c = 2 * math.atan2(math.sqrt(a), math.sqrt(1-a));
        d = r * c;
        return d

    def date_rfcformat(self, dt):
        if dt.tzinfo is None:
            suffix = "-00:00"
        else:
            suffix = dt.strftime("%z")
            suffix = suffix[:-2] + ":" + suffix[-2:]
        return dt.strftime("%Y-%m-%dT%H:%M:%S") + suffix
```

The first method here takes in two sets of geolocation coordinates and calculates the distance between them in miles. This is based on the Haversine formula, and specifically how it works is outside the scope of both this book and my knowledge. This method is based on the JavaScript code found at *http://www.movable-type.co.uk/scripts/latlong .html*. For this method, it was ported to Python and converted to calculate the distance in miles rather than kilometers.

The next method simply takes in a Python `datetime` object and converts it into the format defined by RFC 3339 (*http://www.ietf.org/rfc/rfc3339.txt*) . Implementations of this code can be found on various sites on the Internet. This particular implementation can be found on the official Python website (*http://bugs.python.org/issue7584*).

Building the Game Itself

At this point we've got a pretty good collection of models to help manage the back-end logic of this game. Now let's move on to the game itself and start building some realtime user interactions.

User Authentication

The *models.py* file contains a good deal of the code needed to run the core of this game, but we still have to build the views and start assembling the controller classes to actually interact with the user. We'll be using a single file to handle all of the controller functionality, whether the request originates from an HTTP request, an XMPP request, or even an SMS message. Inside your *appengine* folder, create a file called *main.py* and add the following code:

```python
# standard python library stuff
import wsgiref.handlers
import os, logging, random, urllib, cgi, re
from datetime import datetime

# app engine imports
from google.appengine.ext.webapp import template
from google.appengine.ext import webapp, db
from google.appengine.api import xmpp, users, urlfetch
from google.appengine.ext.webapp.util import login_required
from django.utils import simplejson as json

# import all models:
from models import *

def main():
    # setup the specific URL handlers
    application = webapp.WSGIApplication([('/', MainHandler),
                                          ],
                                          debug=True)
    # run the application
    wsgiref.handlers.CGIHandler().run(application)


# handle the root URL for the site
class MainHandler(webapp.RequestHandler):
    def get(self):

        # load the current user from google
        current_user = users.get_current_user()
```

```
        # the file location of the logged out template
        template_path = os.path.join(os.path.dirname(__file__),
                                'templates/main-logged-out.html')

        # setup the basic template variables
        template_values = {
            "user": current_user,
            "login_url": users.create_login_url('/sync/user'),
            "logout_url": users.create_logout_url('/')
            }

        # If the user is logged in, use the full template
        if current_user:
            template_path = os.path.join(os.path.dirname(__file__),
                                'templates/main.html')

            # load the UserInfo object for this user
            ui = UserInfo().by_user(current_user)

            # add UserInfo data to the template
            template_values["allow_sms"] = ui.allow_sms
            template_values["mobile_key"] = ui.mobile_key
            template_values["mobile_number"] = ui.mobile_number
            template_values["mobile_short_code"] = Textmark.short_code
            template_values["mobile_keyword"] = Textmark.keyword

        # render the template
        self.response.out.write(template.render(template_path, template_values))


# this needs to stay at the bottom of the file
if __name__ == '__main__':
    main()
```

Having built the previous App Engine examples, this code should be pretty easy to understand. We import the modules that we'll need from the standard Python library and from Google's additional libraries. After that, we import every class contained inside our new *models.py* file. After that, we define the main function, which just creates the URL mappings and runs the application. At this point, we've set up only one URL to display. When a user hits the root of the site, /, we'll route them off to the MainHandler controller class, which is the next method defined in this file.

At its heart, the MainHandler class is very simple. Its main job is to check whether a user is logged into the system and load the UserInfo object it's available. We then take that information and pass it on as template variables to help render the view and display it to the user.

Rather than reinvent the authentication wheel, we're just going to use App Engine's users functionality, which has Google handle the user authentication aspect of this application. This allows us to authenticate users and get some basic information about them without having to write any code. It also allows users to log in without creating yet another account on another service. While we can force users to be logged in to access this view, we simply load the user's object from Google and generate URLs for both logging in and logging out. To create the login URL, we simply call the `users.create_login_url` supplied with the URL where we'd like the user to end up after a successful login. In this case, we're going to send them off to a URL called /sync/ user. Next, we check our datastore to see if we can load a `UserInfo` for the currently logged in user. If it exists, we populate a few more template variables and, finally, render the HTML view.

Depending on whether or not the user is authenticated, we need to display one of two different templates. If a user is not authenticated, we'll show her a template called *main-logged-out.html*. In the *appengine/templates* directory, create a file called *main-logged-out.html*:

```
<!DOCTYPE html>
<html>
  <head>
    <meta http-equiv="content-type" content="text/html; charset=utf-8"/>
    <meta name = "viewport" content = "width = device-width; maximum-scale=1.0;
      user-scalable=0;">
    <title>iPandemic</title>
  </head>

  <body>
    <div id="header">
      <h1>iPandemic</h1>
    </div>
    <p>Welcome to the game. Sign in (via google) to get started.</p>
    <a href="{{ login_url }}">Log in with your Google Account</a>
  </body>

</html>
```

When users come to the site and they are not logged in, there isn't much we can do for them. So this template simply displays the header and provides a link for the user to log in. Although also essentially a static HTML page, the logged-in version of this page has a bit more code. Add a file called *main.html* to your *templates* directory:

```
<!DOCTYPE html>
<html>
  <head>
    <meta http-equiv="content-type" content="text/html; charset=utf-8"/>
    <meta name = "viewport" content = "width = device-width; maximum-scale=1.0;
      user-scalable=0;">

    <title>iPandemic</title>
    <!-- for jQuery -->
    <script type="text/javascript" src="http://www.google.com/jsapi"></script>

    <!-- for the maps API -->
    <script src="http://maps.google.com/maps?file=api&v=2&sensor=true&key=YOUR-
      GOOGLE-MAPS-API-KEY"
            type="text/javascript"></script>
```

```
          <!-- the basic CSS for the site -->
          <link rel="stylesheet" type="text/css" href="/static/main.css" />

      </head>

      <body onunload="GUnload()">

        <div id="header">
          <h1>iPandemic</h1>
          <ul id="options">
          </ul>
        </div>

          <div id="messageWindow">
            <form id="msg-form">
              <input id="msg" placeholder="I challenge you to a duel!" />
              <input type="submit" id="msg-send" value="Send" />
              <p>
                Send a message (whatever you want) to challenge the user.
              </p>
            </form>
          </div>

          <div id="map"></div>
          <div id="fullscreen"></div>

          <div id="footer">
            {% if allow_sms %}
              SMS is enabled to {{ mobile_number }}
            {% else %}
              To enable SMS send "<strong>{{ mobile_keyword }} {{ mobile_key }}</strong>"
                to {{ mobile_short_code }}.
            {% endif %}
            <a href="{{ logout_url }}">Log Out</a>
          </div>

      </body>

  </html>
```

We don't have much to do for a user who isn't logged in, but once she does log in, we're going to want to load up the JavaScript files that we'll be using from Google. After the standard includes, this HTML file is just the shell that we'll end up populating with JavaScript. Feel free to change the CSS styles, but the id attributes should be retained because we'll be referring to them directly in the JavaScript.

Starting from the top of the BODY, we've added a header and an unordered list that will contain any number of options for the user at certain points during the game. Below that is a DIV, hidden by default, that will allow a user to send a message to another user during a challenge. Below that we have the map DIV, in which we'll draw the actual map. The fullscreen DIV is used to overlay content across the entire screen when the user takes certain actions.

Toward the bottom of the file, we have a small bit of template logic around whether the user has enabled the SMS functionality of this application. To sign up for this functionality, we ask the user to send in his unique `mobile_key` to our specific keyword. If he has already enabled this service, we simply tell him which number he has on file. We also provide a link to log out this user from the application.

This is a perfectly functioning HTML file that contains most of what we'll need to continue. But in order to make the most out of the small screen real estate on a mobile device, we're going to want to ensure the map is the proper size, that padding sizes aren't too big, and various other minor style adjustments. To take care of these styling issues, create a file called *appengine/static/main.css* and fill it with the following basic style information:

```
BODY { font-family: monospace; }

/* header and options */
div#header { width: 100%; height: 42px; display: block; }
div#header h1 { float:left; margin: 0px; padding: 0px; }
div#header ul#options { float:right;
                        margin:0;
                        list-style:none;
                        text-align:right;
                        font-weight:bold; }

/* the map */
#map { width: 85%; height: 300px; border: #ccc solid 1px; }

/* hide the message window by default */
#messageWindow { display: none; }

/* the "fullscreen" overlay */
#fullscreen { background-color: white;
              top: 0px; left: 0px;
              height: 90%; width: 90%;
              margin-left: 5%;
              z-index: 1000;
              position: absolute;
              display: none; }

/* the big "close button" for the full screen overlay */
#fullscreen .close { width: 100%;
                     font-size: 1.7em;
                     text-align: center;
                     background-color: #ccc;
                     color: black;
                     top: 0px;
                     left: 0px; }
```

We're close to having the ability to log into this application, but we're missing one step between the login page and displaying this fully authenticated template. When we created the `login_url` earlier, we requested that the Google Accounts authentication service redirect the user to our **/sync/user** URL. Let's update the *main.py* file to have this functionality:

```
def main():
    # setup the specific URL handlers
    application = webapp.WSGIApplication([('/', MainHandler),
                                          ('/sync/user/?', SyncUserHandler),
                                          ],
                                         debug=True)
    # run the application
    wsgiref.handlers.CGIHandler().run(application)

class SyncUserHandler(webapp.RequestHandler):
    def get(self):
        UserInfo().sync(users.get_current_user())
        self.redirect('/')
```

After logging into the service, users are directed to the **/sync/user** URL, which is routed through the `SyncUserHandler` controller. This controller calls the `sync` method on the `UserInfo` object, which just ensures that we have a record for this user in our datastore. If this user isn't in our datastore, we generate a new entry; otherwise, it simply returns. When that finishes, we simply send the user on to the main site.

Now we have enough code to handle a number of different aspects of this game, but through the browser we only have the ability to log in. This application can run locally using the App Engine Launcher program. Start it up and direct your browser to the local site. After logging in, you should see a page resembling Figure 10-2.

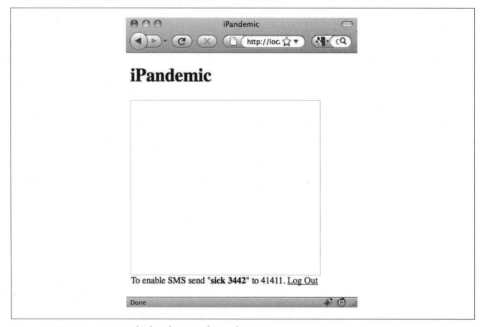

Figure 10-2. Logging into the local copy of iPandemic

Geolocation

Having built the HTML shell of the logged-in view, we can now start building out our application using JavaScript. The first thing we want to do is set up the Geolocation functionality of this application. Let's create a new JavaScript file in the *static* directory called *geo.js*:

```
// ask google to load the jquery libraries
google.load("jquery", "1");

// setup our basic object
var ipGeo = {
    map: false
};

// the function that actually grabs the geolocation information
ipGeo.getLocation = function(successCB, failCB) {
    if(navigator.geolocation && navigator.geolocation.getCurrentPosition)
        navigator.geolocation.getCurrentPosition(successCB, failCB,
                                                 {maximumAge: 300000});

    else
        failCB();
};

ipGeo.initialize = function(map_div_id) {
    if (GBrowserIsCompatible()) {
        // setup the default map using the map div supplied as a parameter
        ipGeo.map = new GMap2(document.getElementById(map_div_id));
        ipGeo.map.setUIToDefault();

        // setup the map
        ipGeo.getLocation(function(position) {
                    // pull out the coordinates and center the map
                    var lat = position.coords.latitude;
                    var lon = position.coords.longitude;
                    var gpos = new GLatLng(lat, lon)
                    // center the map
                    ipGeo.map.setCenter(gpos, 17);
                    // set a marker at the current location
                    ipGeo.map.addOverlay(new GMarker(gpos));
                },
                function() {
                    alert("Your browser doesn't support geolocation");
                });
    }
    else {
        alert("Google doesn't think your browser is compatible with their maps, " +
            "this will be painful without them...");
};
```

Since we're using Google's Ajax API hosting to host our JavaScript files, we ask Google to load the jQuery library. After that, we jump right into setting up our application object, ipGeo. The only member variable that we need at this point is a variable to contain the `map` object, so that it can be easily referenced in the different member functions.

The first of those member functions is `getLocation`, which is a wrapper call for the browsers, own `navigator.geolocation.getCurrentPosition` method. This method is available on most recent mobile browsers and is even available on desktop browsers with increasing frequency. Firefox on the desktop already includes this functionality natively within the browser. Rather than checking to see whether each browser supports this function every time we want to call it, we simply call this `ipGeo.getLocation` method, which wraps up that logic and makes the proper success and failure callbacks depending on what happens. Because locating the exact GPS coordinates of the browser can take some time, `navigator.geolocation.getCurrentPosition` runs asynchronously and executes the proper callback when data is available.

Aside from the success and fail callback functions, we also pass along a small object with a single key/value pair for `maximumAge`. Making a `getCurrentLocation` request is expensive, both in terms of the amount of time it takes to return and the drain on batteries it takes to use a GPS sensor in a mobile device. Setting the `maximumAge` parameter to 300,000 milliseconds allows us to cache the results for five minutes. This amount of cache time will ensure that any geolocation-based action that takes place in a standard session will require only one actual external request. This also stops the result from being cached indefinitely, which is actually the default behavior on some devices.

The next method is `ipGeo.initialize`, which takes in a parameter that is just the ID of the DIV we're going to use to display the map. This method then checks to see whether Google thinks this browser is compatible with their maps API and creates the map object. There are a number of different options (*http://code.google.com/apis/maps/documentation/reference.html#GMapOptions*) that can be used when working with these maps, but we're just going to use the default options and tell the map to use the default user interface. Next, we simply call the `getLocation` method and, upon success, we center the map on the coordinates it returned and add a marker at the current location.

Now that we've built some basic JavaScript functionality into this application, we need to add it to the HTML views. We don't need to add this to the logged-out page, just the page where the user has already been authenticated. Open up *templates/main.html* and make the following adjustments:

```
...

<title>iPandemic</title>
<!-- for jQuery -->
<script type="text/javascript" src="http://www.google.com/jsapi"></script>

<!-- for the maps API -->
<script src="http://maps.google.com/maps?file=api&v=2&sensor=true&key=
  YOUR-GOOGLE-MAPS-API-KEY" type="text/javascript"></script>
```

```
<!-- our local JS and CSS -->
<script type="text/javascript" src="/static/geo.js"></script>

</head>

<body onload="ipGeo.initialize('map')" onunload="GUnload()">
  <div id="header">
...
```

This is all the code that is needed to locate users graphically and pinpoint them on a map. Try heading back to your iPandemic test application. If you're using a browser such as Firefox or even the Safari emulator included in some versions of XCode on the Mac, you should see something like Figure 10-3 for your current location.

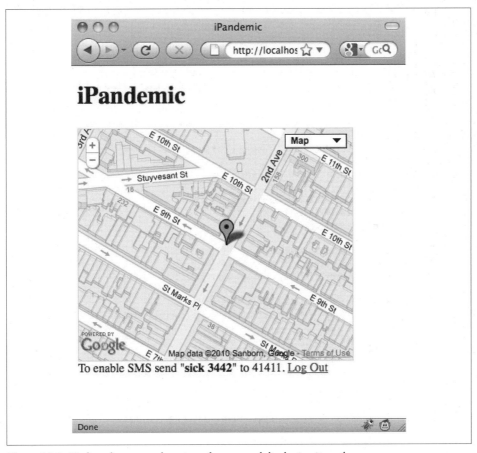

Figure 10-3. Finding the current location of a user and displaying it on the map

Keep in mind that if you're testing this code out using a desktop browser-based implementation of getLocation, the actual coordinates may be slightly off from your actual location. At the time of this writing, most computers lack GPS sensors. Without GPS, the geolocation is accomplished by other methods, such as finding the general location of your IP address, which is much less accurate.

Spreading Germs

The most basic action to be taken in this game is to "cough," which creates and spreads germs in specific locations. We've already built the Germ class, which can load and store the germs in our datastore, and have even written the code to locate the user. So adding the cough action to the game is fairly straightforward. Let's start by adding the controller and URL routing for this action. In the *main.py* file:

```
def main():
    # setup the specific URL handlers
    application = webapp.WSGIApplication([('/', MainHandler),
                                          ('/cough/?', CoughActionHandler),
                                          ('/sync/user/?', SyncUserHandler),
                                          ],
                                          debug=True)
    # run the application
    wsgiref.handlers.CGIHandler().run(application)

class CoughActionHandler(webapp.RequestHandler):
    def post(self):
        # make sure the latitude/longitude are floats
        lat = float(self.request.get('lat'))
        lon = float(self.request.get('lon'))

        # load up the user information
        current_user = users.get_current_user()
        user_info = UserInfo().by_current_user()

        # get the default disease for this user
        d = Disease().get_default_disease_for_user(current_user)

        # instantiate a new germ object
        new_germ = Germ(user=current_user,
                        disease=d,
                        location=db.GeoPt(lat, lon))


        # tell GeoModel that the location has been updated
        new_germ.update_location()
        # save the germ
        new_germ.put()

        # update the disease
        d.strength += new_germ.strength
        d.put()
```

```
# let the command center know
CommandCenter().add_germ(new_germ)
CommandCenter().update()

# finally send the germ back to the browser
germ = new_germ.format_for_json(current_user)
germ['color'] = Game().default_color_friendly
self.response.out.write(json.dumps({'message': '', 'germs': [germ]}))
```

To save a Germ, we only need three different pieces of information from the client. We need to know which user is creating the germ and that user's current latitude and longitude coordinates. Once we have those formatted suitably, we can load up the user's default disease using get_default_disease_for_user and instantiate the new Germ object.

Whereas most of our models extend the db.Model class, the Germ class extends GeoModel. The GeoModel class provides us with various geolocation capabilities, but in order to use them, we must inform the base class whenever the location of a specific object has been updated by calling the update_location method. This generates a list of properties that will be used later to search for germs based on proximity. Once we've updated the location, we can simply put into the datastore like we would with any other model.

This germ is part of a larger disease, and as germs are created and die off, this affects the total strength of the disease. So since we've just created a new germ, we want to add the strength of this new germ to the overall strength of the disease. This information is used in the model class when we want to find out which germ would win if they had to fight.

Once the germ and the disease have been updated and saved to the datastore, it's time to notify the CommandCenter of the new germ. To do this, we call add_germ and then update. This is separated into two steps because adding a germ to the CommandCenter doesn't take any time, but updating the command center is a much more expensive call. This way we can add several germs in a loop and then run the update method across all of the newly created germs.

Finally, we want to respond to this browser request with the newly created germ. To do this, we simply format it using JSON and respond back to the client. Because the current user created this germ, it's considered a friendly germ and we give it the friendly color. This is a useful visual cue that tells the user with a glance which germs on the map are friendly and which are enemies. We're also including a blank message field, which will be used by other methods later.

We now have the ability to add a germ to the datastore, but we don't have anything on the client side that allows us to create a germ, nor do we have any logic to display it on the map. Let's fix that by updating the *main.html* file to have a new link:

```
...
    <body onload="ipGeo.initialize('map')" onunload="GUnload()">

        <div id="header">
          <h1>iPandemic</h1>
          <ul id="options">
            <li><a id="button-cough" href="javascript://" onclick="ipGeo.cough();">
                [COUGH!]
            </a></li>
          </ul>
        </div>
...
```

This new option simply gives the user an interface element to click on and initiate a cough action. Let's keep going and add the client cough functionality. In the *appengine/ static/geo.js* file, add the following method:

```
ipGeo.cough = function() {
    ipGeo.getLocation(function(position) {
                        // pull out the lat/long coords
                        var lat = position.coords.latitude;
                        var lon = position.coords.longitude;
                        // recenter the map
                        ipGeo.map.setCenter(new GLatLng(lat, lon), 17);
                        // post the actual cough request
                        $.post('/cough/',
                                { 'lat': lat,
                                  'lon': lon },
                                 ipGeo.receivedGermData,
                                'json');

                  }, function() {});

};
```

This method keeps all of its functionality wrapped up inside a successful callback from the `ipGeo.getLocation` method. When that method returns successfully, we pull out the latitude and longitude coordinates, recenter the map, and post the results to the */cough/* URL. Once we've made the request to that URL, our cough should be added to the datastore, but we're still not showing anything on the map. To handle that, we request a callback when jQuery's `post` method completes. Let's add that callback method to *appengine/static/geo.js* now:

```
ipGeo.receivedGermData = function(data) {
    // pull out the data sent from the cough callback
    var message = data.message;
    var germs = data.germs;

    // if there is a message, display it to the user
    if(message) {
        alert(message);
    }
```

```
    // if there is a germ, draw it on the map
    for(var i in germs) {
        ipGeo.putGermOnMap(germs[i]);
    }
};
```

This method simply catches the JSON-enoded data that is received from the /cough/ URL. If a message is supplied, we'll display that to the user, but otherwise we simply loop through all of the germs and put them on the map with a method called ipGeo.put GermOnMap. Let's go ahead and add that method, along with a couple of others needed to display the extra germ information on the map:

```
ipGeo.putGermOnMap = function(germ) {
    var lat = germ.lat;
    var lon = germ.lon;
    var spread = germ.spread;
    var color = germ.color;

    // generate a marker that looks different than the default
    var blueIcon = new GIcon(G_DEFAULT_ICON);
    blueIcon.image = "http://www.google.com/intl/en_us/mapfiles/ms/micons/
      blue-dot.png";
    blueIcon.iconSize = blueIcon.shadowSize = new GSize(46, 46);
    var markerOptions = { icon: blueIcon };

    var marker = new GMarker(new GLatLng(lat, lon), markerOptions);

    // allow the user to click and see the data about this germ
    GEvent.addListener(marker, 'click', function() {
                    var d = germ.disease;
                    html = "<div id='"+ germ.id + "'>'";
                    html += "<br><small>";
                    html += "<strong>Strain</strong>: " + d.strain + "<br>";
                    html += "<strong>Host</strong>: " + d.host + "<br>";
                    html += "</div>";

                    ipGeo.fullscreenShow(html);
                });

    // show it on the map
    ipGeo.map.addOverlay(marker);

};

// show and hide the extra germ data
ipGeo.fullscreenHide = function() {
    $('#fullscreen').html('');
    $('#fullscreen').hide();
};

ipGeo.fullscreenShow = function(html) {
    $('#fullscreen').css('display', 'block');
    var a  = $('<div>')
                .click(ipGeo.fullscreenHide)
                .attr('class', 'close')
```

```
                .html('[close]');
        $('#fullscreen').append(a);
        $('#fullscreen').append(html);
    };
```

This adds three new methods to the ipGeo object. The first of these methods, putGerm
OnMap, does the actual work of adding the marker to the map. To do this, we start by
pulling apart the germ that is passed in as the only parameter. Then, we build a simple
marker using Google Maps API's blue icon, and we increase the size a bit to make sure
it's visible around the first marker that we drew on the screen in initialize.

Next, we add a callback function so that we get notified when the user clicks on the
marker itself. When the user does this, we want to show the user extra information
about the germ, such as the name of the strain and the host of the disease. The Google
Maps API actually provides a really nice method of displaying information about a
specific marker, openInfoWindowHtml, but its performance on a mobile phone is quite
slow. To ensure a smoother performance, we use a custom function that just displays
a large DIV on the screen. This performs much better on older phones than the open
InfoWindowHtml, which involves adjusting the map, drawing a shadow, and even downloading new map tiles to display the information.

That faster method for displaying information is called ipGeo.fullScreenshow. Along
with its companion function ipGeo.fullScreenhide, this gives us the ability to quickly
show additional information on the screen with a limited performance hit on mobile
devices.

Let's open the browser again and test out this new cough functionality. When I view
it in the XCode iPhone simulator, the result looks like Figure 10-4.

Drawing the germ itself as a little point on the map tells only half the story of the germ.
Each germ has a different level that affects how far it has spread out over the map, and
we should display that information as well. To do that, let's draw a circle around the
germ that illustrates how far it has spread. For this action, we'll need to add another
method to *geo.js*:

```
    ipGeo.drawCircle = function(center, radius, color) {
        var poly = [];
        var lat = center.lat() ;
        var lng = center.lng() ;
        var d2r = Math.PI/180 ;                    // degrees to radians
        var r2d = 180/Math.PI ;                    // radians to degrees
        var Clat = (radius/3963) * r2d ;           // using 3963 as earth's radius
        var Clng = Clat/Math.cos(lat*d2r);

        var points_in_circle = 10;

        // add each point in the circle
        for (var i = 0 ; i < points_in_circle; i++)    {
            var theta = Math.PI * (i / (points_in_circle / 2)) ;
            Cx = lng + (Clng * Math.cos(theta)) ;
            Cy = lat + (Clat * Math.sin(theta)) ;
```

```
        poly.push(new GLatLng(Cy,Cx)) ;
    }

    // add the first point to complete the circle
    poly.push(poly[0]) ;

    var line = new GPolygon(poly, color, 3, 1, color, 0.2);
    ipGeo.map.addOverlay(line) ;
};
```

Figure 10-4. Viewing the new cough marker and additional information

This code generates a circle and displays it on the map based on a single `center` point and a `radius` of a certain number of miles. Essentially, it figures out how to draw the circle based on how many points we elect to show. Because we're showing this on a mobile phone, and performance counts in realtime applications, we're only going to show 10 points, but this can be increased to be as smooth as you'd like. Once again, this code was not written by me from scratch; it is a modified function based on the work of Jeremy Schneider (*http://jerschneid.blogspot.com/2008/12/simple-way-to-draw -circle-with-google.html*).

To actually draw this for each germ, we need to call it from within the `ipGeo.putGer mOnMap` method. Update that method to have the following changes:

```
ipGeo.putGermOnMap = function(germ) {
    var lat = germ.lat;
    var lon = germ.lon;
    var spread = germ.spread;
    var color = germ.color;

    ipGeo.drawCircle(new GLatLng(lat, lon), spread, color);
...
```

Running the application again and hitting the cough link gives the same approximate results, only this time with the circle drawn around the point of the germ in the color specified by the `CoughActionHandler` (see Figure 10-5).

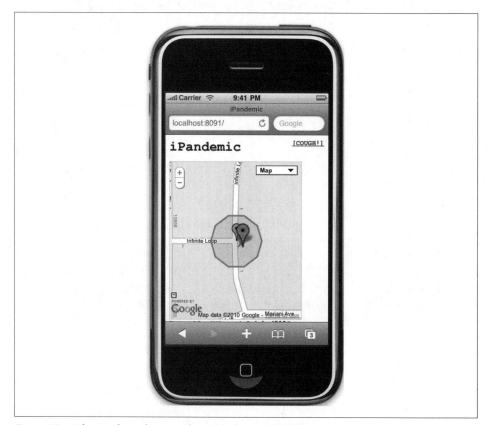

Figure 10-5. The cough marker complete with the spread of the germ

Loading Germs

Now that we're saving, displaying, and showing germs as we cough, we need to start to load them when a user loads the web page. A big part of the game is finding out if your current area is infected and responding to that. In order to add that functionality, we need to be able to load up germs that already exist in the area. We need to add some server-side functionality to get this to work, but on the client side, most of the work is already done. Let's start on the client side. In your *appengine/static/geo.js* file, add the following method:

```
ipGeo.showNearbyGerms = function(lat, lon) {
    $.post('/get/nearby/germs/',
            { 'lat': lat, 'lon': lon },
            ipGeo.receivedGermData,
            'json');
};
```

This method does one thing, so it's fairly simple to understand. When giving latitude and longitude parameters, it simply makes an Ajax request to /get/nearby/germs and supplies a callback method. That callback method is the exact same method that we use in the cough method. It will take any number of germs, loop through them, and draw them onto the screen. This function is ready to load nearby germs, but we need to make sure to actually call this method every time a user loads the page. To do that, let's modify the initialize function to call showNearbyGerms:

```
ipGeo.initialize = function(map_div_id) {
...
                        // set a marker at the current location
                        ipGeo.map.addOverlay(new GMarker(gpos));

                        // show the nerby germs
                        ipGeo.showNearbyGerms(lat, lon);
                },
...
```

This ensures that every time a user loads this page, we'll load up the nearby germs. Now that we can load and show them on the client side, let's move over to the server. We need to add the ability to pull these germs out of the datastore based on their proximity to the current location. Inside *appengine/main.py*, add the following controller and the new URL route in the application object:

```
def main():
    # setup the specific URL handlers
    application = webapp.WSGIApplication([('/', MainHandler),
                                        ('/cough/?', CoughActionHandler),
                                        ('/sync/user/?', SyncUserHandler),
                                        ('/get/nearby/germs/?',
                                         GetNearbyGermsHandler),
                                        ],
                                        debug=True)
```

```python
    # run the application
    wsgiref.handlers.CGIHandler().run(application)

class GetNearbyGermsHandler(webapp.RequestHandler):
    def post(self):
        lat = float(self.request.get('lat'))
        lon = float(self.request.get('lon'))
        germs = Germ().get_germs_near_point(lat, lon,
                                        max_distance_in_meters=1609*3)

        output = []
        current_user = users.get_current_user()

        # loop through each of these germs
        for germ in germs:
            # the same germ in JSON format
            g = germ.format_for_json(current_user)

            # assume this is an enemy
            g['color'] = Game().default_color_enemy

            # if the creator of this germ is us, it's not an enemy
            if germ.user == current_user:
                g['color'] = Game().default_color_friendly

            # otherwise, let's figure ot exactly how far away this germ is...
            else:
                distance = GameUtils().distance_in_miles(lat,
                                                        lon,
                                                        germ.location.lat,
                                                        germ.location.lon)

                # are we within the spread of this germ?
                if distance < germ.spread:
                    g['color'] = Game().default_color_threat
                    g['threat'] = True

                    # this user is threated by this.
                    # log it so we can force them to do something
                    UserThreats().create(current_user, germ)

            # add this germ to the list of germs we'll send back to the client
            output.append(g)

        self.response.out.write(json.dumps({'message': '',
                                            'germs': output}))
```

The point of GetNearbyGermsHandler is to load nearby germs and encode them into JSON so they can be easily displayed by the web browser. To do that, we take the latitude and longitude parameters supplied during the Ajax request and pass them along to the get_germs_near_point method. In this case, we're looking for germs within a distance of three miles. This will allow us to ensure that we show any germs that have grown from their original area toward where the user is currently located. It also gives us enough breathing room to show germs on the map if the user starts to scroll around the map beyond what is immediately available.

The `get_germs_near_point` method takes those latitude and longitude parameters, loads up nearby germs, and returns them in an array. We then want to loop through each of them to format them and take a couple of other actions based on the type of germ we find. First of all, we want to format the germ to JSON. Once we've done that, we want to determine whether the germ is an enemy or a friend. We consider a germ to be friendly if the current user created it; otherwise, it's an enemy.

If the germ is an enemy, we know that it's close to the current user by virtue of it having been included in the results from `get_germs_near_point`. However, we want to figure out whether our current user is inside the **spread** of that germ. If it is, it's a threat to the current user and we want to do a few extra things. First of all, we want to draw the circle around the germ in a different color to make it clear that the germ is a threat and not just an enemy. We also want to mark the germ as a threat in case the client-side script wants to behave differently in light of this fact. We want to actually create a `UserThreats` object for this threat. Any time a threat occurs, we need to put it in the datastore and ensure the user reacts within a reasonable amount of time. Finally, we add this particular germ to the **output** array and send the entire array back to the client. This will then get picked up by the `receivedGermData` method, which will display each germ on the screen.

If you venture out and "cough" in a number of different locations while logged in as different users, you'll be able to see the different types of germs displayed on the screen. Figure 10-6 shows an area with the different types of germs loaded.

Threats

The previous section touched on the idea of the threat concept in this game. There are two types of these threats in iPandemic: a "natural" threat and the "challenge" threat. We started creating natural threats in the previous section. These occur naturally when a user loads the game and is in an area already infected by another user. A challenge threat is that user's direct challenge to the germ already in the area.

Natural threats

Natural threats happen when a user loads the game from a location that is already infected by another user. When this happens, the user must respond to the threat in some way. There are two options to respond to this threat: the user can "cover" up and try to avoid the disease or she can challenge the other user.

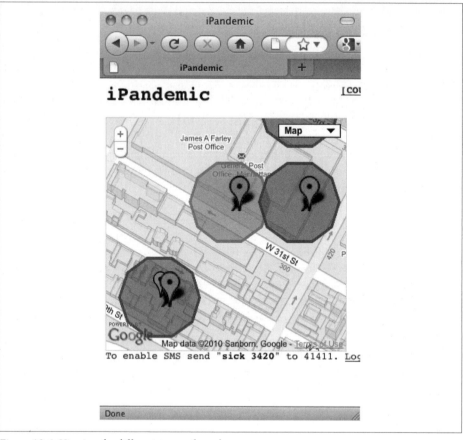

Figure 10-6. Viewing the different types of nearby germs

We are already storing the natural threat types, so let's add some logic on the client side that lets the user know she's been threatened and gives her options to respond. In *appengine/static/geo.js*, let's add a new member variable to the `ipGeo` object that keeps track of the current threat:

```
var ipGeo = {
    map: false,
    current_germ_threat: ''
};
```

On the server side, the `GetNearbyGermsHandler` checks each germ that is nearby and sets the `threat` field to `True` if a specific germ is a threat to the user. When we receive this list of germs on the client side, we can easily set the `current_germ_threat` variable based on which of these germs is a threat. We simply check each germ and set this variable for the germ that is a threat in the `receivedGermData` method:

```
ipGeo.receivedGermData = function(data) {
...
    ipGeo.current_germ_threat = '';
    for(var i in germs) {
        if(germs[i].threat) {
            // setup the current_germ_threat variable
            ipGeo.current_germ_threat = germs[i].id;

            // update the options to illustrate the threat
            var options = "<li><strong>You are Threatened!</strong><br />";
            options += "<a href='#' onclick=\"ipGeo.challenge();\">[CHALLENGE]</a> |";
            options += "<a href='#' onclick=\"ipGeo.cover();\">[COVER UP]</a>";
            $('#options').html(options);
        }

        ipGeo.putGermOnMap(germs[i]);
    }
};
```

Now if any of the germs are threats, we'll store that germ's `id` in the `current_germ_threat` variable. We also update the options at the top of the page. Normally this list gives the user the option to "cough," but when she is threatened we want to warn her about that and give her some new options. In this case, we suggest that she either "challenge" the other user or "cover up" so she doesn't lose points.

Let's start by building the **cover** functionality. The idea behind this feature is that when faced with an infected area, sometimes it makes sense to cover up rather than challenge the germ. This is the easiest of the two features to implement and potentially the safest possible route for the user. On the client side, all we need to do is implement a single Ajax request. Add the following method to *appengine/static/geo.js*:

```
ipGeo.cover = function() {
    ipGeo.getLocation(function(position) {
                $.post('/cover/',
                        { 'target_germ_id': ipGeo.current_germ_threat },
                        function (data) {
                            $('#options').html('Covered Up!');
                        },
                        'json');
            }, function() {});
};
```

This method just makes a request to the **/cough/** URL. The single parameter is the germ that threatened the user and caused her to cover up. Upon successful completion of this request, we update the options menu to let the user know what happened. The server side isn't too complicated, but we're going to need to add two new methods. Let's start by adding the following:

```
def main():
    # setup the specific URL handlers
    application = webapp.WSGIApplication([('/', MainHandler),
                                          ('/cough/?', CoughActionHandler),
                                          ('/sync/user/?', SyncUserHandler),
```

```
                                    ('/get/nearby/germs/?',
                                     GetNearbyGermsHandler),
                                    ('/cover/?', CoverActionHandler),
                                    ],
                                debug=True)
        # run the application
        wsgiref.handlers.CGIHandler().run(application)

    class CoverActionHandler(webapp.RequestHandler):
        def post(self):

            target_germ_id = self.request.get('target_germ_id')
            current_user = users.get_current_user()

            if target_germ_id:
                # load the enemy germ
                enemy_germ = db.get(target_germ_id)

                # you covered up, so your disease strength increases
                disease = Disease().get_default_disease_for_user(current_user)
                disease.strength += Game().default_disease_strength_increment
                disease.put()

                # this threat has been handled though, let's remove it from the datastore
                UserThreats().remove_threat(current_user, enemy_germ)

            self.response.out.write(json.dumps({}))
```

When a user covers up, we want to take a couple of actions. We want to increase the strength of their disease, even though they're not creating any germs. We also want to remove this threat from the datastore. Once a threat expires, the user loses points if it hasn't been addressed. Because this user is addressing the threat by covering up, we want to ensure it doesn't affect the user's score. To remove the threat, we call the remove_threat method on the UserThreats object. Let's create that now. In the *models.py* file add the following method to the UserThreats class:

```
    class UserThreats(db.Model):
        # who needs to respond to this threat?
        user = db.UserProperty()
    ...
        def remove_threat(self, user, germ):
            q = UserThreats.all()
            q.filter('user = ', user)
            q.filter('germ_threat = ', germ)
            threat = q.get()
            if threat:
                threat.delete()
```

To delete a threat from the datastore, we only need two pieces of information: the user who was threatened and the germ involved. We use those variables to locate the germ and, if we find it, we delete it from the datastore.

If you log in as one user, cough, and then log in as another user, you can easily test this functionality. Figure 10-7 shows what it looks like after successfully covering up from a germ threat.

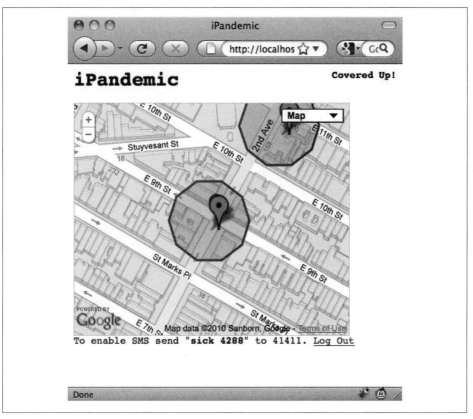

Figure 10-7. Successfully covering up

 For a more complete game experience, the `CoughActionHandler` would be a good place to adjust the scores of both the current user and the enemy user. For brevity, we're not adding it here, but the code available online does update the scores at this point.

Initiating a challenge

When a user is threatened by a natural threat, she can cover up and avoid the situation entirely or she can challenge the user. Challenging a user starts a series of events that involve communicating in realtime with the other user, regardless of whether they are logged into the application, and a race against the clock for all parties involved.

We've already added the link to initiate a "challenge" when a user is threatened. Let's add the JavaScript to handle this action. In *appengine/static/geo.js*, add the following method:

```
ipGeo.challenge = function() {
    // hide the fullscreen viewer if it's open
    ipGeo.fullscreenHide();

    // show the message window and focus the text input
    $('#messageWindow').show();
    $('#msg').focus();

    // listen for a submit event
    $('#msg-form').submit(function() {

            $.post('/message/to/germ/host',
                    { 'target_germ_id': ipGeo.current_germ_threat,
                      'msg': $('#msg').val()
                    },

                    // on successful submit, clear and hide the form
                    function() {
                        $('#msg').val('');
                        $('#msg-send').unbind('submit');
                        $('#messageWindow').hide();
                        $('#msg').blur();
                        $('#options').html('Challenged User!');
                    }
            );
            return false;
    });
};
```

For one user to challenge another, she must send a message to the other user. The application isn't concerned about the content of the message; the goal is to have the users interact in realtime through a variety of methods. To initiate this communication, we wait until a user clicks the challenge link and then provide a small text entry field and a submit button that will allow them to enter a message and send it the other user. We then listen for a submit event on this form. When we receive it, we post a request containing the text of the message along with the germ involved in this threat.

The server side of this action is actually surprisingly simple. We need to create a new threat object and send a message to the user who has been threatened. In your *main.py* file, add the URL mapping and the controller for this functionality:

```
def main():
    # setup the specific URL handlers
    application = webapp.WSGIApplication([('/', MainHandler),
                                        ('/cough/?', CoughActionHandler),
                                        ('/sync/user/?', SyncUserHandler),
                                        ('/get/nearby/germs/?',
                                         GetNearbyGermsHandler),
                                        ('/cover/?', CoverActionHandler),

                                        ('/message/to/germ/host/?',
                                         MessageToGermHostHandler),
                                        ],
                                        debug=True)
    # run the application
    wsgiref.handlers.CGIHandler().run(application)

class MessageToGermHostHandler(webapp.RequestHandler):
    def post(self):
        g = Germ.get(self.request.get('target_germ_id'))

        # a couple of things happened here:
        # by sending this message, the current user has instigated
        # a threat against the enemy user.
        # if the enemy responds in two minutes
        ut = UserThreats().create(g.user, g.key(),
                                expires_in_minutes=2,
                                challenge_user=users.get_current_user(),
                                threat_type='challenge')

        if ut:
            mesg = self.request.get('msg')
            mesg += "\n\nThis is a direct threat! Protect yourself."
            Messenger().send(from_user=users.get_current_user(),
                        to_user=g.user,
                        body=mesg,
                        response_key=ut.response_key)
```

All the logic in creating a threat like this is already handled by the code we've already written. When we receive this type of request, we want to do two separate things. First, we need to create a new UserThreats object. By challenging a user, this threatens the owner of the germ, so we create a threat directed at that user. This threat expires in only two minutes because we want the challenged user to respond quickly. However, this likely happened while the threatened user was not logged into the site. So we must inform that user by sending them a message, complete with the response_key that will enable the user to respond from either SMS or XMPP, whichever method is most convenient. Figure 10-8 shows the flow of threats as they function in realtime.

Updating threats

We're creating and responding to threats, but because they don't expire, there is no reason for the users to respond as they happen. If threats expire without being dealt with, the application needs to penalize the users and tell them what happened. To do

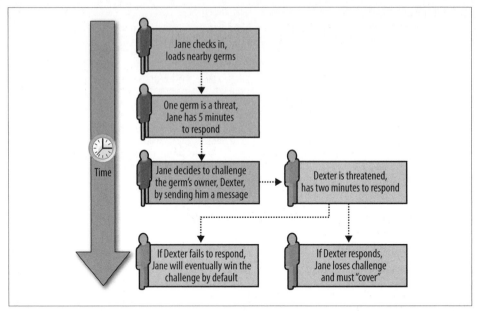

Figure 10-8. How threats work in iPandemic

this, we'll define a cron job that runs every minute and takes action on any threat that has expired. Running cron jobs in App Engine is similar to running them on a standard server. We define a job to run and the schedule for running it. When it's time to run one of the jobs, App Engine makes a GET request to the specified URL, and your application executes anything that needs to be done. To get started, let's define the cron schedule by create a file in *appengine* called *cron.yaml*:

```
cron:
- description: see if there are open challenges
  url: /cron/update/threats
  schedule: every 1 minutes
```

This entry tells Google that we want to run the code at `/cron/update/threats` once a minute. While App Engine's cron jobs can get slightly delayed, having this job run close to once every minute is perfect for our needs. We're not doing anything super time-sensitive; we just want to check to make sure that none of the threats have expired.

On the server side, responding to these cron requests works exactly like responding to any other HTTP request. Let's add the URL mapping and the new controller now. In your *appengine/main.py* file, make the following changes:

```
def main():
    # setup the specific URL handlers
    application = webapp.WSGIApplication([('/', MainHandler),
...

                                        ('/cron/update/threats/?',
                                         CronThreatHandler),
                                        ],
```

```
                                           debug=True)
        # run the application
        wsgiref.handlers.CGIHandler().run(application)

class CronThreatHandler(webapp.RequestHandler):
    def get(self):
        UserThreats().update_threats()
```

When we receive a request for this cron job, we simply call a method on the User
Threats object and return. Although this works perfectly, in a production setting you
may want to ensure that this request originated from Google's App Engine cron system
by checking the header or setting it up to run for a specific user. For now, let's go ahead
and add the update_threats method to the UserThreats class. In your *models.py* file,
add the following code:

```
def update_threats(self):
    # load the expired threats
    timeformat = '%Y-%m-%d %H:%M:%S'
    q = UserThreats.gql('WHERE expire_time < datetime(:1)',
                        datetime.now().strftime(timeformat))

    for x in q:
        if x.threat_type == 'challenge':

            # a local reference to the germ
            germ_threat = x.germ_threat

            # deduct points and send a message to the user
            UserInfo().by_user(x.user).update_score(-3)
            message = "Someone threatened you and you didn't respond. "
            message += "Points deducted! Also, your germs died!"
            Messenger().send(None, x.user, message)

            # update the overall strength of the disease
            germ_threat.disease.strength -= germ_threat.strength
            germ_threat.disease.put()

            # Delete any natural threats related to this threat
            tq = UserThreats.all()
            tq.filter('user = ', x.challenge_user)
            tq.filter('germ_threat = ', germ_threat)
            tq.filter('threat_type = ', 'natural')
            natural_threat = tq.get()
            if natural_threat:
                natural_threat.delete()

            # send a message to the winner of this challenge
            message = "Good challenge. You wiped out the other disease. "
              (Refresh and) cough again to spread yours!"
            Messenger().send(None, x.challenge_user, message)

            # delete the original GERM that caused the threat
            CommandCenter().delete_germ(germ_threat)
            germ_threat.delete()
```

```
        elif x.threat_type == 'natural':
            # this user didn't do anything!
            UserInfo().by_user(x.user).update_score(-3)

            # the other user scared someone off
            UserInfo().by_user(x.germ_threat.user).update_score(+3)

            message = "You were threatened by a disease on your last check-in"
            message += " and didn't cover or challenge successfully."
            message += "Points deducted!"
            Messenger().send(None, x.user, message)

        # delete this threat whether it's a challenge or natural threat
        x.delete()

    # update the command center after the loop has finished
    CommandCenter().update()
```

This method starts by loading all of the expired threats out of the datastore by looking for any threat whose `expire_time` is in the past. For each expired threat we check the `threat_type` and take different actions based on which type we find.

If the expired threat is a `challenge` threat, we need to do a few different things. Suppose Jane sends a challenge to Dexter. After receiving a challenge threat, Dexter must respond in a certain amount of time. If he doesn't respond, we want to inform him that time is up and deduct points. We then want to deduct some strength from the overall disease because the germ involved in this challenge was defeated.

When Jane sent this threat to Dexter, she had been threatened by a natural threat because the place where she checked in had already infected by Dexter's germ. To respond, she sent out this challenge threat, which has since expired. As far as the game is concerned, Jane has addressed her natural threat by challenging Dexter and winning. Because she's addressed her natural threat, we delete it so that it doesn't expire later and send her a message. Finally, this challenge threat all started because of a germ and in losing this challenge, the germ should also be deleted.

Going through that loop, we may also find that the expired threat had a `threat_type` of `natural`. When this happens, a user is checked in at an infected location and didn't properly handle the threat. This means that the user may not have done anything, or it could mean she sent a challenge request but the challenged user responded in time.

If a `natural` threat expires, we want to update the scores for both of the users. Whoever failed to respond to the threat has some points deducted and the other user gains some points. We also want to notify the user by sending her a message about what happened. Finally, whether the threat was a `natural` or `challenge` threat, we want to delete it from the datastore.

Responding to challenge threats: Receiving XMPP and SMS messages

When Jane challenges Dexter, Dexter is notified by instant message and SMS and given a short period of time to respond to the threat. He can do this by replying to either of those messages. At the end of each message sent as a challenge threat, there is a string resembling "Respond with @4 [your message here]." That response key, @4, allows Dexter to respond directly to Jane via XMPP or SMS through the game without knowing any other information about Jane.

Receiving XMPP messages. To get started with this functionality, let's start accepting the XMPP responses. When we set up our *app.yaml* file for this application, we enabled an inbound service called xmpp_message that allows us to receive XMPP messages from users. Receiving these messages is as simple as responding to any other type of HTTP request, only messages are received to a specific URL. Update your *main.py* file:

```
def main():
    # setup the specific URL handlers
    application = webapp.WSGIApplication([('/', MainHandler),
...

                                          ('/_ah/xmpp/message/chat/?', XMPPHandler),
                                          ],
                                         debug=True)
    # run the application
    wsgiref.handlers.CGIHandler().run(application)

class XMPPHandler(webapp.RequestHandler):
    def post(self):
        # parse the message object
        message = xmpp.Message(self.request.POST)

        # clean up the resource name
        email = message.sender
        if email.find('/') != -1:
            email = email[:email.find('/')]

        # the sender should be a user of our system.
        sender = users.User(email)
        body = message.body.strip()

        # pull out the response key from the message
        results = re.findall("@([0-9]+)\ (.+)", body)
        if len(results) == 1:
            response_key, msg = results[0]
            response = UserThreats().respond_to_threat(sender, int(response_key), msg)

            # if we have a message from respond_to_threat, send it back to the user
            if response:
                message.reply(response)
            else:
                message.reply("Message delivered, we'll see what happens.")

        # we couldn't figure out what the resource key was...
        else:
            message.reply("I had trouble dealing with that... sorry :(")
```

Having built the XMPP functionality in a previous chapter, some of this should look familiar. The first thing we do is set up the XMPP message object using the POST data that we've received. Next, because XMPP sender addresses are often in the format of an email address with an additional resource string attached to the end, we want to strip off that additional string. Then, we load the users object based on the email address and clean up the body of the message.

Once we've done all the housekeeping associated with accepting this message, it's time to look at the message body itself and see if we can figure out what the user is trying to tell us. All messages that come into the system are directed at a specific threat using the response_key. So, the first thing we want to do is see if we can pull out the resource key with a simple regular expression. If we load exactly one result, we know we've probably understood this type of message.

We then notify the UserThreats object that sender is responding to the threat identified by the response_key. We'll define respond_to_threat next, but it will return a message to the user, which this method just passes back up the chain. If we don't get a response or we don't understand the request, we notify the user and return.

 It's good practice to allow the user to opt out of receiving XMPP messages through the XMPP interface itself. That code has been left out of this version for brevity, but it exists in the version of the application that you can download from the website.

Receiving SMS messages. Now that we're accepting IM messages, let's move on to accepting SMS messages and allowing users to respond to threats in that way. Still in the same *main.py* file:

```
def main():
    # setup the specific URL handlers
    application = webapp.WSGIApplication([('/', MainHandler),
...
                                          ('/catch/sms/?', SMSIncomingHandler),
                                          ],
                                         debug=True)
    # run the application
    wsgiref.handlers.CGIHandler().run(application)

class SMSIncomingHandler(webapp.RequestHandler):
    def get(self):
        self.response.headers['Content-Type'] = 'text/plain'

        # prepare some HTTP parameters as variables
        uid = self.request.get('uid')
        body = self.request.get('body').strip()

        # try to load the sender of this message from the datastore
        ui = UserInfo().by_mobile_number(uid)
```

```
    # great we found this user in the datastore
    if ui:
        # pull out the response_key, if it's in there...
        results = re.findall("@([0-9]+)\ (.+)", body)
        if len(results) == 1:
            code, msg = results[0]
            response = UserThreats().respond_to_threat(ui.user, int(code), msg)
            self.response.out.write(response)
        else:
            self.response.out.write("I'm not sure what you wanted me to do.")

    # we didn't find this user by UID.
    else:
        # perhaps they're trying to sign up by sending their mobile_key?
        ui = UserInfo().by_mobile_key(body)
        if ui:
            # check
            ui.allow_sms = True
            ui.mobile_number = uid
            ui.put()
            self.response.out.write("OK, SMS is enabled. Good choice.")
        else:
            self.response.out.write("I couldn't find that mobile key.")
        return
```

 This method assumes that we're using the TextMarks service in much the same way as we did previously in this book, setting it up to make a request to /catch/sms whenever an SMS is sent to our keyword.

This method works in much the same way that the XMPPHandler worked. In the XMPP method, we had the email of the user as it exists in our datastore, but when we're using SMS, we have to load each user based on her phone number. If we have the mobile number in our datastore, we load the UserInfo object and run respond_to_threat in the exact same way that we did in the XMPP method.

SMSIncomingHandler's only real deviation from XMPPHandler comes when we are unable to load the UserInfo object for the mobile number. In XMPPHandler, we can assume that we have that user's XMPP address in the datastore because we use that when she logs into the application. With SMS, though, we don't have a user's phone number until she explicitly signs up and gives it to us.

When a user views the application, she's greeted with a message explaining that she can sign up for SMS messages by sending her mobile_key to the keyword. This next bit of code checks to see whether that is happening. If we don't know who a certain user is, we try to load the UserInfo object using by_mobile_key. If the body of the message is the mobile_key for a specific user, we save her mobile number and respond back.

Handling the response. When a user receives a threat, she needs to be able to respond to that threat. That ends up coming through a method called `respond_to_threat`. Add it to your *models.py* file:

```
def respond_to_threat(self, user, response_key, response):
    # load the response using the user/response key combo
    q = UserThreats.all()
    q.filter('user = ', user)
    q.filter('response_key = ', response_key)
    threat = q.get()

    if not threat: return

    # did they respond to a challenge threat?
    # let's increase the strength of the challenged germ
    if threat.threat_type == 'challenge':
        challenge_user = threat.challenge_user

        # increase the strength of the germ that was threatened
        threat.germ_threat.strength += Game().default_disease_strength_increment
        threat.germ_threat.put()

        # update the score of the users
        UserInfo().by_user(user).update_score(3)
        UserInfo().by_user(challenge_user).update_score(-1)

        # the loser should get a response too...
        message = "%s: %s\nYou lost the challenge! You should probably cover up."
          % (user.nickname(), response)
        Messenger().send(user, challenge_user, message)


    # The threat has been responded to!
    # we can delete it
    threat.delete()

    # this is a successful challenge, tell the user who responded
    response_to_sender = "Awesome! You defeated a challenge!"
    response_to_sender += "Points, strength, good looks? All increased."
    return response_to_sender
```

When one user responds to a threat, `respond_to_threat` handles the logic for what follows. This happens when a user checks in at a location that is infected by another germ. That user then decides to challenge the germ rather than cover up. Immediately, a message is sent out proclaiming the challenge. To defend herself against a challenge, all a user must do is reply via instant messenger or SMS. If she does that, she's successfully defeated the challenge. This method handles that logic.

So the first thing we need to do is load the `UserThreats` object based on the `user` object and the `response_key`. Assuming we were able to load this threat, we want to check to ensure it's a "challenge" threat type. If it is, we have a couple of tasks that we need to accomplish. First, we want to increase the strength of the threatened germ as a reward for being successfully defended. Next, we want to adjust the scores of the two players involved. The user who successfully defeated this challenge sees a score increase and the loser receives a slight decrease in score.

Next, we set up and send out messages to the different users. First, we want to notify the user who issued the challenge that his challenge has failed. That user still has the active "natural" threat out there and should cover up, so we advise the user of this. Next, we set up the message that we'll send back to the user who fended off this challenge to inform her that she was successful.

Having responded to a threat means that it's no longer a threat to the user. Because it's no longer a threat, we can get rid of it. To do that, we simply delete it from the datastore. We also want to send a message to the user who responded to this request. To respond, we simply return the response message that we want to send to the user, and the controller class will handle routing the message back to the user. We can't actually send the reply at this point in the code, because it's not clear whether the user sent a response through XMPP or SMS, so leaving this up to the controller is the simplest option.

Responses in action. As we add more of these communication features, it becomes harder to test them out locally. While you can use the App Engine admin section to test XMPP messages locally in your application, testing the SMS functionality requires a publicly facing URL. This means that the easiest path to test some of this functionality is to deploy it to your live App Engine instance and run it from there.

To test a challenge on your application, you'll need two separate Google accounts. Check in and "cough" at one location and then sign out. Using your second account, sign in again, and you should be presented with a threat. If you challenge that threat, you should receive an instant message and an SMS if you've enabled that service. Figure 10-9 shows an example of this communication.

 You can always see examples of how this works by using the live iPandemic instance (*http://www.ipandemic.com*).

Spreading Germs

When we go to display the germs on the map, one of the things we look at is the `spread` of the germ. The `spread` is a variable that dictates the size of the germ on the map and in the game logic. A germ with a spread of `1.0` is drawn on the map as being a mile wide. As time passes, the germs need to grow and expand on the map. To do that, we'll set up another cron job that spreads the germs. Add the following code to your *main.py* file:

```
def main():
    # setup the specific URL handlers
    application = webapp.WSGIApplication([('/', MainHandler),
    ...
```

```
                                    ('/cron/spread/germs/?',
                                      CronSpreadGermsHandler),
                                    ],
                                 debug=True)
        # run the application
        wsgiref.handlers.CGIHandler().run(application)

    class CronSpreadGermsHandler(webapp.RequestHandler):
        def get(self):
            Germ().auto_spread()
```

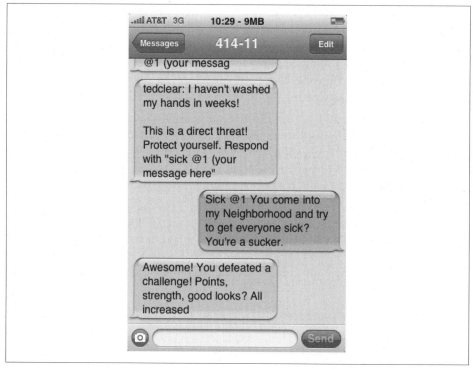

Figure 10-9. Responding to a threat via SMS

Once again, this cron job controller does nothing more than accept the request and pass all of the logic in to a method inside a model class. In this case we call auto_spread in the Germ model. Open up *models.py* and add the auto_spread method to the Germ class:

```
        def auto_spread(self):
            # get all of the germs
            germs = Germ().all()

            for g in germs:

                # each germ increases size by its speed
                g.spread += g.spread_speed
```

```
            # as it grows, it gets slower
            if g.spread_speed > Game().default_germ_slowdown:
                g.spread_speed -= Game().default_germ_slowdown

            # we've updated the germ, notify the command center
            CommandCenter().add_germ(g)
            g.put()

        # update the command center after running through everything
        CommandCenter().update()
```

The purpose of this method is to take every germ on the map and make it slightly larger. To do that, we loop through every germ in the datastore and increase its **spread** property. We accomplish this by incrementing it by the value of its **spread_speed**. The spread speed starts out as a relatively large number, which enables new germs to spread quickly and not die out initially. However, as they grow, they get slower, which is what the next bit of this code does. Once we've increased the spread of the germ and decreased the speed, it's time to notify the **CommandCenter** and save the germ with the **put** method.

We don't run **update** on the **CommandCenter** until after we've completed the loop with all of the germs. Every time this code runs, the germs will increase all across the map. New germs will spread faster than old ones, but they'll all increase by some amount. To test this out, simply load the **/cron/spread/germs** URL in your browser several times in a row. You should be able to notice a jump in the size of the existing germs.

However, we're not going to access this URL manually; we'll be running this through Google's cron service as well. So let's add this to the *cron.yaml* file now. While we're in there, let's also add an entry for the final cron job we'll need for this application:

```
cron:
- description: see if there are open challenges
  url: /cron/update/threats
  schedule: every 1 minutes

- description: make the germs grow
  url: /cron/spread/germs
  schedule: every 10 minutes

- description: should any germs fight each other?
  url: /cron/fight/germs
  schedule: every 10 minutes
```

Once you redeploy this application, Google will start running this cron job every 10 minutes, which means that every 10 minutes, each germ on the map will grow. They're set to grow very slowly, but at some point, they'll all start overlapping. That's where last cron job comes in.

Fighting Germs

As the germs grow behind the scenes, they occasionally step on one another's toes. More specifically, after a while, germs start to grow so big that they are in the same space, even if they weren't when they were created. When this happens, we want them to fight on their own without any user interaction.

We've already added a cron job for this activity that hits the URL /cron/fight/germs every 10 minutes. Let's add the handler code to accept this request from App Engine. In your *main.py* file, make the following additions:

```
def main():
    # setup the specific URL handlers
    application = webapp.WSGIApplication([('/', MainHandler),

...

                                          ('/cron/fight/germs/?',
                                           CronFightGermsHandler),
                                          ],
                                         debug=True)
    # run the application
    wsgiref.handlers.CGIHandler().run(application)


class CronFightGermsHandler(webapp.RequestHandler):
    def get(self):
        Germ().auto_fight()
```

Aside from calling code specific to fighting the germs, this code is exactly like the CronSpreadGermsHandler. So let's move right on to the *models.py* file and add the auto_fight method to the Germ class:

```
def auto_fight(self):
    # keep track of who needs to go
    losers = []

    # get all of the germs
    germs = Germ().all()

    # loop through each germ
    for g in germs:
        # no need to check the losers
        if g in losers: continue

        # test it against all the othr germs
        for x in germs:

            # no need to check the losers
            if x in losers: continue

            if x.key() != g.key():
                distance = GameUtils().distance_in_miles(g.location.lat,
                                                          g.location.lon,
                                                          x.location.lat,
                                                          x.location.lon)

                # are they close together? They should fight
                if distance < g.spread:
                    if g.would_defeat(x):
                        losers.append(x)
```

```
            else:
                losers.append(g)

    if len(losers):
        message = "I hate to be the one to tell you this, "
        message += "but one of your germs was outmatched."
        for loser in losers:
            # send a message to the user...
            Messenger().send(None, loser.user, message)
            # notify the command center
            CommandCenter().delete_germ(loser)
            # delete the germ
            loser.delete()

    # let's update the command center
    CommandCenter().update()
```

The purpose of the `auto_fight` method is to look at each of the germs on the map and determine whether any of them are overlapping. If one germ overlaps with another in some way, they should fight it out. The strongest germ wins and continues to exist, while the weaker germ dies out.

So to get started with this, we create an empty array to keep track of which germs have already fought and lost. Then, we just start looping through the germs. Any time we run into a germ that has already lost, we skip it and continue. Otherwise, we take that germ and compare it against every other germ in the datastore. We then figure out the distance between the germs to see whether they are overlapping. If the spread of the germ is greater than the distance between them, it's time to fight.

Fighting the germs is actually very simple. We just look at one of the germs and see whether it would defeat the other. The losing germ is then appended to the losers array and we keep going with the loop.

Once we make it through all of the entries in the loop, we check to see whether there are any losers. If there are, we have a couple of things to do. First, we want to quickly send a message to the user who created the germ that says he just lost a germ and might want to get out there and "cough" or challenge another user. After that, we notify the `CommandCenter` that a germ has been deleted. After deleting the germ and any other germs that lost their fights, we call `update` on the `CommandCenter` object. Figure 10-10 shows the result of this action.

Realtime Syndication

Many different parts of the code have notified something called the command center after taking action, but it hasn't actually done anything other than keep track of the germs as they come and go. Let's start using this data to work in some realtime syndication, which will lead the way to realtime analytics and a fully multiuser chat application.

Figure 10-10. Receiving a message from the game

To start with, we're going to take the knowledge that the command center has about the current state of our application and create an Atom-based XML feed that can be used by other applications to monitor, visualize, and expand on this application. To do that, we need to add a new controller and view to this application. Let's start with the controller. Inside the *main.py* file, add the following controller:

```
def main():
    # setup the specific URL handlers
    application = webapp.WSGIApplication([('/', MainHandler),
                                          ('/feed/?', FeedHandler),
                                          ],
                                          debug=True)
    # run the application
    wsgiref.handlers.CGIHandler().run(application)

class FeedHandler(webapp.RequestHandler):
    def get(self):
        # grab the germs from the command center
        germs = CommandCenter().get_germs()

        # generate a nicely formatted array including JSON formatted germs
        output = []
```

```
for x in germs:
    germs[x]['json'] = json.dumps(germs[x])
    output.append(germs[x])

# set some template variables
template_values = {
    'germs': output,
    'url': 'http://' + os.environ["HTTP_HOST"],
    'updated': GameUtils().date_rfcformat(datetime.now()),
    'title': 'iPandemic'
    }

# render the xml
path = os.path.join(os.path.dirname(__file__), 'templates/atom.xml')
self.response.headers['Content-Type'] = 'application/atom+xml'
self.response.out.write(template.render(path, template_values))
```

To generate our XML feed, we simply need to get the list of current germs from the command center. Although we're using the Atom format to contain all of this data, the actual payload for the entry will be JSON formatted. To prepare for the template, we format the germ into a JSON-encoded string here in the controller.

Once we have all of the germs assembled into an array, we set up the other template variables that we'll need when rendering the Atom output. We'll be using the current URL in several spots in the file, as well as the `title` and the `updated` date of this file. Since we're always generating this file on the fly, we'll just use the current time for the `updated` field.

We have the germs and the other template variables all sorted out, so the only thing left to do is actually render the XML. We do that using App Engine's `template` system. All that's left to do is create the template itself. Create a file called *appengine/templates/atom.xml* and fill it with the following code:

```
<?xml version="1.0" encoding="utf-8"?>
<feed xmlns="http://www.w3.org/2005/Atom">

  <title>{{ title }}</title>
  <updated>{{ updated }}</updated>

  <id>{{ url }}/</id>
  <link rel="alternate" href="{{ url }}/" title="{{ title }}" type="text/html"/>
  <link rel="self" href="{{ url }}/feed" title="{{ title }}"
        type="application/atom+xml"/>
  <link rel='hub' href='http://pubsubhubbub.appspot.com/' />
  <author><name>{{ title }}</name></author>

  {% for germ in germs %}
    <entry>
      <id>{{ url }}/#{{ germ.id }}</id>
      <title type="text">Germ {{ germ.id }}</title>
      <link href="{{ url }}/#{{ germ.id }}" rel="alternate" type="text/html"/>
      <updated>{{ germ.updated }}</updated>
      <published>{{ germ.timestamp }}</published>
      <content type="text/plain" xml:base="{{ url }}">
```

```
        {{ germ.json }}
      </content>
    </entry>
  {% endfor %}

</feed>
```

This is a pretty standard Atom-based XML file. We define the title and all of the fields required and expected by a proper Atom file. We even advertise a `hub` property for people who wish to subscribe via PubSubHubbub.

Inside the `entry` tags, we supply an automatically generated title based on the ID of the germ. That's fine because we don't expect end users to actually see the title of this entry. Germs don't have permalink style pages, so the `link` specified here just links to a fragment on the main index page of the site.

The most important part here is the `content` entry. In this case we're printing only the JSON-encoded germ and nothing else. This allows for any application that wants to use this data to import this file, look at the content fields, and get all of the data it needs.

Publishing the feed

Since we have a proper Atom XML file that we can use for syndication, we can publish it using PubSubHubbub. Combining this protocol with our command center, which is notified about every minor action that affects a germ on the site, third parties can get a total realtime view of what is happening in this application. It's also extremely simple to implement on this end.

Every time we called the `add_germ` or `delete_germ` method on the `CommandCenter` object, we followed it up with a call to `update`. This means that we can enable realtime syndication for all the germ activity on the site just by pinging the Hub from that one method. Inside *models.py*, add the following method to `CommandCenter`:

```
class CommandCenter(object):
    cc_memcache_key = 'cc-germs'
...
    # notify everyone of the changes
    def update(self):
        url = "http://pubsubhubbub.appspot.com"
        data = urllib.urlencode({'hub.url':
                                'http://' + os.environ["HTTP_HOST"] + '/feed',
                                'hub.mode': 'publish'})
        logging.info(urlfetch.fetch(url=url, payload=data, method=urlfetch.POST))
```

This simply changes the `update` method to ping the hub instead of the `pass` statement that it was running before. Because we already defined the `update` method and were calling it at all the right spots, enabling realtime syndication is as simple as adding those four new lines to the `CommandCenter` object.

The Command Center

The application that we've built at this point runs on Google's App Engine platform and exists almost entirely on the mobile phone. It has realtime components that allow the application to reach users when they're not currently looking at the site, and even via SMS, when they're not actively doing anything on the phone or the computer. However, now we that we have realtime access to the germs as they are built and destroyed, we can build a full-featured front-end to view everything while not actively participating in the game.

This part of the game will be built using Tornado so that we can take advantage of its support for long polling. This will also require us to run the game from a separate server, which will enable us to use PubSubHubbub in the same way that any other subscriber would use it.

The basic site

To get started, let's create a file in the *ipandemic/tornado* folder called *server.py*. Start if off with the following code:

```
import os, logging
import tornado.httpserver
import tornado.ioloop
import tornado.web
import tornado.auth
import simplejson as json
import time, re, uuid
from tornado.options import define, options
from tornado.escape import url_escape
import urllib, urllib2
from xml.dom import minidom

# Define options that can be changed as we run this via the command line
define("port", default=8088, help="Run server on a specific port", type=int)

# a basic controller to load the default template
class HomeHandler(tornado.web.RequestHandler):
    def get(self):
        # see if we can load the user info from a cookie
        user_json = self.get_secure_cookie('user')

        if user_json:
            user = json.loads(user_json)
        else:
            user = None

        self.render("command-center.html", user=user)

class Application(tornado.web.Application):
    def __init__(self):
        handlers = [
```

```
            (r"/", HomeHandler),
        ]

        settings = {
            "static_path": os.path.join(os.path.dirname(__file__), "static"),
            "template_path": os.path.join(os.path.dirname(__file__), "templates"),
            "cookie_secret": "you-cookie-secret",
            "login_url": "/login",
            }
        tornado.web.Application.__init__(self, handlers, **settings)

if __name__ == "__main__":
    tornado.options.parse_command_line()
    http_server = tornado.httpserver.HTTPServer(Application())
    http_server.listen(options.port)
    tornado.ioloop.IOLoop.instance().start()
```

This is essentially the same base Tornado application that we've used in previous chapters. We import what we need, build an application class, and start the application. There are only a couple of things to notice here. In this particular instance, we specify a default **port** of 8088. While it's not strictly necessary to use this port, this application must run on a port that can be accessed from App Engine, which has restrictions on the ports it can access. We're using the reference PubSubHubbub hub located at pubsubhubbub.appspot.com, which runs on App Engine. Also, we specify a **cookie_secret** in this code. This will allow Tornado to secure the cookies against forgery.

HomeHandler, the controller class that handles the root URL of the domain, just does two quick things. First, HomeHandler tries to load the user information out of the secure cookie. Then, it simply renders a template called *command-center.html*. Let's define that file now. Create a file in your **tornado** directory called *templates/command-center.html* and add the following code.

```
<!DOCTYPE html>
<html>
  <head>
    <meta http-equiv="content-type" content="text/html; charset=utf-8"/>

    <title>iPandemic - Command Center</title>
    <!-- for jQuery -->
    <script type="text/javascript" src="http://www.google.com/jsapi"></script>

    <!-- for the maps API -->
    <script src="http://maps.google.com/maps?file=api&amp;v=2&sensor=false&key=
YOUR-GOOGLE-MAPS-API-KEY"
            type="text/javascript"></script>

    <!-- our local JS -->
    <script type="text/javascript" src="{{ static_url('cc.js') }}"></script>

  </head>

  <body onload="cc.initialize('map', false);" onunload="GUnload()"
                                    class="control-center">
```

```
    <div id="header">
      <h1>iPandemic - Command Center</h1>

      <ul id="options">
        {% if user %}
          <li>Logged in as {{ user['name'] }}</li>
        {% else %}
          <li><a href="/login" >Log In with your Google Account</a></li>
        {% end %}
      </ul>
    </div>


    {% if user %}
        <div id="footer"><a href="/logout">Logout</a></div>
    {% end %}
  </body>

</html>
```

This template simply loads up the different JavaScript files that we'll need and defines
a basic shell of a page. We also check to see whether the user is logged in and present
either a link to log in or out, depending on the status. Part of that HTML code involves
including a local JavaScript file and defining a DIV that will be used for a map. Let's
add that JavaScript now to show that map. Create a file in *ipandemic/tornado/static/*
called *cc.js* and add the following code:

```
google.load("jquery", "1");

var cc = {
    map: false,
    default_lat: 40.730521,
    default_lon: -73.984337
};

cc.initialize = function(map_div_id) {
    if (GBrowserIsCompatible()) {
        cc.map = new GMap2(document.getElementById(map_div_id));
        cc.map.setCenter(new GLatLng(cc.default_lat, cc.default_lon), 13);
        cc.map.setUIToDefault();
    }
    else
        alert("Google doesn't think your browser is compatible with " +
                "their maps, this will be painful without them...");
};
```

The first thing this file does is ask the Google Ajax APIs to load the jQuery library. After
that, we start defining our Command Center, or cc, object. The first variable that we
need is map, which will hold a reference to the GMap2 instance that we'll be interacting
with throughout this application. The next two variables, default_lat and
default_lon, simply define the default position that we load on the map. These two

numbers center the map on the lower part of Manhattan, so feel free to change that to whatever makes sense for your user base.

Then, we add a method called `initialize` that just sets up the map by centering it on the default location and loading the default user interface elements. This method is actually called from *command-center.html* through the `onload` tag on the `body` element.

We've now got the shell of an application ready to run. Let's start up the server and ensure everything is working. From your terminal window, start the server:

```
~ipandemic/tornado $ python server.py
```

Now if you point your browser to *http://localhost:8088*, you should see a page similar to Figure 10-11.

Figure 10-11. The basic command center

Authentication

By default, Tornado ships with the ability to authenticate through a variety of third-party sites, including Google, Facebook, Twitter, Yahoo, and FriendFeed. Since we're already using Google Authentication on the game side of this application, let's continue with that and use it here. Inside *server.py*, add the following controller:

```
class Application(tornado.web.Application):
    def __init__(self):
        handlers = [
            (r"/", HomeHandler),
            (r"/login/?", GoogleLoginHandler),
            ]
...

class GoogleLoginHandler(tornado.web.RequestHandler, tornado.auth.GoogleMixin):

    @tornado.web.asynchronous
    def get(self):
        if self.get_argument("openid.mode", None):
            self.get_authenticated_user(self.async_callback(self._on_auth))
            return
        self.authenticate_redirect()

    def _on_auth(self, user):
        # if we're authenticated, set the cookie, otherwise try again...
        if not user:
            self.authenticate_redirect()
            return
        else:
            self.set_secure_cookie('user', json.dumps(user))
        self.redirect("/")
```

This code adds the routing from the /login URL to the GoogleLoginHandler class. There are many different options to choose from when authenticating through third-party sites, but we're only interesting in the most basic form, which is identifying the users. To do that, when we get a login request, we simply forward the user along to Google with the authenticate_redirect method. When Google sends the user back, the request will get routed to the _on_auth method. When we receive this request, we simply dump the user object into a JSON-encoded string and set it as a cookie.

This code uses the @tornado.web.asynchronous decorator. Decorators in Python are analogous to macros in most other languages. In this case, adding this bit of code before the method definition extends the method itself. For a thorough look at decorators in Python, view Bruce Eckel's great post entitled "Decorators I: Introduction to Python Decorators" (*http://www.artima.com/weblogs/viewpost.jsp?thread=240808*).

Now that users can log in, let's give them the ability to log out. To do this, we can simply clear the cookie. In your *server.py* file:

```
class Application(tornado.web.Application):
    def __init__(self):
```

```
            handlers = [
                (r"/", HomeHandler),
                (r"/login/?", GoogleLoginHandler),
                (r"/logout/?", LogoutHandler),
                ]
    ...
class LogoutHandler(tornado.web.RequestHandler):
    def get(self):
        self.clear_cookie("user")
        self.redirect('/')
```

With Tornado, when you enable third party authentication, you can fully authenticate with the actual service, even if you are running the application locally. Whereas App Engine only allows you to authenticate using test users, Tornado allows you to do the real thing. Try starting up the server now and logging in. When you are redirected to Google, you should see a screen resembling Figure 10-12.

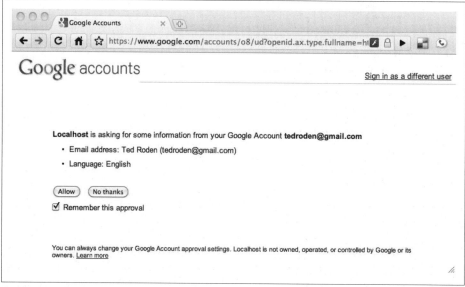

Figure 10-12. Authenticating a local Tornado application on Google

Consuming PubSubHubbub

On the game side of this application, we spent a lot of time notifying the Command Center class of different germ activity and setting up the update method to ping the PubSubHubbub server. Let's take advantage of that work now by subscribing to the PubSubHubbub updates.

To get this feature moving, the first thing we need to do is actually request the subscription from the hub. We can do that by modifying the Application object to subscribe whenever we launch this server. In your *server.py* file, append the following code to the end of the __init__ method on the Application object:

```
app_host = 'http://cdc.ipandemic.com:%d' % options.port
topic_url = "http://www.ipandemic.com/feed"
hub_url = "http://pubsubhubbub.appspot.com"
callback_url = app_host + "/catch/germs"

# set up the different urls we need to know
logging.info("Subscribing to the HUB")
data = urllib.urlencode({'hub.topic': topic_url,
                         'hub.callback': callback_url,
                         'hub.verify': 'async',
                         'hub.mode': 'subscribe'})

try:
    response = urllib2.urlopen(hub_url, data)
except (IOError, urllib2.HTTPError), e:
    if hasattr(e, 'code') and e.code == 204:
        logging.info("204: No Content")
    error = ''
    if hasattr(e, 'read'):
        error = e.read()
    logging.info('%s, Response: "%s"' % (e, error))
```

This should look vaguely familiar from when we subscribed to a hub way back in Chapter 3. Before we can contact the server and request the subscription, we have to define some variables to explain where everything is located. The first variable, app_host, is the endpoint of this Tornado-based command center application. This host must be publicly accessible because the hub is going to make HTTP requests to it. For this variable, enter in the final URL that you'll be using.

The next variable, topic_url, is the URL of the Atom feed to which we want to subscribe. This would be the Atom feed built previously in this chapter. After that, you can safely leave the variables as they are in the text. We're just defining the URL of the hub that is shared by multiple applications. Finally, we define the callback_url, which is the endpoint URL used when the hub has new data.

Subscribing to a hub is a two-step process. The first part is requesting the subscription, which we've just defined. The second part of the subscription process is responding to the challenge request sent by the hub. This challenge request is used by the hub to ensure that the URL we provide is actually expecting to receive updates. To define this, we need to add a new URL route and a controller class. Let's define that now:

```
class Application(tornado.web.Application):
    def __init__(self):
        handlers = [
            (r"/", HomeHandler),
            (r"/login/?", GoogleLoginHandler),
            (r"/logout/?", LogoutHandler),
            (r"/catch/germs/?", CatchGermsHandler),
            ]
...
class CatchGermsHandler(tornado.web.RequestHandler):
    def get(self):
```

```
    if self.get_argument('hub.mode', False):
        self.finish(self.get_argument('hub.challenge'))
```

This new controller class, `CatchGermsHandler`, will be used to accept publish requests from the hub. However, before we can receive any published messages, we'll have to respond to the challenge request. To do that, we simply check to see whether the server sent the `hub.mode` parameter along with the request. If it was sent, we then take the `hub.challenge` parameter and write it out as our response. This informs the server that we are expecting publish requests and that the subscribe request was valid. If you want to start the *server.py* script from your publicly accessible server, you should see some traffic into the Tornado console similar to the following:

```
~ipandemic/tornado $ python server.py
[I 100217 23:31:41 server:78] Subscribing to the HUB
[I 100217 23:31:41 web:714] 200 GET /catch/germs?hub.challenge=
WfVLMg1RlBCbv1ktrk3OrOpZ7_EZYpakg5_yF6o5eUbghf4bDOIMy4FkABt_aY66m
W6uPe6XwIfy8LGV8wc4OL6VPkGUG9Z8ZjciSPUPXYlFSPFEakDL6xodwh-sFDYl&hub.
topic=http%3A%2F%2Fwww.ipandemic.com%2Ffeed&hub.mode=subscribe&hub.
lease_seconds=2592000 (66.249.85.65) 0.92ms
```

The first thing you can see here is our logging message announcing that we're about to try to subscribe to the hub. It may take a few seconds, but at some point after that you should see the challenge request come in from the hub. Our script responds to that just fine and you're subscribed. There is no final check in from the Hub telling you that everything worked, but everything should be fine.

Now that we're subscribing to the hub and responding to the `hub.challenge`, we're all set to actually accept the published data from the hub. To do that, let's add another method to the `CatchGermsHandler` class.

```
class CatchGermsHandler(tornado.web.RequestHandler):
    def get(self):
        if self.get_argument('hub.mode', False):
            self.finish(self.get_argument('hub.challenge'))

    def post(self):
        # parse the XML with the minidom module
        dom = minidom.parseString(self.request.body)
        ATOM_NS = "http://www.w3.org/2005/Atom"

        # loop through all of the content nodes
        for node in dom.getElementsByTagNameNS(ATOM_NS, 'content'):
            germ = json.loads(node.firstChild.data.strip())

            # add them to the notifier class
            self.application.notifier.add_germ(germ)

        # update the notifier class
        self.application.notifier.update_clients()
```

This adds some new functionality to the same /catch/germs URL. When we receive a POST request from the hub, we immediately start parsing the XML payload using Python's `minidom` module. This XML payload may be anything from the entire Atom file with hundreds of germs to a single entry tag informing us of one change. Whatever the extent of the data, we can easily ignore everything in it aside from the content tags, which contain JSON-encoded germ. We simply loop through each of those content tags and run a method called add_germ on an object called notifier. Once we're through with the loop, we take that same notifier object and run a method called update_clients.

Notifying users

Previously, in the CatchGermsHandler class, we referred to an object called notifier. Although it hasn't been defined yet, its purpose is probably clear. The Notifier class is what keeps track of the germ data on this end and publishes it out to the web clients watching the command center home page. Let's add that class now. In your *server.py* file, add the following code somewhere above your Application object:

```
class Notifier(object):
    # the connected web clients
    listeners = []
    # the list of germs
    germs = []

    def add_listener(self, callback):
        self.listeners.append(callback)

    # send the
    def notify_listeners(self, messages=False, germs=False):

        # call the callback method on each of the listeners
        for callback in self.listeners:
            try:
                callback(messages=messages, germs=germs)
            except:
                logging.error("Error in listeners callback", exc_info=True)

        # we've just sent something to each listener, clear the list
        self.listeners = []


    def add_germ(self, germ):
        x = 0
        # if we already have this germ, update the data and return
        while x < len(self.germs):
            if self.germs[x]['id'] == germ['id']:
                self.germs[x] = germ
                return
            x += 1

        # otherwise, just append the germ to the list
        self.germs.append(germ)

    # a convenience method to notify the listeners
    def update_clients(self):
```

```
# notify everyone about the germs
self.notify_listeners(germs=self.germs)
```

Parts of this code are quite similar to the `Tweet` class defined in Chapter 5. Before we get started, we set up two variables to keep track of both the list of connected clients and the current list of germs. Then the first method, `add_listener`, simply adds the listener to the list. In this case, when a client starts a long polling request with this server, the controller class will call this `add_listener` method with a `callback` method as the only parameter. We store this `callback` in the listeners list and use it when we have data available.

The next method, `notifier_listeners`, is the method that we call when data becomes available. When this method is called, the caller specifies which type of data has been updated, and then we simply loop through the list of listeners, calling the callback method for each one. Once we've updated all of the listeners, we clear out the list because we know that everybody just received data and no one is currently waiting for anything. However, in practice, the clients will all reconnect immediately and the process will start anew.

The next two methods are those that we already referenced in `CatchGermsHandler`. The first of the two, `add_germ`, takes in a parameter called `germ`, which is a dictionary representation of the germ data itself. We just check to see whether we already have this specific germ by comparing its `id` field with the `ids` that we currently have in the `germs` list. If we don't have it, we simply append it to the list.

After that, we have a method called `update_clients` that is provided as a convenience method to users of this class. This class allows other objects to notify the listeners of the new data without requiring the classes to know about the internal workings of this class.

Now that we've added this class to the application, we have to instantiate it in a way that will allow us to access it from all of the controllers. We can just do that from the `__init__` method on the `Application` object. In *server.py*, add the following line:

```
class Application(tornado.web.Application):
    def __init__(self):
        self.notifier = Notifier()
        handlers = [
...
```

Because we added the `notifier` object as a member variable of the application class, we're able to access it from any of the controller methods. It's available through `self.application.notifier` in each of those classes.

Handling long polling on the server. This part of the application is going to use long polling to ensure that the clients always have the latest data. On the server side of things, adding this functionality is fairly straightforward. We just have to add another URL mapping and a small controller method. In *server.py*:

```
class Application(tornado.web.Application):
    def __init__(self):
        handlers = [
            (r"/", HomeHandler),
            (r"/login/?", GoogleLoginHandler),
            (r"/logout/?", LogoutHandler),
            (r"/catch/germs/?", CatchGermsHandler),
            (r"/updates/?", UpdateHandler),
        ]
...

# wait for updates and return them when available
class UpdateHandler(tornado.web.RequestHandler):

    @tornado.web.asynchronous
    def post(self):
        self.application.notifier.add_listener( \
            self.async_callback(self.handle_updates))

    def handle_updates(self, messages=False, germs=False):
        if not self.request.connection.stream.closed():
            self.finish({'germs': germs})
```

This method uses Tornado's `tornado.web.asynchronous` decorator. This decorator means that this method will return, but the connection to the client will not be terminated until explicitly `finished`. So inside this method, all we need to do is add a new listener via the `add_listener` method and supply a callback method.

This callback method, `handle_updates`, will be called when new data is available to send to the client. When that happens, we'll check to make sure that the connection is still open and then `finish` the connection by sending the JSON-encoded `germs` object. The JavaScript side of this application will then take those germs and display them on the map.

Long polling on the client side. The server side of this application is all ready to go. We're accepting long polling requests from the clients, waiting for data to become available through PubSubHubbub subscriptions, and sending the data back out to any number of clients. However, the client side of this application isn't doing anything more than displaying a map. Let's set it up to handle the germs as they come in.

This application uses long polling to get the latest realtime data from the server. To do that, we must start polling the server continuously. Let's update the `cc.initialize` method in *tornado/static/cc.js* to start this process:

```
cc.initialize = function(map_div_id) {
    if (GBrowserIsCompatible()) {
        cc.map = new GMap2(document.getElementById(map_div_id));
        cc.map.setCenter(new GLatLng(cc.default_lat, cc.default_lon), 13);
        cc.map.setUIToDefault();
        cc.commandCentralPoll();
    }
...
};
```

```
cc.commandCentralPoll = function() {
    $.post('/updates/',
        {},
        function(data) {
            cc.receivedData(data);
            cc.commandCentralPoll();
        },
    'json');
};
```

Adding this method simply starts the process of polling the server. We make a POST request to /updates, and when it returns, we send the data along to a method called receivedData. Then, we call commandCentralPoll again. This Ajax request may return instantly or it may take several minutes before any data is available. However, once that data is available, we act on it quickly and immediately request more.

Asking for the data is only a small part of the issue; we also need to do something with it once it's returned. To do that, let's define the receivedData method:

```
cc.receivedData = function(data) {
    if(!data) return;
    var germs = data.germs;

    // put the germs on the map
    if(germs) {

        // clear the current map
        cc.map.clearOverlays();

        for(var i in germs) {

            // only draw germs that aren't deleted
            if(!germs[i].deleted)
                cc.putGermOnMap(germs[i]);
        }
    }
};
```

The data returned from our long polling request is a JSON-encoded object. The only key inside that object is called germs, which contains the array of germs that the server knows about. So the main point of receivedData is to take those germs, loop through them, and display them on the map unless they are marked as deleted. To do that, we simply clear all of the existing germs off of the map, loop through the ones we have, and put them on the map using putGermOnMap. That method is a simpler version of the one used for the mobile phone:

```
cc.putGermOnMap = function(germ) {
    var geo_pt = new GLatLng(germ.lat, germ.lon);
    var spread = germ.spread;
    var color = germ.color;

    cc.drawCircle(geo_pt, spread, color);
```

```
            var marker = new GMarker(geo_pt);

            // allow the user to click and see the data about this germ
            GEvent.addListener(marker, 'click', function() {
                                var d = germ.disease;
                                html = "<div id='"+ germ.id + "'>";
                                html += "<br><small>";
                                html += "<strong>Strain</strong>: " + d.strain + "<br>";
                                html += "<strong>Host</strong>: " + d.host + "<br>";
                                html += "</div>";

                                marker.openInfoWindowHtml(html);
                        });

            // show it on the map
            cc.map.addOverlay(marker);

    };
```

This version of `putGermOnMap` is a stripped-down version of a method with the same name from *appengine/static/geo.js*. Because it's designed to work on a desktop browser, it uses Google's `openInfoWindowHtml`. Although that method works on mobile devices, it tends to slow the application down too much for it to be useful. However, on a desktop browser, users expect it.

The only thing missing from drawing these germs on the map is drawing the spread of the germ. Just like on the mobile phone, we want to draw a circle around each germ to show the relative size of the germ. Add the `drawCircle` method now:

```
    cc.drawCircle = function(center, radius, color) {
        var poly = [];
        var lat = center.lat() ;
        var lng = center.lng() ;
        var d2r = Math.PI/180 ;            // degrees to radians
        var r2d = 180/Math.PI ;            // radians to degrees
        var Clat = (radius/3963) * r2d ;   //  using 3963 as earth's radius
        var Clng = Clat/Math.cos(lat*d2r);

        var points_in_circle = 90;

        // add each point in the circle
        for (var i = 0 ; i < points_in_circle; i++)      {
            var theta = Math.PI * (i / (points_in_circle / 2)) ;
            Cx = lng + (Clng * Math.cos(theta)) ;
            Cy = lat + (Clat * Math.sin(theta)) ;
            poly.push(new GLatLng(Cy,Cx)) ;
        }

        // add the first point to complete the circle
        poly.push(poly[0]) ;

        var line = new GPolygon(poly, color, 3, 1, color, 0.2);
        cc.map.addOverlay(line) ;
    };
```

The only difference between this version of `drawCircle` and the version we made in *appengine/static/geo.js* is that this one draws far more points in the circle than the one designed for the mobile phone. Again, it's important to tailor the code for the device on which it will run.

If you run this application from a publicly accessible location, you'll be able to see the germs on the screen. If a germ gets deleted from the iPandemic application, it will disappear from this screen in a matter of milliseconds. That event would have triggered a `delete_germ` call on `CommandCenter` on the game side of the application. That call would have been followed by a call to `update` on the same `CommandCenter` object. That method would ping the PubSubHubbub server, which would grab the feed and immediately notify this application. If you start this server, you should see something like Figure 10-13.

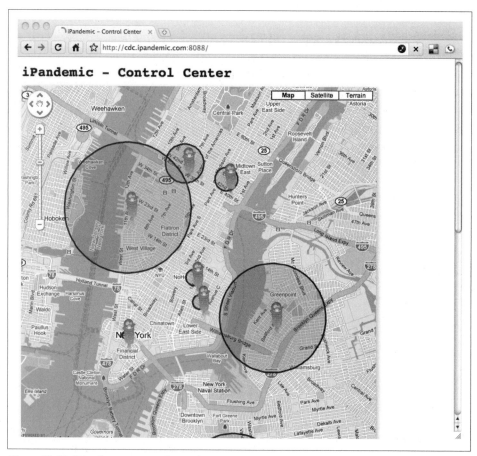

Figure 10-13. Watch germs spread in realtime

Chat

Although a good portion of this game exists entirely on a mobile phone, the command center does push out realtime updates to any number of connected clients. When users arrive at a location, they should be able to continue to interact with the game and each other. Knowing that we always have a good number of users connected who are watching their germs spread and die out, it's a good place to allow more realtime communication. In this case, we'll add a chat interface to allow all of the users to communicate with one another.

The chat application that we built in Chapter 6 allowed users to communicate privately with each other. For this game, we'll build a public chat where each user can see the messages sent by every other user. This simplifies things in some ways because we do not have to worry about managing user interface windows or routing the messages from one user to another. However, we can't just add all new functionality; we want to continue to use the existing long polling system that we set up to monitor the germs.

Server side. To get started with this, let's update the main template to have a space for chatting. In *command-center.html*, add the following code:

```
<!DOCTYPE html>
<html>
...
    <div id="map" style="width: 700px; height: 700px; float: left;"></div>

    <!-- something to hold the whole chat UI -->
    <div id="chat-container" style="float: left; width: 200px; width: 200px;">

      <!-- A simple input to accept new messages -->
      <div id="chat-form">
        {% if user %}
          <input type="text" id="chat-input" placeholder="Say something..." />
        {% else %}
          <em>Log in to join the chat</em>
        {% end %}
      </div>

      <!-- A container to hold the existing messages -->
      <div id="chat" style="height: 700px; overflow: auto;">
      </div>

    </div>
```

This just adds the interface elements that we'll need for chat. We build a container DIV, chat-container, with a style attribute that will allow it to sit next to the map. Then, we build the form and the chat DIV that will hold all of the messages as they arrive.

Moving along, let's set up the Notifier class to handle messages along with the germs. Parts of it are already set up for this, so it's not a big deal to add in this new functionality. In *server.py*, update the Notifier class to have the following code:

```
class Notifier(object):
    listeners = []
```

```
        germs = []
        message_cache = []           # a list of recent chat messages
        message_cache_size = 20      # the amount of recent messages to store

        # send a message to the other users.
        def send_message(self, text):

            # build the message object
            message = {'text': text,
                       'id': str(uuid.uuid4()) }

            # send it out to the clients.
            self.notify_listeners(messages=[message])

            # and update the message cache
            self.message_cache.extend([message])
            if len(self.message_cache) > self.message_cache_size:
                    self.message_cache = self.message_cache[-self.message_cache_size:]
```

The first thing we do here is create some new member variables to hold the existing message cache. We want to keep a small cache of the most recent messages so that clients can catch up if messages arrive while they're reconnecting after receiving data. This will also allow us to send the most recent messages to a user when she connects for the first time, allowing her to get caught up with the current state of the chat.

Then, we add the send_message method, which is what we'll use in other Python code to actually send a message to all of the users. The first thing we do is build the message object, which consists of the text of the message itself and a unique uuid. This id field will be used by the client when requesting new messages to signal the last message that was received. After that, we simply call the notifier_listeners method, supplying a messages parameter instead of the germs parameter. That method will actually send the message to each of the clients.

Once we've sent the message, we want to add it to the existing cache, which we do by calling extend on it. Then, we clean up the cache to ensure it doesn't grow too big. This cache is used to send to the new clients as they connect, or it's used to send any new messages to users if they fall behind for some reason. To do that, we need to update the add_listener method to check whether the user needs to see new messages. Let's update the add_listener method in the *server.py* file to handle this:

```
    def add_listener(self, callback, cursor=None):
            # if they've supplied a cursor, send them any messages since that cursor
            if cursor:
                index = 0
                for i in xrange(len(self.message_cache)):
                    index = len(self.message_cache) - i - 1
                    if self.message_cache[index]["id"] == cursor: break
                recent = self.message_cache[index + 1:]
                if recent:
                    callback(messages=recent)
                    return
```

```
# if they haven't sent a cursor, send them everything in the cache
if not cursor and len(self.message_cache):
    callback(messages=self.message_cache, germs=self.germs)
    return

self.listeners.append(callback)
```

Previously, this method simply added the callback to the `listeners` list and returned. We still have that line of code, but now we want to check whether any messages are immediately available. We start that by accepting a `cursor` variable. This variable is the `id` field that is saved by the client and tells us the last message a particular client received.

If we have a `cursor`, we want to see whether it matches up to the latest message sent to the server. If it doesn't, gather up all of the messages sent since `cursor` and send those messages immediately. We do that by simply searching the `message_cache` for the `cursor` and running the `callback` function if we find any new messages.

If the client doesn't supply a `cursor` variable, we can just assume they've never seen any of the messages, so we simply run the callback and send all messages to the client. If we end up making it to the end of the method, the client supplied a `cursor`, but it's the most recent message, so we simply add them to the listeners array and wait for any new messages to arrive.

Whenever the server has new content to send to the client, it calls the `callback` method stored in the `listeners` list. In this particular code, that method is always the `handle_updates` method of the `UpdateHandler` controller. Let's update that to send the chat messages as well as the germs:

```
# wait for updates and return them when available
class UpdateHandler(tornado.web.RequestHandler):

    @tornado.web.asynchronous
    def post(self):
        cursor = self.get_argument('chat_cursor', False)
        self.application.notifier.add_listener( \
            self.async_callback(self.handle_updates), cursor)

    def handle_updates(self, messages=False, germs=False):
        if not self.request.connection.stream.closed():
            self.finish({'chat_messages': messages, 'germs': germs})
```

The first change here is that we listen for a parameter called `chat_cursor` and add it as a parameter to the `add_listener` method. This will be used in that method to check whether we're all caught up with messages or need to send previous messages immediately.

To send the messages back, all we need to do is add the `messages` parameter and send it back out to the client when we're closing the connection. We do that by adding another field to the dictionary called `chat_messages`. With that, the client-side Java-Script can simply look for another object as part of the dictionary it receives as a parameter and pull the messages out of that.

However, before we worry about handling things on the client side, we still need to add some code to send messages using the `send_message` method. First, let's start with the obvious method of accepting chat messages from users. Add the following URL route and controller to *server.py*:

```
class Application(tornado.web.Application):
    def __init__(self):
        self.notifier = Notifier()
        handlers = [
            (r"/", HomeHandler),
            (r"/chat/say/?", ChatSayHandler),

...

class ChatSayHandler(tornado.web.RequestHandler):

    def post(self):
        # figure out which user is sending a message
        user_json = self.get_secure_cookie('user')
        if user_json:
            user = json.loads(user_json)

            text = self.get_argument('text').strip()
            if len(text):
                # assuming we have a message, format it and send it!
                text = "<strong>%s</strong>: %s" % (user['first_name'], text)
                self.application.notifier.send_message(text)
        # send a response to the client
        self.finish({'status': 'ok!'})
```

This method accepts a post request from the client and immediately tries to load the user object from the cookie. If we do have a user object, we grab a parameter called `text`, clean it up, format it, and send it using the `send_message` method. To format it, we simply add the username of the sender before the message to let everyone know who sent the message. Once we've handed the message off to `send_notifier`, we don't have anything else to do, so we just return a response message.

Sending messages that users explicitly send is useful, but we should also let the existing users know when another user has joined that chat. To do that, we just need to add a line to the login handler. Inside *server.py*, update `GoogleLoginHandler` to send the message on behalf of the newly authenticated user:

```
class GoogleLoginHandler(tornado.web.RequestHandler, tornado.auth.GoogleMixin):
    ...
    def _on_auth(self, user):
        if not user:
            self.authenticate_redirect()
            return
        else:
            self.set_secure_cookie('user', json.dumps(user))
            self.application.notifier.send_message(user['first_name'] + " joined")
        self.redirect("/")
```

In this code, just before the user is redirected to the home page after successfully completing the login process, we send a simple message announcing the user's arrival.

Client side. As it exists now, the JavaScript we've written for this application is already polling the /updates URL, which now provides both the germs and the messages that we need to display on the screen. So now we need to update the methods that receive data to do something with those messages and then add the ability to send them back. To get started, let's update the main cc object to keep track of the current chat cursor variable. In *tornado/static/cc.js*, update the following member variable:

```
var cc = {
    map: false,
    default_lat: 40.730521,
    default_lon: -73.984337,
    chat_cursor: ''
};
```

This additional variable allows us to keep track of the last message that we've seen and send it back to the server when we are in the process of polling for new updates. Let's go ahead and add that parameter now:

```
cc.commandCentralPoll = function() {
    $.post('/updates/',
        { 'chat_cursor': cc.chat_cursor },
        function(data) {
            cc.receivedData(data);
            cc.commandCentralPoll();
        },
        'json');
};
```

This simply takes that new variable and sends it along to the server whenever we poll for new updates. Now let's start keeping track of that cursor. To do that, we want to monitor each and every message that comes in and save the id of the latest one that we receive. We can easily do that as soon as we receive a message and start the process of displaying it on the screen. Let's update cc.receivedData to handle the messages and, in turn, this cursor variable:

```
cc.receivedData = function(data) {
    if(!data) return;
    var germs = data.germs;
    var chat_messages = data.chat_messages;

    if(chat_messages) {
        for(var x in chat_messages) {
            cc.chat_cursor = chat_messages[x].id;
            cc.addToChat(chat_messages[x]);
        }
    }
    ...
    // put the germs on the map
    if(germs) {
```

The first change we make here is to check the data parameter for both the `chat_messages` field as well as `germs`. If we find any messages, we loop through them one by one and save the id to the `chat_cursor` variable. When we get to the end of the loop, that will always be the most recent message. Once we set that variable, we pass the message along to a method called **addToChat**, which will add it to the screen. Let's define that now. Inside your *tornado/static/cc.js* file, add the following method:

```
cc.addToChat = function(message) {
    var span = $('<div>');
    span.attr('class', 'single-message');
    span.html(message.text);
    $('#chat').prepend(span);
};
```

This method simply takes the `message` parameter, which is just a string of the message itself, and adds it to the DIV identified by having `chat` as an `id`.

If you restart the server now, you'll be able to see users join the chat as they log in. Figure 10-14 shows what this should look like.

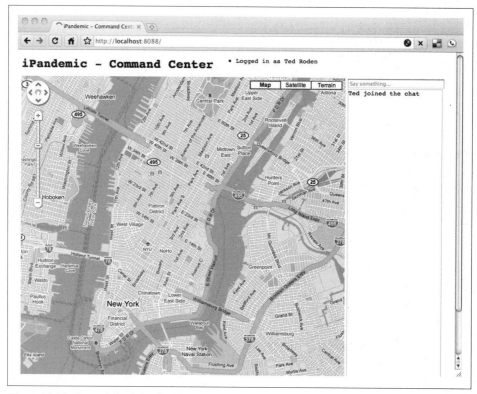

Figure 10-14. A user joined the chat

The only thing missing now is the ability to actually send out a message. To do that, we need to listen as users type into the form and then send the messages when it's appropriate. To do that, let's update the `cc.initialize` method to listen for this event.

```
cc.initialize = function(map_div_id) {
    $('#chat-input').bind('keypress', function(e) {
                            var code = (e.keyCode ? e.keyCode : e.which);
                            if (code == 13) { cc.sendChat(); }
                     });
    ...
```

All we do here is bind a callback function onto the keypress event of our `input` field. This method ignores every keypress until the user presses Enter, which has a `keyCode` value of 13. When the user does press Enter, we call the method `cc.sendChat`. Let's define that now:

```
cc.sendChat = function() {
    // get the value of the text input
    var text = $('#chat-input').val();

    // send it to the server
    $.post('/chat/say',
        { 'text': text },
        function(data) {
            // upon success, clear the text input field
            $('#chat-input').val('');
        },
        'json');
};
```

This method simply takes the value out of the text input field and sends it in a post request to the server at /chat/say. Assuming that the request is successful, we clear out the text input field so that the user can send another message.

This method is all that's needed for the complete chat functionality of this application. Populating the `chat` DIV will be handled when the polling to /updates comes back, which will probably occur within a few milliseconds. Figure 10-15 shows a few people chatting, along with updates from the germs.

In Review

This application takes a good number of the technologies that we've discussed in this book and puts them together in one more or less cohesive application. While we started from scratch to build this application, there is no reason why a developer couldn't take a single part and incorporate it into her application.

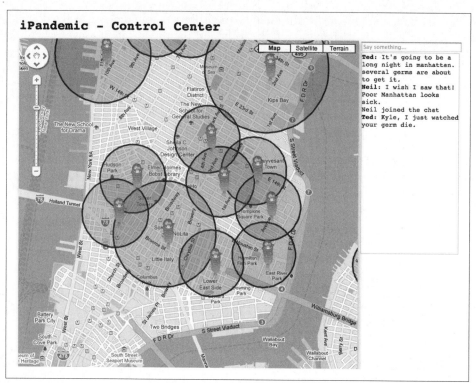

Figure 10-15. Viewing the completed control center

Adding a chat based on long polling can be done from almost any server setup; if it's not directly supported, firing up a simple Tornado web server on a separate port will certainly do the trick. The SMS integration on this application is a small extra feature—the application would certainly work without it—but having it there enhances the user's experience. Likewise for Instant Messaging, this addition can easily be done by firing up an App Engine instance and responding to a few API calls.

Having these technologies in your application is pretty easy—small steps, but the end result is that users can interact with your application in drastically different ways. As the web increasingly moves away from the desktop computer, it's important that your application can respond in every way your users expect. Depending on your application, there is a good chance that users would start interacting with your application more frequently, and hang around longer, if you gave them the means to do it on their own terms.

Index

Symbols

$HTTP_RAW_POST_DATA variable (PHP), 35

% (percent signs), enclosing Tornado flow control statements, 92

. (period) in hub parameters, 33

@login_required decorator, 134

@property decorator, 104

@tornado.web.asynchronous decorator, 86

_ (underscore) in HTTP requests, PHP handling of, 33

{ } (curly braces), enclosing arbitrary expressions in Tornado, 92

A

active users list, obtaining from enjoysthin.gs, 13

active.users API call, 17

advice statement (Bayeux protocol), 60

Ajax libraries API, 67

Amazon
  EC2 server, 220
  Web Services developer website, 220

AMIs (Amazon Machine Instances), 220

analytics on realtime Web, 185–216
  Chartbeat service, 186
  customized, 189
    catching statistics on server, 193–198
    making sense of traffic, 198–201
    sending SMS alerts, 214–216
    sending tracking pings with JavaScript, 189–193
    tracking backend traffic and custom data, 208–214

viewing traffic, 201–208
  Woopra service, 187

Apache, httpd server, 55, 77
  (see also Cometd server)

APISendHandler class, 149

App Engine, 6, 130–151
  authentication logs on Dashboard, 180
  creating application with the SDK, 131
  dashboard, 137
  Deploy button in Launcher, 136
  instant messaging application extended for SMS, 158–160
  iPandemic game, 218
  making web request with urlfetch module, 147
  memcache implementation, 228
  modifying main.py file for instant messaging, 133
  receiving instant messages, 139–141
  responding to instant messaging user commands, 143
  sending instant messages, 141
  setting up an API, 149–151
  setting up Google account, 130
  signing into your application, 136
  taking advantage of Google, 133
  urlfetch class, 230
  weather information from instant messenger, 146–149

app.yaml file, 132
  changing for SMS, 158
  XMPP services, 139

Application class (Tornado), 104
  URL handler for typing messages, 123
  __init__ method, 117

We'd like to hear your suggestions for improving our indexes. Send email to *index@oreilly.com*.

logs, viewing in App Engine dashboard, 137
long polling, 58
    browser two-connection limit and, 72
    client side (iPandemic game control center),
        285–289
    handling on server (iPandemic game), 284
    timeout parameter, 64
    Tornado support for, 81

M

mail command, 154
main.py file, 133
    adding IMUser class, 135
    adding XMPPHandler class, 139
    importing simplejson module, 146
    main function, API request handler, 149
    modifying for instant messaging, 133
MainHandler class (example)
    App Engine application, 134
    chat application, 104
    Tornado application, 83
        changing to specify template, 93
Maven, 61
    instructing to start server for live blog, 76
    pom.xml file, 65
measuring user involvement (see analytics on
        realtime Web)
memcache, 228
message-serving platform, Web as, 56
messaging, 2
    (see also instant messaging; SMS)
    Bayeux protocol, 58
    standard HTTP message delivery, 58
Messenger class (example), 230
/meta channels, 60
mobile devices, web browsers, 4
Model-View-Controller (MVC) framework, 81
modules section (pom.xml file), 66
MySQL
    creating database and tables, 14
    entries table, syndication_test database, 36
    users table (example)
        updates for user bookmarks, 21
        updates to last_update field, 24

N

namespace, Java source code in cometd-java,
        63

natural threats in iPandemic game, 253–257
notification
    defining notification object and function
        (chat example), 109
    notification function (chat example), 104
    Notifier class (iPandemic command center),
        283–284

O

offline data storage, 4

P

pass statement (Python), 108
passwords, 89
    (see also authentication)
    collecting and passing along with publish
        request in live blog, 75
    requiring for live blog, 73
period field (SUP file), 12
PHP
    defining PubSubHubBub class (example),
        30
    json_decode function, 18
    list function, 19
    SimpleXML extension, 18, 20
    substr function, 22
    superglobal variable,
        $HTTP_RAW_POST_DATA, 35
pinging server when no new content available,
        55
pings
    catching tracking ping statistics on server,
        193–198
    sending tracking pings with JavaScript, 189–
        193
    updating and analyzing data from user
        pings, 198–201
    Weblogs.com, 10
<plugins> tag (XML), 65
polling, 64
    (see also long polling)
    chat server for updates, 115
    long polling in server push, 58
pom.xml file (Maven), 61
    changes to, 65
POST requests (HTTP), 36
    (see also HTTP)

$HTTP_RAW_POST_DATA variable in PHP, 35
    hub subscription requests, 28
    hub subscription verification, 29
    posting to hub URL and adding parameters, 31
    publish POST requests from hubs, 34
proxy module, installing on Apache httpd server, 77
publish/subscribe services
    publishing with SUP, 21–26
    subscribing with SUP, 13–21
publishing
    content to server in live blog feed, 68
    in live blog feed, limiting to authorized users, 73
    messages to clients in live blog feed, 71
PubSubHubbub protocol, 26–38
    publishing with, 36–38
    subscribing to feed updates, 280–283
    subscribing with, 30–36
    subscriptions, 27
pull versus push, 4
push
    pull versus, 4
    server push, 57–60
Python, 6
    chat-server.py script, 103–105
        chatting on server side, 117
        login process, 107–112
        LoginHandler class, 107
        URL handler for typing messages, 123
    decorators, 86
    flow control statements, mapping in Tornado, 91
    FriendFeed validator, 25
    Google App Engine SDK, 131
    main.py file in App Engine, 133
        modifying for instant messaging, 133
    pass statement, 108
    pycurl and simplejson libraries, 80
    Queue module, 85
    re (regular expression) module, findall method, 91
    simplejson module, 90
    sms.py script, 159
    SMSSendHandler class (example), 181
    SMSService class (example), 160–161
    Textmark class (example), 168

Thread class, 89
Tornado, 79
uuid, 108
Zeep class (example), 174

Q

queue, setting up to store Twitter tweets, 85

R

re (regular expression) module (Python), 91
realtime user experience
    definition of realtime, 2
    prerequisites for building, 4
regular expressions
    matching items commonly found in tweets, 90
    searching for images, 53
    for URL routed to SMSIncomingHandler, 165
RequestHandler module (Tornado), 104
retweets, 90
river of content feed, 57–77
    integrating Cometd into your infrastructure, 77
    realtime live blog, 66–72
        posting content to, 67
    server push technology, 57–60
    server-side filters, 73–77
    setting up Cometd environment, 60–66
rot13 command, 144
RSS, 9
RSS feeds, 18
    (see also syndication)
    published to hub, 27
    validators for SUP data in, 26
rssCloud protocol, 10

S

SendHandler class (chat example), 117
server push, 57–60
    Bayeux protocol, 58
    long polling, 58
server-side filters (with Java), 73–77
    FilterPasswordCheck class (example), 74
servers
    designed old way, 55
    EC2 or other hosted server, 220
    new design to handle use of HTTP, 56

About the Author

Ted Roden was the first full-time developer hired on at Vimeo.com, and currently works in the Research and Development group at *The New York Times*. His work researching and prototyping topics closely related to the content of this book has been profiled by Harvard University's Nieman Journalism Lab (*http://bit.ly/f7rdJ* and *http://bit.ly/YzELI*). At the *Times*, he has also worked on bringing election night coverage, maps, and updates to the mobile website, as well as March Madness fantasy brackets. He is also the creator of a popular social bookmarking site: enjoysthin.gs.

Colophon

The animal on the cover of *Building the Realtime User Experience* is a common hill myna (*Gracula religiosa*). Myna birds (sometimes spelled mynah) are not a biological group: instead, humans applied the term to species of the starling family that are native to India and surrounding areas. These are very social animals, and are typically found in forested areas in groups of around six individuals. Mynas are omnivorous, with a diet of insects, nectar, and fruit.

Common hill mynas have glossy black plumage with white patches on their wings. Their bill is colored orange fading into yellow (rather like a piece of candy corn), and their legs are yellow. They have distinctive yellow wattles beneath their eyes and on the back of their neck. The position and shape of these wattles are the easiest way to distinguish between the various hill mynas of the *Gracula* genus. Rather than walking with the jaunty gait common to other starlings, hill mynas hop from branch to branch in the treetops.

Myna birds are famous for their talking ability, and the common hill myna in particular is renowned for mimicry. In the wild, this species has a large repertoire of calls shared by neighboring groups—local dialects that change completely between different areas. In captivity, if training begins at a young age, these mynas are able to imitate a wide range of phrases and sounds with uncanny accuracy and pitch. Myna owners should remember that these birds are intelligent, will only learn phrases that appeal to them (an enthusiastic tone of voice usually catches their attention), and are *always* listening to conversation around them. Check out Johnny Carson's interview session with a myna bird at *http://bit.ly/bWJFYu*.

The cover image is from Johnson's *Natural History*. The cover font is Adobe ITC Garamond. The text font is Linotype Birka; the heading font is Adobe Myriad Condensed; and the code font is LucasFont's TheSansMonoCondensed.